I0478564

A True Free Market

Market

CONVERSATIONS ON GAINING LIBERTY AND JUSTICE THROUGH ECONOMICS

STEPHEN TAFT

OPEN BOOK EDITIONS
A Barrett-Koehler Partner

iUniverse®

A TRUE FREE MARKET
CONVERSATIONS ON GAINING LIBERTY AND
JUSTICE THROUGH ECONOMICS

Copyright © 2015 Stephen Taft.

Author photo by Benjamin Brundrett Wright

All rights reserved. No part of this book may be used or reproduced by any means, graphic, electronic, or mechanical, including photocopying, recording, taping or by any information storage retrieval system without the written permission of the publisher except in the case of brief quotations embodied in critical articles and reviews.

iUniverse books may be ordered through booksellers or by contacting:

iUniverse
1663 Liberty Drive
Bloomington, IN 47403
www.iuniverse.com
1-800-Authors (1-800-288-4677)

Because of the dynamic nature of the Internet, any web addresses or links contained in this book may have changed since publication and may no longer be valid. The views expressed in this work are solely those of the author and do not necessarily reflect the views of the publisher, and the publisher hereby disclaims any responsibility for them.

Any people depicted in stock imagery provided by Thinkstock are models, and such images are being used for illustrative purposes only. Certain stock imagery © Thinkstock.

ISBN: 978-1-4917-6347-6 (sc)
ISBN: 978-1-4917-6349-0 (hc)
ISBN: 978-1-4917-6348-3 (e)

Library of Congress Control Number: 2015904623

Print information available on the last page.

iUniverse rev. date: 07/08/2015

Fellow citizens—a wise and frugal Government, which shall restrain men from injuring one another, shall leave them otherwise free to regulate their own pursuits of industry and improvement, and shall not take from the mouth of labor the bread it has earned. This is the sum of good government, and this is necessary to close the circle of our felicities.

—Thomas Jefferson's first inaugural address

Contents

Entrance—Introduction

We have erred in our practice of economics. The most prevalent symptom of it, although mostly unrecognized as such, is our ongoing political battling between capitalism and democracy. Many among us find each doctrine to be threatened by perfections of the other. Rampant capitalism is feared as a threat to democracy, and unbridled democracy is feared as a threat to capitalism. Good citizens have splintered across a deepening divide where politicos toss legislative bombs designed to undermine and recast their enemy's preferred ideal. Unfortunately, this is not a case of "Whatever doesn't kill you will make you stronger." Either ideal's failing will leave our nation weaker. It is deeply mistaken policy that has created fuel for this destructive debate. Free markets and free elections are two of our nation's founding liberties, yet they are at odds, because we have blindly structured our economy to put us at odds about them. We can't collectively decide whether a parent enduring financial hardship represents a failure of the economy or a failure of the parent. We can't agree on how much access to the voting booth is enough. And underlying this harsh political division are hopes for bringing incompatible partisan visions of what a fair opportunity is to economic life. This maddening, enduring conflict will rage until we start practicing economics with aplomb.

Free-market supporters see equality of opportunity growing as the role of government shrinks. Their dream is for people to act on their entrepreneurial ideas, to trade and hire with as little interference from government as possible. The mechanics of capitalism, as they see it, are uniquely able to bring discipline and efficiency to the use of society's resources. It logically follows that any government spending, beyond what's needed for our most basic requirements, is allocating resources less effectively than the free market would and is hindering our collective quest to maximize the nation's strength, productivity, and wealth.

However, this philosophy is vulnerable to its inevitable results. A competitive system is going to yield more losers than winners. If victory in economics is defined as the attainment of financial freedom, relatively few can win at our game of capitalism, for the poor and middle classes will always comprise the bulk of us. But, to the free marketers' chagrin, democracy is also being played here, and majorities can dominate in games of politics.

When the practice of economics spurs a community to see its own as winners or losers, defined by income and assets, a tart politics is enabled. Parties divide over rightfully pursuing the preservation of or the distribution of individual wealth. We side between those two choices—sometimes bickering, sometimes enraged—while the argument affects the entire population of a nation.

Here is where the conflict becomes palpable. Many of us are using one government program or another for day-to-day living. According to capitalism's champions, aid-dependent people and their supporters represent a threat to our economic strength simply by acting as a voting majority. They demand from government expansive programs for food, welfare, health care, education, and retirement—the very existence of which drain our capitalist energy and add to our national debt. These confident capitalists believe that if the economy were only left alone, without such government interference, the unchained brilliance of a free market would find cures for our economic ills, including sufficient charity for the needy. Therefore, free-market idealists require citizens to take care of themselves, to be responsible for themselves, so that government can be as small as possible.

These wealthy free marketers and their supporters, being a natural minority, have only their accumulated capital to drive politicians to protect the system that works so well for them and to counter the greater number of nonwealthy voters. While they encourage our representatives to vocally support the unhindered accumulation of wealth, they support both bold and surreptitious efforts to suppress the vote of those who would redistribute it. Their political journeymen will rarely hesitate to twist democracy's technical operations: gerrymandering, limiting voting hours, creating inefficiencies to make select voting lines unbearably long, intimidating those uncertain of their rights with bogus legalities, or demographically challenging the validity of names to shrink voter registration lists, all in attempts to guide the outcome of elections. Free marketers will also buy vast quantities of advertising across all effective outlets to make their point known or to drown out the points of their opposition, and they will defend that spending with the right and glory of free speech. Their motivating good intention is to achieve greater purity in capitalism in order to maximize our economic freedom.

But then there are those who see moral injustices in the cold machinations of capitalism. Such folk demand a leveling of market outcomes, for they believe the uneducated, unskilled, or unemployed are more unlucky than undeserving. They see most financial need arising from unfairness in our system, like short straws given for circumstance, and feel that our community, through government, has an obligation to address such misfortune. These outcome levelers see government programs as critical to bringing economic justice to the nation, righteousness rising as government defines and addresses people's needs. They, too, will gerrymander and advertise to fight their opponents' fire with fire, but they will generally support the unhindered voting rights of their natural majority. Such doubting capitalists believe that the free market, if left alone, would run roughshod over all but the wealthy. So they tender most responsibility for compassion to the state, supporting a calculated fairness by having government offer what a coldhearted free market is incapable of delivering. The purity of capitalism is their fear. A robust democracy is their cudgel against it.

Thus, the battle lines for the betterment of the nation are drawn. One side is willing to sacrifice the purity of democracy; the other side is willing to sacrifice the purity of capitalism. Yet both claim to be acting for the sake of economic justice. There's no agreement on what economic justice means, even though both sides define it with opportunity, nor on how it should be achieved. War for the political upper hand rages ominously, with the two sides striving for seemingly incompatible goals. Successes for one side become diminishments for the other.

This conflict is not a passing fad. It will not be a mere footnote to our age; it will become our contribution to history. We have unwittingly programmed it into our society. So it will remain with us until we choose to upgrade the code to what a better economics offers. Whatever flaws the two sides see in our capitalistic practices, the ironic truth is that this war between free marketers and outcome levelers is not over our fundamental problem. All the time, conversation, and expense of it, will one day be seen as a fool's errand.

While the drama of politics is what's most visible through popular media, the roots of our current two-party tensions are found in economics. Most of our domestic issues boil down to debates over taxes or spending. And most of us feel drawn to one camp or the other by our relative confidence in the free market to address the relevant issue. Whether it's poverty, education, or health care, we either trust the free market to solve it or we don't.

This book argues that both our confidences and our doubts are misplaced. Our warring politics is not over the merits of a true free market but over the merits of what we have: a poorly designed market. The real issue, the one we don't debate, is that our very idea of capitalism has been tainted by mistakes made in creating it.

It's not so unreasonable to think we fervently believe something in error. We used to think the Earth was flat, that the sun revolved around the Earth, that gods threw lightning bolts, that money could be made of wood, and even that under a dependable climate, the value of a tulip bulb could equal the value of a home. Clearly, ours is not an immutable reality. Our constant power and obligation is to newly understand and then alter our path.

It's therefore quite common to wonder what might be wrong with the world we've given ourselves. So, what if capitalism doesn't have to be an enemy of the poor? What if democracy doesn't have to be an enemy of the rich? What if the rich could gain greater wealth without concern for others placing claims on their success? And what if the poor could take care of themselves while needing nothing extra from the state? Could it be that the flaws causing capitalism's weaknesses are rote adaptations from so long ago that they only seem to be economically natural, and that we are now blind to the humanity and freedom that capitalism can actually offer?

As the dialogue to follow explains, our acceptance of taxing capital is what will continually pressure our economy to fray and our politics to splinter. It creates an economic desperation in some of us that is a source of unwitting exploitation by the rest of us. And because it perpetuates cyclical instability, it's not an efficient way to fund government. Taxing the result of work is a de facto distortion to our economy. It distorts both the relative value of products and the relative value of work. Obviously, taxation is necessary to allow government to function, but a tax becomes part of the economic playing field. Therefore, it can only be economically neutral when it falls on the field; that is, the earth on which our competition is played. Yet taxing capital, what results from our work, is not today seen as a problem.

The other unseen flaw that will be explained is our concept of ownership. We see ownership in anything that our laws allow to be sold. But economic principles are clear in that, of the three economic building blocks—land, labor, and capital—only capital can be individually owned. What existed prior to work belongs to our community, to all of us. Laws that lack appreciation for this cause capitalism its stresses and stumbles. Individual claims on land, for example, are critical to allow our economic imaginations to flourish, and government's clear role is to manage and protect this right. But when laws misidentify the proper recipient of land's value, significant economic distortions occur that become costly to all of us, owners and nonowners alike.

It's as if our economic lives today are floating on the ceaselessly chaotic and churning wake of a great ship named *Economy*. We bob up and down almost randomly, almost helplessly. We can see the ship, but we're blind to its design below the surface that creates the wake on which our economic fates are riding. We can't even see the steering mechanism to glean what recessionary course we might be taking until a downturn is already fact. We can absolutely do better.

Good design stems from human will, smartly applied to the laws of nature. A building, for example, cannot stand for long when designed in ignorance of physics. When physics is misapplied, the building crumbles. A farm cannot thrive when it is run in ignorance of agriculture, for when the basic needs of plants are not tended to, crops die. And a free market cannot thrive when constructed in ignorance of economics. When its fundamental forces are unappreciated in our lawmaking, the market fails. We have seen buildings collapse, and we have learned to build them better. We have seen crops die, and we have learned to better understand their needs. We have also seen markets fail, but we have not yet learned the nature of a true free market. We have tweaked our economic rules or applied new laws from political expedience, intuitive habit, or fear. Then we have proclaimed that great lessons have been learned. But in reality, we have only learned to wait for markets to fail again. We have not been quick to understand why cycles of economic dread persist among us or why our birth circumstance, more than anything, determines our economic fate.

If economics is the dominant means by which we interact with strangers, then economics is the framework for society's freedom. Freedom's economy must embody two conditions: that opportunity not be a zero-sum game and that every transaction can be declined without incurring harm to one's household. *Harm* is not the rejection of an opportunity to make a million dollars; rather, it is the possibility one won't then be able to feed one's family or keep them warm on a winter's night, without accepting help. Such concern is a form of desperation that has no place in a true free market.

Economic freedom doesn't mean that the successful must provide food or heat to the able-bodied poor. It does mean that the designers of a free economy, our lawmakers, must make sure that all able-bodied persons can care for themselves without requiring payments from a boss or a government. Economic freedom means that one can choose to have a boss or not, choose to be a boss or not, without needing welfare for saying no or from failing.

This might sound to some of us like pining, idealistic pabulum. Others might react viscerally at the perceived impossibility. But there is a history to human thought that as strongly disagrees. There are currents of optimism in our chronicles that lean toward the potential for freedom. These are the currents I have sought to follow and to expand upon.

Soulful economists have long been concerned with maximizing our overall well-being. Adam Smith, David Ricardo, Henry George, Karl Marx, Ludwig von Mises, and John Maynard Keynes are some who have held legitimate concerns for our human dignity. And they arrived at some starkly different conclusions on how to best address it. Mises is seen by some as a capitalist's capitalist, who saw capitalism as a pathway to freedom. Marx is often seen as a communist's communist, who saw capitalism burdening men with suppression. Both rightly define capital as something of potential economic utility. But they also accepted as fundamental that taxes are equally valid on what capital we have made as on what we have not. So they missed a major distinction. Rather than having seen beneath the common practice concocted by our foilable beliefs, what they each saw as fundamental was not fundamental enough.[1]

It is when we form a rudimentary community, and begin to depend on each other for goods and services, that economic forces first emerge. We secure food. We build shelters and gathering spots. We learn to hone different talents among us. The recognition of efficiency and need reflects a drive to improve our lives. It's in our essence as people. So we trade, seeking greater ease and variety for our days.

As the great power in trade was appreciated, we learned that the conditions for it could be tweaked for the sake of favor. Nations formed different economic systems by altering rules over its very potential, yielding dramatically varied results. Still, our human attributes are universal and constant. They will flow between us when we live with any dependence on each other, irrigating our interactions with an economic water that

---

[1]   Mises writes in *Human Action*, published in 1949, "Today there is, among businessmen and accountants, unanimity with regard to the meaning of capital. Capital is the sum of the money equivalent of all assets minus the sum of the money equivalent of all liabilities as dedicated at a definite date to the conduct of the operations of a definite business unit. It does not matter in what these assets may consist, whether they are pieces of land, buildings, equipment, tools, goods of any kind and order claims, receivables, cash, or whatever." Foundation for Economic Education, Inc. edition, 1996, p. 262.

Marx, in *Das Kapital*, first published in 1873, writes, "We have seen that even in the case of simple reproduction, all capital, whatever its original source, becomes converted into accumulated capital, capitalized surplus value." Waxkeep Publishing edition, 1886, from chapter 24.

Neither man questioned whether the origin of capital was to be considered when determining appropriate taxation.

takes the shape of whatever legal container it is given and leaks where that container has pores or cracks.

These basic human attributes, when given critical mass by the formation of community, become fundamental economic forces, operating as tendencies in every economy we can imagine:

1. All human work uses what land offers—its material or location.
2. When a trade is not for love or charity, the incentive is to profit from it.
3. When traded from need, the price paid can be more than the value received.
4. Some people will lie or cheat to meet their needs.
5. There is a narrower acceptable range for public behaviors than private ones.
6. Most people find comfort in the choices of crowds.

Understanding the interplay of these forces is what is needed to construct a true free market. Wise economic designers can read them as a map. But when the efficient route is ignored or unseen, the forces reflect like signposts warning of problems ahead. Our laws can steer us clear of, or right into, those problems.

The laws we choose reconcile the demands of social living with our individual freedoms. Idealized capitalism is approached by subjugating communal strengths to the needs of the individual. This is what we call a free market. The opposite, subjugating individual strengths to the needs of community, points to an idealized communism. This is a centrally planned market. Most nations have made choices that fall somewhere in between. But at every point on the scale in our world, there has been less-than-enduring success. Social systems have required regular amending or have folded. People have persistently been left hungry or without opportunity. Every nation has tried various blends of approaches, without any satisfying their populations for generations at a time. And all have taxed human-made capital.

We might then ask: Would more freedom be available to us today had better choices been made in the past? And what do we mean by freedom in the first place? Must the state and the individual be adversaries? In effect, are the ideals we hold ideal to hold?

Everything mankind does begins with questions, and then conversation. Whether large as an economy or small as a molecule, anything we've designed or invented begins with conversation about the possibility. The conversation might be held behind closed doors with a single loved one or reverberate in the world at large, but it precedes all further actions. The bulk of this book is a conversation between two believers in free will who are seeking their fullest freedom.

Economics is held high throughout these pages. It is only one of three bodies of law that prescribe our freedoms, but for most of us, it is the most influential in daily life. The other two, politics and morality, will be addressed only as they touch upon economics.

While economic law becomes mere fodder for our political wars, it remains a crucial tool for community design, particularly versatile and powerful. Just as hammers can be used to build a home or to take a life, economic law can further develop us or diminish us. It matters that it is forged from truth. *A True Free Market* is named for this ideal.

Three principles can guide our lawmaking through the map drawn by the six fundamental forces:

1. Freedom always allows for the choice to participate or not.
2. Capital—the result of labor—is not to be taxed.
3. Honesty is economically efficient for communities, but it can be inefficient for individuals.

These principles unite the forces into good economic design. They stem from a reverence for the wide breadth of aspiration inherent in community and the necessity of tending this little speck of the universe in which we're born. They draw from the heart and the mind in the same way the survivor of a highway wreck draws a renewed appreciation for life.

Economics teaches us that such appreciation doesn't have to be relegated to brief moments of national tragedy or national joy. Our entwined passions are part and parcel of the freedom in a truly free market. Perhaps we have yet to live in its marketplace because we have yet to experience a collapse iconic enough to spark us to begin a proper economic reengineering.

The Great Depression inspired us to change, but for all the agencies and programs implemented to fix the economy, we never addressed the flaws. They remain today.

We can find comfort in knowing that freedom doesn't arrive perfected. Freedom comes in waves to cultures, accepted only in fits and starts. We are always learning what is possible. Our political conversation can evolve to allow for more possibilities.

This book is dedicated to not waiting for another ominous crash to force our understanding. Existence on Earth, a miracle in the face of extraordinarily long odds, deserves to be cherished now with laws that structure our living with appreciation for our good fortune and honor for our myriad ambitions. Our capitalism can be made inclusive, without requiring a driving financial ambition to live securely, and without issuing penalties or resentment toward those who relish its competition. A true free market can be erected. We need only understanding and desire.

Sam Rueul and Jorge Olduvai are friends who share a passion for economic understanding. Beginning with the nature of fairness and freedom, their conversation methodically explores the fundamental forces that float our economic ship. Their words, chapter by chapter, slowly sketch an economic design using those three guiding principles to better the wealth of nations and allow us all, as individuals and communities, a new potential.

CHAPTER 1

Playing the Game, or Not

Two men in the city's Central Park offered each other a welcoming hug, meeting for what might have been the thousandth time in their middle-aged lives. From their initial introduction, soon after graduating from different universities, they shared a dual bond: respect for each other and dissatisfaction with the world around them.

"Mr. Olduvai, I've been looking forward to this conversation since you pissed me off last time."

"Well, I can't promise it won't happen again, Mr. Rueul. But really I'm just glad Ada is giving up her time with you today. She's okay? And Marga?"

"Ada's fine … thanks. She's been liking her alone time, so it's no problem. And Marga's back at school now. She left last Sunday. Her last semester."

Already!

"We're getting old, Jorge."

We are. And that makes time precious. So …?

"Go for it."

The last thing we were talking about, Sam … was … freedom, I think.

"Exactly when you were pissing me off."

Without warning or rustle, a dozen starlings flew from a hackberry tree beside the asphalt path. Sounds of joyful children spilled from a playground nearby. But the two men were determined to hash out ideas of economic delusion that had percolated in their talks. Their challenge this day was that

1

while they agreed there was delusion, Jorge saw delusion in society at large, while Sam saw delusion in Jorge.

How can freedom annoy you, Sam? I was trying to make the point that the only limit to it is fairness. Then you had to leave.

"Well, I have time now. And what you don't understand is that one man's fairness is another man's oppression."

Fairness is an equality of opportunity …

"See? That's oppression. I'm already annoyed."

I didn't say anything oppressive!

"You said 'equality of opportunity.' Equality—economic equality—means taking from someone who has and giving to someone who doesn't. And that has nothing to do with fairness. But it has a lot to do with the oppression of success."

Well, now you're not being fair.

"Why not?"

Because you had asked me last time we met what I mean by fairness. And now you're using your own definition to assume what I mean.

"That's what it usually means."

So you're assuming the usual …?

"You're right … I shouldn't assume, especially with you, Jorge. Forgive me?"

I might.

"So, what do you mean?"

Fairness is an equality of opportunity, nothing else. It has nothing to do with taking what belongs to someone to give to someone else. It's the potential in every moment of economic life. It's like sports that way.

"Economics is like sports?"

A good sport provides the opportunity for excellence to each competitor at every moment they play. That's a fair game, Sam. Otherwise, it will lack integrity and won't hold our interest. The same goes for a good economy; it also provides opportunity for everyone who's in it. That's a fair economy. Without the right rules for equal opportunity throughout, dishonor will infect its politics. People with the means will just jockey for advantage instead of honing real skill. Making the rules then becomes more important than playing the game.

"When you talk about equality of opportunity in sports ... are a person's advantages in skill or height or whatever still valid, without compensating competitors?"

Of course. Personal advantages are natural. Some athletes are going to be better than others—quicker or stronger, as you say. But when the game is good, the rules themselves won't favor one player over another. And the referees don't give anyone special treatment. A game with integrity simply gives uniform opportunity to all. It doesn't equalize ability.

"So it's the same in economics, I hope. Natural advantages, like stamina or brainpower or strength, don't need compensating either, right?"

Absolutely. Our differences actually make for good drama; they create favorites and underdogs and give us something to root for. It helps make our economic system popular.

"I don't think of economics as being popular."

Well, it needs to be, Sam. Everyone is part of the economy. So if the system isn't popular, the system is in trouble.

"A lot going on with fairness in sports, isn't there?"

Well, it needs to work, to keep people interested. It's why when stones or bottles are on the field, they're removed. It's all about fairness—keeping luck to a minimum so talent and skill can dominate. That's why games are cancelled in bad weather; heavy rain or wind can erase a difference in ability, or can change the skill set needed to win.

"Okay, but what does this have to do with economics?"

Everything.

"We're going to cancel the economy if it starts to rain?"

Very cute.

"Jorge, it's your analogy."

The point is that it's the rules and conditions for a game that have to be fair.

"I realize that. It's still a bad analogy."

Why?

"For the same reason we don't cancel the economy when it rains. Sports can be postponed. But economic needs don't go away no matter the weather. In fact, some needs grow because the weather's bad."

Sam, unless there's a huge event, like a hurricane or a flood in a place that doesn't normally get them, weather doesn't make economics unfair. But a muddy field can ruin a sport.

"Still, sports is entertainment. Economics is about the nitty-gritty of life. Professional sport is more of a fantasy job that only a few of us get to do. And we only get to watch while we're not busy earning a living. So it seems to be apart from real life for most of us. I mean, when you're watching a game, and a player runs and gets near to scoring, and the fans cheer louder as he goes, if only for a second nothing else matters. It's a transporting moment. I don't think about my mortgage. I don't think about the chores Ada has waiting for me in the house. I don't get occupied with whether my Marga's done her homework or not. But when I'm doing my job, those things occur to me all the time."

Sam, sports are reality. And we've been playing them for a very long time. Ask the ancient Greeks. They're a part of us.

And economically, sports are very serious. Just think of all the human time and energy we devote to games. Beyond the athletes and judges, think of all the manufacturers who make the equipment and souvenirs, the molded glass and concrete and metal in the stadium, or the cameras, microphones, and lights and the people to work them. And the electricity ... all the people and equipment at the power company. Sam, think of the human effort devoted just to watching at the stadium as you and Ada do, with the mass transportation systems or roads built to get you there.

"I get it."

Or think of watching at home as I do—all the video screens around the country needed to satisfy couch potatoes like me and the sports bar crowds. And all the food and drink we consume that has to be harvested, packaged, shipped, prepared, and served. Think of all the deals cut as part of a media broadcast ... with the talent and crew, the sponsors and advertisers, and the people who make their products.

"I get it, Jorge."

One sporting event can generate as much economic value as a small city does in a year. So how is it not part of real life?

"It's big business, no question. But there's a difference between being a big business and being a serious part of life. Athletes just happen to have some talent to entertain. It's not like they're thought of as being major contributors to society. They're just lucky to be skilled at whatever sport is paying big money when they're young."

The fact that one happens to have the skills demanded by their time doesn't mean they're a lesser contributor to society. Suppose someone invents a better-cooking, easier-cleaning line of pots and pans that makes chefs happier. Ten years earlier, the technology for it didn't exist. Ten years later, and someone else would have already invented it. So that person with that skill set is lucky too, just like an athlete. Are they also unimportant in their contribution?

"No, of course not. But there are degrees of contribution. You say 'demanded by our time,' but you can't equate cooking, or say what doctors, nurses, and emergency responders do in saving lives, with people who play a game for a living. You can't. Yet the athletes can be paid so much more."

So, why not equate them?

"They're not contributing anything real, Jorge. It's just entertainment."

Contribution is a matter of perspective, isn't it, Sam? Person-to-person, yes, doctors have the greatest impact, far exceeding that of athletes. However, an athlete who has become wealthy from his sport has likely inspired others to find their own abilities or has elicited joy in many, many fans. Could the huge impact on a single person by a doctor be equaled in significance by an entertainer's smaller impact on millions?

"Okay, suppose that instead of doctor, I said research scientist. And he discovers a drug that can help millions or even billions of people. The impact on humanity would be gargantuan, and he'd probably still make less than a top athlete."

He'd still be lucky to have an intellect to fit the demands of his day. It's just not for economics to sort through the morality of relative rewards. Money flows according to desires and rules. Market forces judge profitability, not morality.

But that scientist would be honored in his time and remembered in history. Jonas Salk gave us a cure for polio in 1955. The same year Roy Campanella was a baseball MVP. Don't you think more children are learning about Jonas Salk than Roy Campanella, by far? It's not economics' place to assess what history will remember. Historians do that. Economics is concerned with the present. And only part of the present—our ability to create or trade in products and services. All else, for the most part, is outside of economics.

Just as morality doesn't guide calculations of economic value, the judgment of history is not guided by profit. Many cultures used slaves to achieve economic success. And many business empires rose in violation of laws. Sam, influence and wealth are not the same. Economics and history are two separate and distinct judges.

Anyway, it's mostly leaders who are making choices that affect our many lives. And I'm not even talking about going to war. I can see by your face that I need to explain ...

"No, I get it. I just don't want to assume I know where you're going."

Good. Let's think of life as being divided into economic events, like when you as an individual are engaged in buying or selling a product or service, and noneconomic events, which would be every other moment of your day. And to keep it simple, let's also assume that everyone is good; evil doesn't exist.

"If you're not going to make a realistic example, Jorge, what's the point?"

Simplifying can make a point easier to see and not get lost—like viewing a single root in isolation on the forest floor instead of intertwined with scores of others. Evil's real, but it's an extra and twisty root when it comes to seeing how laws affect people.

"Uh huh ... we're saints now. Got it."

I'm not saying that. The point, Sam, is that we can be masters of our own individuality. We can come and go as we please with whomever we like. We are free in our activities.

"Now that's an ideal!"

But it's all potential. Leaders can impose rules on us whenever they desire. For example, I might not be allowed to gather with you and neighbors on the street to voice a strong opinion. Or we can be put under a curfew. We can be told whom we can't marry. We can be drafted into military service. And we could not say no to any of these things without significant consequences. Saying no to our leaders in the wrong time and place could get our freedom pulled from us altogether.

"Jail ... it certainly happens."

Even in the best societies, people are subject to such decrees from the top. So, in life outside of economics, we are not necessarily masters of our own fates. The opportunity to forge your own path is not always available. It depends on our leaders. Are you with me, Sam?

"So far."

Good. Now, within the—

"Wait."

What?

"If a war is fought for economic purposes, and I'm drafted, isn't my military service within the economic realm? You just said being drafted is noneconomic."

Our leaders determine the purpose of war. They can decide that the greater good is for our economy. And war itself will have a direct impact on different industries within our economy. But you, as a soldier in a war, are not engaged in economics. You're not buying or selling goods or services. Your needs and your chores are given by the military. You follow orders. Your individuality is mostly stripped away for the sake of the team. The larger thrust of a war can be about one thing, while the impact upon an individual can be something else. So when I mention freedom, I'm talking about the individual. That's where freedom, or its lack, is felt—in each of us individually. That's where freedom matters.

"Funny how soldiers have to sacrifice their freedom in order to protect ours. But I'm with you."

Any government is entrusted with power to do as it sees fit. The people's freedom wholly depends upon how wise and paranoid the government is in exerting its power. A dumb and trusting government effectively allows the strong to dominate the weak, so most people wouldn't be any freer under that regime than under a government run by a savvy but paranoid dictator. Freedom is molded by whoever holds power. So, outside of economic life, freedoms are regularly subdued or even trampled upon for the sake of a government preserving what it believes needs protecting—sometimes its own power, sometimes the needs of favored citizens, sometimes the needy.

And it's not necessarily immoral. It's just rare that a government can act in a way that treats everyone equally, except perhaps in establishing a national holiday. And even then, not everyone can have a day off at the same time. Politics and morality are messy within a community. Outside of economics, equality is hard to achieve. But that makes anyone's effort to promote freedom vital, especially in economics, where it can be achieved.

"So that was your point the other day."

Economics is different than politics or morality. From government's point of view, an unthreatening freedom can be found in it, because economics doesn't depend on individual character but on collective belief. Economic freedom comes from our working together. That's what trade is, after all. There's a logic to it that politics and morality don't share. And because a robust economy will actually strengthen the government that oversees it, a good economy can safely be the goal of any political leader. So freedom through economics can definitely be achieved. There's never a reason an individual shouldn't have the ability to forge their own path economically. But one born into dire poverty can't afford to even try. Without some luck, they're stuck trying to not starve. If economics is about individuals making a living, then economic freedom means no leader can ever tell an individual how to earn that living, as some nations have. But it also means no leader in power due to a democratic vote—assuming we, the people, understand our freedom—will make policy that steers us away from it.

"But leaders do steer us, and we do believe in freedom!"

It feels like a contradiction, doesn't it?

"Tax rates affect investment. Inefficient programs waste money and rack up debt. We're steered all the time. You're right. It is a contradiction. It's like they punch holes in the freedom jug, and it's leaking out. Those things eventually dry up the whole works."

That's because we don't know true economic freedom.

"Last time I checked, we live in capitalism. It's a free market. And how do we not even know what freedom is? Every election cycle, that's all we talk about! What do you think we've been talking about this whole walk, so far?"

For our full potential of freedom to exist, there has to be equality of opportunity at every moment, just as in sports. That's what we don't have. And it seems like we don't know how to achieve it.

"Of course we have opportunity. Everyone has opportunity here."

Yet you feel our leaders hold your economic fate in their hands?

"Well …"

So, what I'm saying is … if you feel that way, then you don't know true economic freedom.

"I don't understand how I could feel any other way. They're our leaders, our representatives. What they decide is always going to impact all of us."

Their impact is powerful today because they have little understanding of economic freedom and less for the nature of economic opportunity. So they make rules based on assumptions of how things work. Their misunderstanding becomes codified in our system. Stresses begin to show, then cascade, but in economic time, which can be decades. With a better foundation of rules to run the community, your life wouldn't be as sensitive to their decisions.

"Are you still talking about a free market?"

Yes, of course. But I'm talking about a true free market. It's where everyone's fate is in his or her own hands, with far less influence from political policy. Every presidential election needn't be about the future of freedom and the fate of the free world. It's misguided economic assumptions that force those issues to the fore.

The two men eyed a well-groomed, white Havanese prancing in red rubber boots along their pathway, its owner tethered a few steps behind. On the grassy commons were readers and sunbathers warm under clear blue sky.

"If politicians would just leave the market alone, everyone could control their own fate for the most part."

Not really.

"Of course they can. Everyone has choices in their lives. And they make them. Maybe extremists could potentially take it away from us, but that's not mainstream. And okay, maybe wealthy people will suffer less from a bad choice, but everyone has choices."

The wealthy not suffering for a lack of choices is just what I'm talking about—not that they should suffer. No one should. Opportunity means you're free to attempt a path through life. And that freedom is in the structure of the community, across the whole community; it's not a distinction between rich and poor. A bad break today can consign a poor or even middle-class person to desperation. Today, someone without assets is also without choices. Even a person with a job, but one that doesn't pay enough, can have to choose between food or medicine. Where's real choice in that situation? There's a growing number of desperate poor. And except for the temporary impact of some government programs, it's been that way for over a century. That's a persistent state of poverty. It's unnecessary. And it's not up to the rich to fix it.

"Who then?"

We all put the rules in place. Bad rules create economic desperation and, intentionally or not, typically shift economic power to the already powerful. I don't like bloated government any more than you, Sam. Shrinking government, however, is not about simply cutting spending. It's about cutting the need for spending. And needs depend on the laws that define society. We have to agree on how bad it should be for the poorest of the poor. Because that decision determines what government needs to spend. The infrastructure we provide will define the rock-bottom lifestyle that we'll let people live. Then, after that, the only thing everyone must be entitled to is fair opportunity. Are they entitled to infrastructure that brings water, electricity, or wireless communication? Are they entitled to sewers or roads?

"So you're talking about redistribution! So disappointing ..."

I'm talking about basic infrastructure. Fairness is not about equality of wealth, like you think I think. Fairness is about equality of opportunity. Rich or poor, we are due choices about our lives. Bad choices—taking a risk and losing—shouldn't lead to desperation, not even for the poor. No one with or without a job needs to be hungry or cold. In a true free market, people can maintain their dignity ... have choice over their fate, even after putting everything into a failure. When the right infrastructure is in place and the right laws, that's what happens.

Sam, a true free market will benefit both rich and poor together, not one over the other. The rich will keep their earnings—all their earnings—while the poor don't ever have to be without hope. Look, free markets, even flawed ones, have brought more choices to humanity than we've ever known before. And this will continue. Some semblance of freedom can thrive even under bad rules because it's natural that the societal contribution of winning ideas will outweigh what losing ideas lose. After an economic collapse, even the collapse of an empire, new leaders start making new rules, but it's not like crops stop growing and water stops flowing.

"I'm sorry, Jorge. I mean, your passion is terrific. I feel it too. But I'm sure I don't really understand you. I can't understand how you give the poor hope without giving them money. And money can only come from people who already have it."

The poor only need the opportunity to sustain themselves. They don't need money.

* * *

"So, when empires collapse, is that because of bad laws? Rome passes a bad law, and the whole thing goes to pot, from Lisbon to Constantinople?"

Well, over time, bad laws do drive bad policy. I know some empires have been said to have collapsed from debt. But debt, in and of itself, is not a bad thing. It's misuse of debt that is a bad thing—like using it to buy favor with the masses. And the need for buying favor on such a scale is driven by bad law. Leaders also know military might makes people feel better. And they know that giving away wealth to the powerful makes potential rivals feel better. But economies suffer when too much of the people's productivity is used to support realms outside of economics. Economies need reinvestment in themselves in order to flourish.

"I agree with reinvestment. But you're saying debt, government debt, isn't always bad?"

I am.

"Does government debt affect borrowing in the private sector?"

Yes. Always. There's only so much borrowing our productivity can sustain.

"Then by definition it's a bad thing."

Not always.

"Of course it is, Jorge. When would that kind of distortion be good?"

When it's necessary. Government debt might be necessary to help our recovery after a natural disaster or to fight a war. It might be used to meet our needs when the private sector doesn't, but that should be rare. If debt is growing year after year after year, then that's a bad thing. It's a symptom of something wrong with the system.

"How do you define what needs the private sector doesn't meet?"

Whatever is needed that the free market can't do, like military protection, assuming its funding is based on need, not favors. Or care for those who can't care for themselves—adults with mental or physical maladies, or orphaned kids.

"Except for the military stuff, charity can do the rest. Why should government?"

If charity reaches everyone who needs help, wonderful. But charities are free to make choices. So, because of limited resources or whatever reason, they don't necessarily help everyone. If charity is helping some but not all, that can be seen as unfair to those who aren't getting it. Government's role is to maintain a fair playing field.

"Not everyone is guaranteed good care in life."

No, not guaranteed. But we need to offer what we can to the needy, and to the best of our ability. Morality is what separates us from the animals. To get primal about it, when push comes to shove, we're all in a fight for survival. What separates us from animals is our spreading a blanket of communal morality over the struggle that affects even strangers. All people can expect some dimensions of fairness. Most animals can only hope to survive.

"There's a lot of needy out there. Caring for everyone is going to bankrupt us. Or else make government programs so big we'll become socialist."

Wow, Sam. It must be scary to think those are the only possible futures. There are other possibilities.

"I don't know what."

Look, I agree that government needs to be as small as possible. But the right size of government, if it's an uncorrupt government, is in accord with the needs of its people. So the key to having small government is to have a system that doesn't create unnecessary needs.

"Our system creates unnecessary needs?"

Absolutely.

"Why, because some people fail at capitalism?"

No. It's not about failing. Almost everybody fails; just ask a successful person about their failures that came before success. Failure's in the game. So people don't fail at capitalism; governments fail at capitalism. Like when a system consigns some people to a lesser life than anyone deserves, they don't even get a chance to fail or succeed, and society is cheated out of hopes and ambitions that never find a chance to spark.

"Then what would you replace capitalism with, Jorge?"

Please … you still doubt my being a fan of capitalism? When you brought up the collapse of empires, didn't I say that economies need reinvestment in themselves to flourish?

"Yes. Okay. But coming from you, that sounds like socialism."

Then the question becomes how to make that reinvestment … how to find the winning ventures that make an economy grow. So tell me, are they more efficiently found in a free contest among products and services or by being government selected?

"By the free market, of course."

I totally agree. See, Sam? I'm as capitalist as you. Capital—every product we make or payment we earn—should be controlled by the people who create it or earn it, so long as it's not to harm others. The imagination in the masses is always going to be greater than that of the finest central planner. The key is to unleash our imagination without threatening the stature of government.

"What does that mean?"

Government always has a role in civil society. That blanket of morality makes for a civil society. Only religion or government has the authority to impose it. So, for those who don't ascribe to religion, only government is able to enforce morality. It also protects us from those whose religion proactively opposes differences in others.

In the economic community, morality is only about fairness. It's the idea of maintaining a level playing field, so we economic athletes can, in a fair game, sort out for ourselves who are competitors and who are not. Fair opportunity is what's moral. And it accrues to all of us, because only equal opportunity allows every imagination to be voiced and tested. Who knows what wonderful thing someone else will come up with?

But because of the rules we use today, we'll never benefit from the many thousands of minds born into desperate situations—those who need to find any available job because their only reasonable dream is to put the next meal on the table. Many will never find a way to avoid taking orders from a boss for minimal pay and cannot think of saving for their future. Others are born rich, without having created any product or service. Some of us own valuable land. Others can't even afford cheap land.

"Hold on. Children of rich people do have natural advantages over the children of poor people."

Of course.

"So why does it need fixing? You agreed it's natural. I feel for the poor. You know I do. But the market brings out the best in us, overall, when it's left alone. You even said the free market is better than central planning."

I've no interest in taking away the natural advantages to being wealthy. But the way we practice capitalism gives disadvantages to the poor that they shouldn't have to endure.

"That's your equality of opportunity?"

Practicing a capitalism that doesn't systematize disadvantages. Yes.

"Then where's the money to help the poor supposed to come from if not from the rich? I knew you were going to piss me off. Every entrance to this park is also an exit, you know."

Why is it so hard to believe that I'm not advocating taking anything from the rich? A man's production is for the man to keep. I'm only saying there's an unnatural poverty with us. The fearsome forms of poverty shouldn't exist. There are flaws in our system—

"So you said. What are they?"

We tax capital for one. We tax everything we make or do that can be sold.

"What else?"

We don't allow people free access to land.

"Who gets free access to land?"

Anyone who wants it.

"The poor?"

If they want it. Or the rich, if they want.

"Whose land do they get?"

Whatever land the free market doesn't want to use. Land that you and I don't want to use.

"Why wouldn't the free market use all the land?"

In a true free market, it wouldn't be worth it.

"Geez, Jorge! Anything else, flaws-wise?"

No, just those two. But they cause the bulk of our problems. They act as giant nails that have split a great crack into our national playing field. This crack allows economic clout to leak from the lower classes to the upper classes. They're two pretty big mistakes.

"Mistakes! I can't imagine ... we've pretty much always taxed capital and owned as much land as possible. Why are they mistakes?"

That's why we're having this conversation—to understand our own economy. It's a class-altering transfer of wealth engrained in our system, that causes the problems we're forever fixing ... the problems we fight over in our politics ... hurling slings and arrows while debating whether it's nobler to free the markets or to help the needy.

"Yes, Shakespeare, that seems to be an eternal debate. But don't change the subject."

I didn't. We're destined to a politics of debating tax rates and programs because of these mistakes.

"So you think the rich don't deserve what they have?"

Not because they're rich! If one can earn a billion dollars, kudos. I'm in awe. More power to her. But the crack distorts things economically. It makes our poor greater in number and poorer than they otherwise would be, and our rich are correspondingly richer. Sam, if we're going to admire billionaires, then the flip side is what, disdain for the poor person who is working but whose family is hungry every day? How does he deserve that?

"There are plenty of reasons for people to be rich or poor, Jorge. Who knows what people do, or likely don't do, to be poor. But I can tell you stories of people who came from nothing—nothing—and became rich, even before they bought their first property."

No doubt.

"And there are stories of rich people who had big estates and then lost them. So when you talk about land, for one, it doesn't sit right. There's more to wealth than that. People have become rich by designing electronics in their family garage! Basically, out of a shack with electricity! Owning property is kind of the least of it, nowadays anyway ... don't you think?"

The fact remains, in our capitalism today, because of bad law, the circumstance of one's birth is way too powerful in defining economic freedom. And by freedom I mean the ability to choose one's path. Choices are severely limited for the poor, especially when compared with choices available to the middle class and, particularly, the wealthy. Escaping poverty today requires either a terrific talent or lots of luck.

"I'm not so sure of that ..."

Have you ever had a bad boss?

"You know I did. The job I had before this one. Remember? He was awful, a clinical narcissist. He's the reason I left there, mostly."

Right. Imagine being stuck with that boss, with that job, because the wages are too low to let you save, and being responsible for a family won't let you quit. And if you take a day off to find another job, you lose a day's pay. If you're poor, only the availability of government aid lets you stand up for yourself and risk getting fired.

"That sucks. But it's also a risk that comes with a free market. I'm not saying the government aid is natural. But having a bad boss is. And honestly, I hadn't thought of that."

The freedom that government aid provides?

"No. That unemployment benefits allow people to act up enough to get fired. I tell you, when the government gets involved, things go from bad to worse."

Sam, you only had the choice to quit because you have assets. Isn't there dignity in self-responsibility, regardless of your amount of assets? I know you'll agree that government shouldn't be in the business of restoring people's dignity. But the government definitely is in the business of maintaining a playing field that allows for that dignity in the first place. It means hope and dignity need to be available to all, in every walk of life. Dignity comes from choosing one's path, not from desperately holding what one considers an unsuitable job. Our laws have drained dignity from the system. Every free man knows he has to take care of himself. But a truly free man doesn't have to work for another man to do it. That's the hallmark of real freedom, and most of us don't get to make the choice.

"You say you're a capitalist, yet it's starting to feel like, when it comes to economics, we have nothing in common. I don't recognize what you're describing. People don't have to get a job? Give land to the poor. And don't tax capital? What then? And what does your government even do? It sounds like a mess, my friend. It doesn't sound like a free market at all."

I promise you, it is. Just give me three minutes to convince you to continue having this conversation with me.

"Only because Ada likes you ..."

Look at our economy today. The rich tend to stay rich. The poor tend to stay poor. Some move up, but not most. Most tread water—or actually slip down. We hear stories in the media, and I'm sure you can tell me one, of people who have pulled themselves out of poverty. But aren't these stories worth telling because they're rare? If it happened all the time, the stories wouldn't be so interesting or newsworthy. There's a kind of class stagnation with us that's not natural.

"Do you have something against rich people?"

Sam … not at all. I'm not judging the fact that there are rich and poor. I'm talking about the fact that the opportunities available to the rich are so different from the opportunities available to the poor. That was your own point a moment ago.

"My point was it's natural and doesn't need fixing. You're the one who wants to fix it. And I don't know how, except to take from the haves and give to the have-nots!"

Well, the situation we have is not natural. And it does need fixing, but not the way you think. Look, a true free market would let the rich and everyone else keep everything they earn. Yes, having money will have advantages. The poor won't have those advantages. Fine. But the poorest don't have to be so poor. The rules we've used to create our so-called free market have forced a hopeless sort of poverty to exist. These laws are mistakes sapping capitalism of its inherent freedoms and efficiencies. The consequences we've given ourselves are a large national debt and political tension between the rich and poor. Fundamental economic forces were not appreciated when we structured our economy. Poverty doesn't have to exist—not in the dire way it does. There can actually be comfort and dignity in being poor. And the rich person's money is not needed to fix it. The national debt doesn't need to exist. What does need to exist, for all of us, is some control over our path in life.

"Jorge, I love you, but are you dreaming?"

Did you ever have a dream that seemed like it could have happened? Even after waking, it felt real?

"So this is a dream of yours. That's all I need to know. The mistaken laws, how do they sap our freedom?"

I shouldn't have used a dream analogy. It's actually a possibility, based on logic.

"How?"

First we need to agree on the goal of a free market. If it's freedom, we need to be clear about what economic freedom is.

"We don't know?"

I'm sure you have an idea. As I do. But we may not agree. We need to understand each other before we talk about our economy's flaws. But before freedom comes the idea of fairness.

"You do realize, Jorge, I'm giving you the benefit of the doubt to give you my time. And I'm skeptical. I'm not the richest guy on the block, and I'd like to keep what I have."

I understand. Just realize I have to start explaining at a very basic level.

"Well, the clock's ticking."

So … we're social beings. We typically like living with other people around us. I warned you; this is very basic.

"Not a problem."

As more and more people live nearby, we learn that we have different talents and desires. One knows how to make clothes. Another can make furniture. One is strong and likes to be active. Another is weak and likes to talk. So we learn to trade, to take advantage of each other's abilities. Trade makes life easier and more interesting. With ongoing giving and taking from each other, we grow a community of economic interdependency.

Economic interdependency means that all active participants in the economy make a vital and respected contribution to society. And it carries through the generations to come. That brilliant researcher you mentioned before would never have had the time to apply his talents if he had to make his own clothes, dispose of his own household waste, harvest or slaughter his own food, build his own shelter, or make the comfortable furnishings inside it. What would he have done if he couldn't simply flip a switch for electricity or turn a knob for gas? Or if he had to invent his own lab instruments? Would the great athlete have had time to practice to be so good if he had to do these other things? Imagine a businessman if he had to design and build his own computers? Or create and haul his own inventory? In a good economy, every successful person is standing not only on the shoulders of giants but also on the shoulders of every market participant. A fair economy recognizes and respects these contributions. Garbage collectors, sewage system designers, architects, electrical and mechanical engineers, farmers, miners, drivers, computer programmers, painters, cooks, service attendants, doctors, athletes, and researchers all uphold a respected part of the community. A good economy finds fair economic recognition for everyone and, therefore, a dignity for everyone. This dignity is not dependent on the good will of employers, and it's not dependent on heartfelt politics in government. It's just part of a system built on choice. The rules define how widely economic dignity is felt.

"Don't we have that now?"

I wouldn't say so, not if some people don't feel free to quit the job with the abusive, narcissistic boss—not if able-bodied people are unable to find work and then have to depend on the government to feed their families. I wouldn't say so if people not taken with competition are nonetheless required to live in a competitive environment.

"Not taken with competition? What are you talking about … you mean the lazy? Or are they Thoreau-like nature lovers who want to commune with the woods?"

Let's not label like that. It's more basic. There's just no reason to think the talent or desire for economic competition is born into us in any less of a way than is athleticism or scientific brilliance. It means that while most people are naturally well suited to competing for work or creating new products, some are not.

"And you think your free market accommodates them?"

It's not my free market. It's simply a properly designed free market. And it does accommodate them.

"They become freeloaders on government handouts."

No. In a true free market, they don't.

"Then what happens to them?"

If they're able-bodied, they live their lives without help from the government.

"How?"

There are areas that are determined—

"Is that what the land is for? The available land?"

Yes.

"If anything sounds like central planning, that's it!"

Sam … it's determined, as I was going to say, by the free market.

"But—"

No "but." It's determined by the free market.

"No, Jorge. There's no free land in a free market."

What do you mean when you say "free market"?

"What do I mean? The same as anybody. The same as you ... well wait ... not you."

No. Not me.

"So how's yours different from everybody else's?"

Okay ... what is the most fundamental aspect of a competitive market?

"One can buy or sell whatever they want, if they can afford it."

That's already being in a competitive market. It's before that.

"Before buying and selling? I don't know."

Do you believe in free speech?

"Of course. We all do. Where'd that come from?"

What's the most fundamental aspect of free speech?

"You can say whatever you want, as long as it isn't unfairly harming others ... like yelling 'Fire!' in a crowded theater when there's no fire."

Don't you have a choice before choosing to speak in the first place?

"Choosing not to speak?"

Bingo. Fundamental to free speech is the ability to not speak. Would there be free speech if one had to unveil every thought?

"No. Oh my, that would be awful. Ha! Divorce lawyers would be billionaires."

Governments and politics would also look very different.

"Scary different. But wait. You're saying what's fundamental to a free market is the ability to not participate in it?"

To not have to compete in it ... yes.

"I should have brought my blood pressure pills to talk to you. You're saying that someone can just choose to drop out of society, get some land, and not take care of themselves? And that's fundamental in a—as you say—'a true free market?' Who's supposed to take care of these people? Me? You? Why should I, especially if it's their choice? In fact, I'd refuse to."

Actually, I said little of what you just stated.

"You just said someone could choose to not compete in a free market!"

In the competitive part of a free market, yes. But that's not saying, as you've inferred, that the choice means dropping out of society and not taking care of themselves.

"How not?"

It's a fundamental responsibility of everyone to take care of themselves and their loved ones.

"That's great. But how does one not compete and take care of himself . . . without taking handouts? How can someone choose to not participate?"

We know fundamentally that we are interdependent. Trade provides much of what's good in life. So someone of able mind and body cannot easily drop out of society. Even in living alone, connections to society are not completely eliminated. But with the right laws in place, one can choose not to participate in the competitive market, just as one can choose not to speak.

"I get what you're saying. But how is that easy without government handouts? How is it possible?"

As we've been discussing, what I mean by free market and what you mean by free market are not the same.

"Clearly not."

If I were to ask you the difference between the free market and society at large, what would you say?

"I'd say there are personal things that are not part of the free market. But the job I have, the home I have, and everything in it, including the food, is all a result of it."

By personal matters, you mean family and friends? Things like that?

"Yes."

So, aside from personal matters, your feeling is that society and the free market are more or less the same?

"Pretty much."

So that's your version of a free market. It's what we already have. I'm telling you there's far more freedom in a true free market, because a true free market has a competitive part and a noncompetitive part, in the same way that speech can be said or unsaid. Having that choice to be in one or the other will add immeasurably to our freedom. The effects will cascade into every single life, regardless of economic status.

While one cannot remove oneself from society, one can live outside of the competitive market. What adorns your home does not have to result from competition. Someone can take care of himself and his family by tending a piece of land, perhaps trading periodically with neighbors. He will not need the government to supply his next meal. He'll find self-respect and satisfaction in providing for his loved ones, without financial pressure. He'll be living a dignified version of poor. And still, he can choose to enter economic competition as fundamentally as he can choose to speak—or not.

"I'm beginning to understand what you mean about the idea of having a choice. But I'm sorry, Jorge; I just don't see how it works. I can't imagine how part of a free market can be noncompetitive.

"And also, how could someone unambitious like that even get land in the first place? You want him to just be given land? Then who's giving it up? It's one thing to have a dream. It's another to be crazy. Please don't turn out to be crazy, Jorge."

Sam, no wonder Ada loves you. Those are good questions. They get right to the fundamentals. But you'll have to decide if I'm crazy or not. We've only begun to discuss it. And I know … the clock is ticking.

CHAPTER 2

The Unfettered No

We still need to establish a common idea of freedom. Tell me if you disagree with this: freedom of speech is primary, including the freedom of people to practice their religions without hindrance or favoritism from the state, the freedom of the press to report on what it sees fit, and the freedom of people to assemble, petition, and criticize. But we also now include the ability to not speak.

"I'm not saying a word."

They walked into a shadowed stretch that sparkled from sunlight finding shifting holes in a breeze-blown canopy of leaves.

It makes sense then that freedom includes saying no in general. If one cannot decline something without harmful repercussions for declining it, then that action is clearly a forced one, not a free one. And I'm not talking about making a bad choice or a mistake. I'm talking about a situation where the one who says no can expect dire physical or financial harm for saying it.

"Like a protection racket."

Yes.

"Or slavery."

Exactly. Saying no to either is almost asking to be injured or to have your property ransacked. In either case, there is no "no." For there to be economic freedom, there always has to be a choice to be outside the competitive market. There are many less obvious examples in society where the choice is forced—where one must participate in an economic interaction, and so it robs us of freedom.

"Like what?"

Well, let's suppose a—

"Wait. Sorry, Jorge. You said people can live outside the market. How? Where is that?"

Outside the competitive market. It's like a suburb to the economic city that appears when the right laws are in place. It allows no to be said to anything economic except self-support. Self-support is every able person's moral responsibility, for otherwise you are taking from others. But we must have the right to say no to everything else in an unfettered way. If it's a constant presence as an option, it gives us fair opportunity.

"Everything? Huh. It's impossible to say no to everything, Jorge. Sometimes you have to suck it up and do what you have to do."

Even so, it can be everyone's choice to trade for a living, or work for another, or not. Those choices needn't depend upon having preexisting wealth to make it a viable choice. What's key with any exchange of goods or services in a free market is for both parties to find the exchange willful and fair. And that sense can only arise when both parties are free to say no without preordaining harm to themselves. Today, someone who is without assets and is hungry likely doesn't have that choice. There can't be a true free market if there is no unfettered no within it. I can't emphasize it enough.

"Poor people can say no to making money and still support themselves? Where are they? Mars?"

Not quite so far. We just have to be clear about the unfettered no first.

"Good thing I put you on the clock."

Suppose a major storm was approaching, and people needed plywood or plastic sheets to shield their windows and doors. The vendors selling those sheets could easily raise prices dramatically.

"They'd be gouging if they did. But it's supply and demand."

Yes. And barring a law against it, they could do it because people who wanted to protect their homes risked significant damage by not buying the protection. So customers can't reasonably say no. Their fear for harm means extra money can be demanded from their pockets. So a gouger is really stealing part of the customer's future. It's not the amount of money taken that's the point; it's the concept of taking extra. This is the pure economics, inherent when there's no reasonable way to decline.

"Why did you say pure?"

It's a raw economic force, a force that is ever present. Someone who can say no to a transaction always has the upper hand over someone who can't.

"Supply and demand. Of course. The coming storm creates a surge in demand for protective materials."

Except it is gouging, because the playing field itself has shifted due to the looming disaster. Supply and demand is more about the permanent conditions that establish ebbs and flows in a marketplace. A price from supply and demand is the result of the rules of the regular field. And a price, by the way, is not just about money.

"What then?"

It's the specifics of the agreed-upon exchange. If you agreed to sell me a first-edition book for a hundred dollars, then the price of your book is a hundred dollars. But the equivalent price to you for my hundred dollars is the book.

We might have haggled over it for days, or reached such a quick agreement that it seemed there was hardly a thought to it. Either way, once we agreed, there is a contract between us, which provides that we each receive what we have identified from the other—you offering the original printing of a book, and me offering money. And we both are likely satisfied, as both of us can feel we got fair value from the other. That's because neither of us felt forced, in any way, to participate. Either of us could have said no.

"I'm glad you think people still buy books. And a first edition too. That's rich."

I guess that doesn't mean much anymore, does it?

"Not really. Not when the first edition is a digital file that can be hacked and copied. Are we almost done with this basic stuff? I'm about to let you run out of time."

Just two minutes more, Sam. Do you see that economic freedom requires our ability to say no to any transaction?

"I suppose. But it's always going to happen. If you lost or broke your phone in a desolate area, the next person to come along could easily charge you money to use theirs."

Of course, Sam, incidents will happen. But I'm trying to get at the larger picture where a choice to say no is built into the system by the very rules that make the system—where people's life plans are at stake, not just dinner reservations.

We're talking about maximizing freedom. Since economic freedom means there's a choice to participate in the competitive market or not, the no has to be easy, or else saying no isn't valid. Even today, in our society, there are places that are clearly outside the competitive marketplace, where no is freely said. These places are where we perform communal actions. They're actions usually driven by personal caring or charity. No exchange is expected; nothing is given in return. The trouble with our capital-taxed economy is that people can't completely avoid the quest for profit unless one is already rich.

"Communal action?"

If I give an apple grown on my property to a friend, then that's a communal action. If I sell it, that's economic. If I choose to clean my son's wound after he falls from a bicycle, it's not economic. I might use hydrogen peroxide that I previously purchased, and a Band-Aid from a box bought long ago, which would have been economic activities when I originally paid for them. But my actual act of cleaning the wound is a communal action. It's not negotiated. I might hope he stops crying, like any parent would, but my applying antiseptic is not contingent upon that. In the broadest terms, it's an act of charity that stems from my caring for him. Communal actions are done without asking anything in return.

"What if Carom said no to you? Would that make your cleaning his cut an economic event? Would that rob him of freedom?"

Carom's in no position to say no to me with any force of reason. And not just because he's my son. Any young boy's no can be ignored in that situation. A small child doesn't understand that the harm from infection could overwhelm the brief sting from an astringent. He can only think of avoiding pain. He doesn't understand the value a little sting might bring him. He has no thought of future consequences of his actions. So he'll get treated. The wound gets cleaned.

"But you're not respecting his freedom if he can't say no."

My child is part of a community. So he must learn there are limits to his choices. He can't be allowed to make decisions that have a cost to the community. For example, he must learn it is dangerous to sneak up behind an elderly person and shout. He must learn it is wrong to throw objects aimed at a neighbor's window. And he must learn about cleaning a wound. He must learn to properly take care of himself.

"Why? Economically speaking, what's a wound got to do with it?"

Isn't the whole community best served by it?

"The whole community? Where's the economics?"

When a child's whims are left unchecked, the community suffers. He could easily, joyfully peel the wallpaper off your wall. He has to be taught not to. Carom once thought he could pick flowers from a public garden. But he learned it was wrong. A child has to learn that living in a community requires having respect for others. A child learns what can be a hard lesson, that your own freedom isn't allowed to encroach on that of others.

Suppose, Sam, I give in to his crying, and the cut is never properly cleaned and dressed. Then his leg gets infected. I'd need a day off from work to take him to a doctor. That means my coworkers would suffer by having to cover for me. The doctor would have to squeeze me in while her waiting room backs up with other patients. Suddenly, waiting to treat Carom comes out of their time—time they might have used to get back to work or to care for their families. Now Carom's infection, so easily preventable, is affecting a lot of people. You can start to see how the burden to the community is avoided if I just ignore the boy's cries and do what is right in the first place.

"Some religions don't allow using an astringent to clean the wound. Some might not even use soap. Are they entitled to their beliefs?"

Of course. But, presumably, those families won't end up in a doctor's office when the infection grows. So they won't be taxing the community's routine and resources. We must embrace such believers as members of our community, if freedom is what we're after.

"It's hard for me when I hear about such families. I almost want to kidnap the kid."

I understand. But our community decides when a child is old enough to be independent of parents. I realize it's hard. Emotions are in play when we happen upon deep disagreements. But freedom only exists when we are allowed to disagree with another, and another with us. True freedom exists only when we can disagree with each other and not be harmed for doing so.

"You always have to fight for freedom. Our country was founded on that."

And it's when we're arguing that we know we're free. But if we're fighting for our freedom, physically fighting, then we're not. Ideas need free reign in a free society. That means no harm can come to a person for having an idea.

"If their idea is communism, it's a threat to me."

Someone believing in communism is someone worth hurting?

"Well, not just for having the idea. But if they started to take over and move the country that way, I'd have to consider it."

Wouldn't the way to stop them be to make a better argument? Capitalism is a powerful force, or can be. It's certainly a beacon of freedom. How hard could it be to win the argument over communism, where government is very intrusive, and your choices are very limited?

"Well, it doesn't work that way. Communism's like a cancer. It spreads. As people start getting needs met by the government, they start to become dependent on the government. Eventually, that's all most people want. Life seems easier. You don't ever have to make big decisions. But there's a cost to that, a big cost. Communist ideas can easily take root here, or at least push us to where socialism could seem like a good thing. It eats capitalism from the inside out, and our freedom goes with it. So you have to stop it while it's small. I'm not saying as small as one man. But he'd be worth watching. It'd be worth being leery."

If there's a threat to capitalism, it's because of the way we practice capitalism. We're rotting ourselves from the inside out. It's bad rules that lead the government to try to fix things. And the more the government gets involved in the economy, the more you see your creeping communism. Like you said, it's a slow government takeover that gradually eliminates your choices over your own life. The very poor experience it already; they have few choices.

"So, you understand! But I'm a bit surprised to hear you say it."

Is it so hard to believe that I'm a capitalist at heart? Sam, I'm just trying to understand how an economy works from the ground up. And it happens to work far better when saying no is everyone's option. The nation would be better off, with better finances and more freedom, if we could choose to say no to economic competition. If we practiced capitalism better, creeping communism or socialism wouldn't be your concern.

"What would be? There's always got to be a concern."

If we had a true free market today? You'd be concerned with and taking care of your family and maybe with finding politicians who were sincere in protecting the economic playing field.

"That's what I care about now. What's the difference?"

When a true free market is allowed in practice, you won't be concerned about creeping communism because the government will have less to do. Most of the problems of poverty go away. So, too, does the government's need to fix them. And with a smaller, less involved government, politicians have less to fight about.

"You're saying if we practiced capitalism better, communism would go away?"

It's only big government programs that cause the fear of it. So I don't know that it would completely go away, but communism could never gain any traction here if we didn't have flaws ingrained in our economy.

"So what's the secret, Jorge?"

Okay, so we agree that communism is bad because it leads to removing choices from life, yet we've determined it's okay for Carom to not have choices, because he's a child and is still learning skills needed to fit into society.

"You're not comparing communism to a cut knee, are you?"

Well, no. But in some ways, even as adults, we're like Carom. We're ignorant about some things ... like a child is.

"This is why I like our friendship. Sure. We're both dumb kids. I'll own that."

So then how can we, as adults, make economic decisions when we don't know much about something? Should those choices be taken away from us?

"No, of course not."

How could there be a fair trade? I mean ... doctors and lawyers and car mechanics. I use them when I need to, but I'm pretty ignorant about all three fields. I wouldn't know if C134 was a part number, a drug, or a law. I'm really like a child to those professionals. Is that fair?

"People are allowed to be stupid. I mean, not you ..."

Appreciate it.

"But it's a free market for a reason; you can make a good choice or a bad choice. That's the nature of the beast."

Yes. But if that's all there was to it, every doctor, lawyer, and mechanic would be rich off of people like me. They'd choose what's financially best for them, but many of them don't take advantage. They maybe make more than average pay, sure, and some even get rich, but most do not. Why not?

"The invisible hand."

Yes. Okay. But what guides that hand?

"An invisible arm?"

Ha ha. Thanks for a smile. It's no that guides the hand. The possibility of saying no. Because even if experts don't respect our knowledge, what they need to respect—especially the lawyer and the mechanic—is our ability to say no to them. Someone can generally find another lawyer or mechanic to work with, and so we can say no to an egregious price for a service. Or we can say no if we suspect shoddy service. That's the key to fair pricing. That's what keeps everyone with a superior knowledge from getting rich off my ignorance.

With the doctor, however, there might be circumstances in which I can't say no because the timely delivery of her skills is critical to my very life.

"You can get a second opinion. Then you could say no to at least one of them."

If I'm conscious, I could. And if they disagree, I could say no to one. But then my no will be no more confident than a coin toss. How much must you be expected to know to choose wisely?

And there are those times you can't get a second opinion. It's tough to say "I'll think about it" to a doctor when you're in the middle of a heart attack. Aside from the exceptionally devout, who, when trying to hang on to life, would say no to timely medical help, if one could even talk at the time?

At other times, though, you can say no. For an annual checkup, for example, a doctor's services are akin to those of the mechanic ... economically speaking.

"Akin ... because we can say no without harming ourselves. It's just a checkup."

In terms of the pricing only. You probably shouldn't say no to a prescription if you get one.

"But that's why there are insurance companies—to set the prices with the doctors for you when you can't talk."

If the treatment you need is covered. But even then ...

"So it seems like there's a timing issue."

Timing?

"I'll use Carom again, if you don't mind."

Of course not, Sam.

"If you buy a box of Band-Aids while you don't need a Band-Aid, you can say no to it without harm. That is a free-market exchange. Right?"

Right.

"But if you buy the Band-Aids after he has fallen, then you can't realistically not buy them ... not while he's crying. That's why timing matters."

So, it's like the storm scenario. There's no freedom in the market when another takes advantage of my stress. Assuming the drugstore is privately owned and not part of some big chain, when I enter with Carom screaming, the owner could change the price. With no competing store near, he'd know I wouldn't say no to a modest increase. The question is ... would he use the power?

When I walk in with Carom like that, the drugstore owner has three choices; he can raise the price for Band-Aids, he can keep the price the same, or he can lower the price ... to the point of giving me one for free. But of course, each choice has consequences. If he chose to raise the price of Band-Aids, there's a good chance he'd make me angry. I'd probably post snarky messages on the Internet to make him lose standing in the community. I'd tell anyone who would listen. And I might never return to his place of business. His selfish, insensitive act, while following natural market forces, violates the very idea of community.

"That seems harsh, Jorge. I mean ... it might be stupid for the reasons you said. But to say it violates the idea of community? That seems harsh."

Well, let's see how harsh. First of all, we've established that being able to say no without harm resulting is the crux of economic freedom. Second of all, we know there's a whole realm of activity outside economics called communal actions, which stem from some sort of caring for others.

They're the glue of a community. If we don't care about each other as parts of a community, then freedom for the less fortunate disappears. When someone can't say no, he or she is vulnerable to anyone who can. Yes, I'm mostly going to care about family and friends. And I realize the storeowner has his too. So I don't expect to be treated like his family. But there's no reason I shouldn't be treated like a part of his community.

Sam, if I see a stranger stumbling and dizzy, and I stop to take her to the emergency room, am I then going to charge her for the ride? No, because we're part of a community. It's why gouging is wrong too. With this hypothetical bloody knee, an exchange happened. And the drugstore owner took advantage of my situation. But taking care of oneself does not require the harming of another. Even without conditions for a proper market, one is still within a community. Community is in whatever we do. When caring is so cavalierly dismissed, absolutely, the idea of community is violated. I wasn't being harsh at all. We're always in a community. A true free market demands that that be understood.

"I thought you said market forces are amoral."

I did.

"Then how is there morality in the market?"

Because a moral market is one in which people are free to live their lives as they see fit. While economic forces aren't moral or immoral, the laws that channel them certainly are. Any laws we write that limit choices for any of us are immoral, unless that choice is to harm another. And no is half of the choices available to a free person.

"Honestly, I'm still a bit lost. But it feels like you've earned your time. So I'm hiring you as my economics mechanic. How about that?"

Great! I'm very glad. We've got a lot of imaginary work to do on this vehicle.

"It won't be the first thing you've imagined."

Well, the fundamental forces are real. Eventually, we'll harness them better.

"What about the other two choices the drugstore owner has?"

Other choices?

"To keep the price of Band-Aids the same or to lower their price?"

Ah ... sorry, I thought we'd talked about it. Keeping the price the same is doing what, as reasonable people, we'd expect. By doing so, even though Carom is crying and bleeding, the owner is holding raw economic forces at bay for the sake of fairness. He may not be conscious of it, but he's respecting a true free market. He is valuing community, along with economics.

And his last choice … lowering the price? Say he hands me a Band-Aid for free. I would say at that moment he was placing community above economics. He has met my need with only a few cents of sacrifice. He engaged in a communal action, expecting nothing in return.

"You wouldn't know that."

Why not?

"You're not in his head. Maybe he did it hoping he'd get some free promotion? If you're going to blab about him when he screws up, wouldn't you talk about him when he does some good?"

Then your point is that he really wasn't doing a good thing, because he was expecting something in return. Sam, you might be right. But that wouldn't change his appearance of easy generosity or my feeling about it. To reach out to another in need is a fundamental communal action. If the one who offers it benefits, that doesn't alter its fundamental goodness. He's not asking for my promotion. It's just that he might receive it in the regular course of story swapping that people like me engage in. It would be newsworthy for us.

"Newsworthy? Band-Aids? I didn't realize you were such a gossip, Jorge."

CHAPTER 3

Honestly . . .

"Anyway, I'm not so sure I agree with you. Just because someone does a good thing doesn't mean they did it for a good reason. People can be very manipulative."

That's why it would be better to have basic laws that embrace the way we are. Our laws for business and economics are way too specific, given our nature. We're not robots.

"Our nature is what needs laws in the first place. We overdo it, though, with the specifics."

That's because we seem to only pass laws to plug leaks as we find them. But an economy can be designed that won't leak. As we've said, the economic forces don't know of morality. Economic forces will allow the strong to dominate the weak, with no regard for the source of that strength—violence, lies, blackmail, insider trading, or whatever. But those same forces can power a fair and moral system if the laws used to design their playing field are fair and moral.

We've discussed how laws prescribing the unfettered no allow price negotiations to be fair. It's also up to government to make rules about manipulations and lies. Being able to say no helps, but it's not enough. The free market, even a proper one, is lousy at ferreting out misrepresentations and fraud.

"Wait. How true does true have to be before you start this government intervention? And what happens to caveat emptor? I don't know about your free market, but my version can sort the honest from the dishonest, especially today. In this day and age, why would the market be lousy at finding dishonesty? Anyone can easily look up just about anything they want to know, on the spot. Isn't that enough?"

Sam, I actually agree with you there. As consumers, we have to do our homework. Taking personal responsibility keeps us free and the free market working, with as little government as possible.

But you're actually raising a few issues here. One is of economic efficiency. Another is the ability of an individual to find the truth, even when armed with the Internet. But first, we must be careful about this idea of "government intervention." Rules are required to form the game in the first place. In any decent competition, there is a governing body to create, review, and revise the rules, and field judges to enforce them. Just pick a sport; some combination of those will be there. If this is to be called intervening, then let's understand what we mean. Because creating, reviewing, revising, and enforcing laws are exactly the government's chores in supervising our economy.

If the chores aren't done, over time there is no free market. The game disintegrates into a mess. We're clearly not all saints. Without rules, there is anarchy. There is no freedom then, because anarchy isn't respectful of rights. Market forces would run amok. Guns and muscles would become legitimate negotiating tools; the market price could go to nothing, with goods being extorted on a whim. Thieves would win. Evil thrives without strong sanctions for the right laws.

Unfortunately, crime has been around for as long as people have. So, regardless of the form it takes—fraud or theft or violence—it's reasonable to consider it part of human nature. It's another fundamental force: people can choose to lie, cheat, or bully to meet their needs. We learn early in life how it works. We've had run-ins with bullies at school. And we learned mechanisms for crime from fairytales, movies, games—even the day's news. Cinderella's stepsisters lived better by conspiring against her. The wizard of Oz puffed himself up to command people by intimidation. But at the same time, we learn that we each have a conscience. And as a community, we draw upon the collective conscience embodied by our laws to keep our evil tempered.

"The wizard of Oz was evil?"

Well, not evil. But he was in over his head as emperor of Oz. His tactics to compensate, before Dorothy showed up, could be seen as an evil ruler's game.

"I always thought that."

So, by embracing the dark of our true nature and finding rules that work on a rudimentary level, we can guide economic forces toward a market that maximizes our freedom and minimizes our chances of getting taken. If we make that our foundation, then anything else is intervention. And I'd agree with you. When rules don't apply on a general level, but only to specific products or companies, that itself is intervention; the market is being manipulated. Even good intent can be harmful when rules cause market imbalances.

"Why do you say crime is an economic force when it seems more like an intervention? It only targets specific products or companies, right? You can't rob every bank, just a chosen few."

Crime is not dictated by laws of the state. That's why it's not an intervention. Unless government is corrupt, crime comes from outside the law. But the motivation behind it is the economic force of profit. If you're stealing bread to eat, or stealing multimillion-dollar art, the idea is to come out ahead by doing it. And the force doesn't much care how that happens. Some people will take what seems an easier path. They can choose to rob banks. People have made that choice ever since banks existed. Some become pirates and steal for treasure or ransom. And that's been a choice ever since traded goods began to cross the oceans. These choices are part of humanity. If cheating has always been part of sport, it will always be part of economics. Some of the wealthiest families in our nation first achieved their wealth through criminal activity. The families were robber barons or bootleggers or financial schemers, and the finances worked out handsomely for them.

"Yes. But that's not how economics works. That's crime."

Do you believe that markets move toward ever-greater efficiency?

"Yes."

Then it follows that some people will see a criminal path as most efficient. Economic forces are present wherever there is a trade. It might be fair, like trading money for some books. Or it might be unfair, like trading money for your life. The economics in these trades is simple; all parties are seeking the best possible price. The only difference is that the fair trade has an unfettered no built into both sides' situation, and the unfair trade does not. When the whole economy is structured so that no is always a legitimate option, yes is never said out of desperation, and we are truly free. The incentive for people to choose crime in order to profit shrinks drastically.

"People suddenly become good?"

No. People will be people. But if there's dignity in being poor, and opportunities to succeed are plentiful for those who want to try, there's less incentive to cheat. I'm not saying that crime goes away. Just that there would be less of it.

"That's a big if, Jorge, bringing dignity to being poor. But if that's there, then sure. I suppose I can see what you mean about crime."

You also brought up a question of efficiency …

"Efficiency? I did? I only mentioned using the Internet to research before we buy."

Exactly so. Imagine thousands, or even millions, of Internet-using truth-seekers, independently burrowing through all the files and memory banks out there; the reams of information that mix the honest with the forged, the statements and claims that need verification, even the omissions and oversights. Think of the tremendous effort of rummaging through all that to determine whether to buy something or not, and realize that each person doing it could as well be creating, innovating, or improving efficiencies.

"That's a free market. People choose how to spend their time."

They do. But now imagine another effort, with far fewer people, working out of a centralized, coordinated institution devoted to policing the market. They would take tips from us to help guide them, just as street police do now. Having this professional organization doing the bulk of the work to ensure that the facts about a product are really facts would demand far less effort from society overall. Making society more efficient is the government's task.

"You want the government to test products like *Consumer Reports*? That's socialism."

Not like that. I wouldn't want the government telling me what to buy. But it would be helpful if they made sure what a seller said about a product was true.

"Come on. Government already does too much!"

I want the government to do less too. But what it needs to do is what the free market can't. Part of this conversation is to understand that and where to draw the line.

Sam, I realize there's a romantic notion to having independent people—masses of noble truth-seekers, busy like ants, striving to find answers for the rest of us, especially in a democracy. It certainly presents a feel-good scenario, us looking out for ourselves. But a free market, profit-driven as it is, can be steered to mislead us. We are gullible creatures, almost eager to latch onto falsehoods. In any type of society, from fascist to free, humans can believe en masse what simply isn't true. A big verdict makes the news, and without having heard all the evidence, we decide the jury was wrong. We often believe that no news is good news, when no news can be hiding a crime. We believe in the simpler solution, because it's easier than understanding complexity. We like to believe that successes are pure and failures are pure, when reality involves many shades of gray. But appreciating shades of gray requires an effort that most of us will not allocate time for.

Naivety leaves us with emotions to guide us and model the world. Emotions are simple and usually understood quickly. They are given high importance in our decision making. The more emotional a story is, the easier it is to invest our efforts, or our money. But when we act on emotion, we have lost touch with the true economic forces. Because they are immune to our feelings—don't even know we have them. So the moment we react with our heart, we have begun to react in a way that pulls us away from economic reality.

We cannot win the fight against dishonesty as independent actors, no more than a sport would be clean if players were to call fouls on each other, or if individual teams hired their own referees. To regulate a market effectively and efficiently, there need to be police disinterested in making profit, just as sports require judges who are disinterested in collecting wins. This is a natural role for government.

Yet look at our politics: we'll work up a huff of passion to pass a law that helps fix a problem. Then we're generally satisfied, in the majority anyway. But the new law only prolongs or exacerbates the problem … until our feelings rise once more, and it's time to fix things again.

This is why, over time, regulations fall in and out of favor. It's why, over time, poverty programs are expanded or contracted. A financier wants to get richer, and so he works to change a rule to ease the pathway. A family is hungry, so taxpayers give them money to buy food. But wait, we decide the financier is now too rich, and so we put in a rule to rein him in. And then, what's this? There are too many families getting help to put food on the table, so let's cut back on the program. We're an impulsive community in our reactions to economic situations. We want something done before we really know what to do. We have to work our economics at a different level to find workable, lasting fixes to our problems.

This is why politics and the impact of dishonesty on an economy are so important. Would you be surprised, Sam, if your Band-Aid story was retold to you one day, but changed so that Carom had actually hurt himself inside that store instead of before we entered?

"You mean it got twisted, like in the telephone game? It wouldn't surprise me, no. But how is that economics?"

A false story can affect a vendor's profitability. If a rumor has emotional soundness, people will take it as truth. You and I and the drugstore owner would know the truth, but that wouldn't matter much. Once a falsehood is believed en masse, it affects markets. However innocently it might have first been told, the false story would hurt the storeowner's reputation. It diminishes his actions in every single scenario. If the story were that Carom fell inside his store, and then he raised the price of Band-Aids, it would make the vendor seem evil. If he keeps the price of Band-Aids the same, he'd suddenly be seen as an insensitive dullard instead of a decent guy. Or if he gave me one for free, his action could paint him as a sort of sweet-talking briber, betraying his fear of legal repercussions after my child fell on his floor. The lie wouldn't let him win. Some customers would avoid him. The longer a falsehood persists, the more economic distortion it causes.

"I see that."

In this age of quick judgments and instantaneous media, the stories we tell each other matter. Business can be harmed by a story that, while more dramatic than the truth, is nonetheless a lie.

But there is a larger issue at stake. This was a casual lie that had a real economic effect; a mere skinned knee and the rumor's emotional resonance easily replaced truth in the public mind. Just imagine the incentives for speech in the commercial realm, in marketing products and services for profit, where big money is involved. The rewards from a fabrication can be alluring, life changing. Larger incentives will provoke more deliberate manipulations of a truth.

The term "snake oil salesman" arose because lies were, and always will be, effective marketing tools. We even have a countering wisdom that has passed through the ages: "If something sounds too good to be true, it probably is." We are taught from an early age to expect and to deal with lies.

"But you're saying the government should deal with lies."

Some lies. Only some. When a pizza joint claims to have the best pizza in town, that's just free speech at play. It's a subjective statement, an opinion, and an integral part of free dialogue. This is where caveat emptor can operate without government getting involved. It's where social tools online can have a powerful effect. There are countless instances of companies lying through exaggeration, understatement, or silence to protect or enhance their reputations. And their advertisements present bold or exaggerated illusions. But it's not like we're all ever going to agree on who or what is best, anyway. I mean ... we have the statistics from sports—unquestionable facts—yet context always provides fodder for people arguing over who was the greatest. We have to accept our posturing and even see the bright side: opinions bring pizzazz to everyday engagements. They're a direct reflection of our humanity.

It's when commercial statements or omissions go beyond subjectivity, to mislead us from facts, that the government has a role—or two, actually—as censor and prosecutor. Misleading statements sap our economic energy by making us search for truth instead of producing. They can also be dangerous. False statements about the health benefits of a product or about the financial benefits of an investment can inflict real harm. People can get sick or die from false claims about food or drugs. Financial falsehoods cause people to waste or lose their money. These harms are often inflicted well before the market can sort out the truth. So government needs to establish rules for truth telling in vulnerable markets and establish a means for verifying company statements before their product is brought to market.

"Aren't people allowed to lose money on bad investments?"

Of course. People are allowed to be mistaken or stupid. But misleading people with a false choice is something else. It's only slightly less alarming than taking their money by gunpoint. Economically speaking, there is little difference.

Socially and morally, of course, lies and guns are very different. Lies offer a false choice. Guns offer no choice. But economically, they yield the same result. Whether it's a lie or a gun in your face, you can be made to choose against your own self-interest.

"Hmmm."

Lies can also come from corporate fictions of financial soundness, or from confident assertions of a company's preparedness for potential accidents, or within their response, or lack of it, to criminal threats. It rings true, doesn't it, that we are often told understatements, along the line of "don't worry about it," in the wake of a corporate faux pas? Few businesses, I think, would find it in their best interest to talk about their own chemical spill or a data theft incident. Most wouldn't tell a consuming soul if they felt they could keep the secret. Now, just because the history of commercial activity is rife with false promises, shoddy service, untruths, half-truths, and material silences is not to say all businessmen act in such immoral ways. Many have understood how to act and profit honestly. But the darker impulse is prevalent in our nature, without question.

The truth-seeking ants among us may find the smaller sins of our commercial nature. But the larger, more impactful secrets of business, the ones promulgated with a mask of normalcy that affect our bodies or the safety of our hard-earned savings, really need the force of state to uncover them. Even math and science can be abused when they're configured for profitability. So a neutral eye, an untempted eye, is critical to see the truth. Because the state is nonprofit and naturally in the role of referee, it makes sense for the state to police corporate claims. Food inspections matter. Drug efficacy reviews matter. Financial transparency matters.

Government's dispassionate investigations can allow legislatures, agencies, and courts to be as untainted as possible by the desire for profit.

"Are you kidding? Why would I ever believe the government is neutral? They're going to have an agenda just like anyone else."

That same flaw in our system that I'm asking you to wait to talk about …

"Yeah, yeah … taxes on capital. And free land."

Yes. Those flaws, in addition to creating intolerable outcomes, also create more temptation to corrupt government.

"But I'm not even talking about corruption, Jorge. I'm talking about an agenda. A government is political by definition. And controversies are going to be decided with politics in mind."

That's true. But just like the referees in sports, government employees can be incented to be neutral. I'm not saying there would never be bad apples in the bunch, but incentives play a big part in how fair the referees are.

"So what are you saying? The role of the state with your market in place would be different from how it is now?"

Both the role of government and of us would be different. If government is double-checking important claims, it frees us to devote more time to innovating and profiting. Productivity is lost when people are forced to wade through a morass of misinformation. From an economic point of view, lies are harmful; honesty is efficient. Certainly, some people see their own situation differently, and they end up sapping efficiency from the rest of us. It's government's role to make sure that companies place their product facts—all the facts, and just the facts—into public light and make them easy to access. Then the free market can interpret them.

"You want government checking all the facts? From every company? That's ridiculous."

No. No. Not everything. Most products are harmless, so not most companies. But food and drug producers present an obvious governmental role. I mean, who wants to risk getting sicker by taking a pill for a cold? Or dying from a tuna sandwich? Beyond that, it's only companies asking for extended contracts with customers that need the honesty police. They need to put in public view an unvarnished accounting of their financial status. These are banks, insurance companies, automobile companies offering multiyear warranties, companies seeking public financing, and situations like that. Because they need our trust over time, they need to show they've earned it. If we're going to give a bank our money, are we not entitled to know a true accounting of the risks that bank is taking? Are you not entitled to assess for yourself its financial soundness? It's no different than knowing the construction of a vault before deciding to keep your family heirlooms in it. Someone can call it a safe, but if it's a box made of balsa wood and painted gray, it wouldn't be a safe worth using.

Only government can ensure that a complete, unedited, and timely representation of the financial truth is produced and made readily available to the public. Essentially, an audit is a policing action. So it requires the same force of law as policing does to conduct an investigation. Unfortunately, because no one wants to upset the person paying his or her salary, a privately hired auditor is no more likely to produce the truth than a privately hired police force is likely to produce justice. Neutrality is something only a good government can represent.

"I can't wait to hear what incentives you think will keep a government honest."

Our conversation won't be over without it.

"At least we found a nice day for this."

They began to hear potent crisp riffs of pop music wafting from a distant stage.

"Wouldn't the desire for a good reputation tend to keep auditors honest?"

Yes and no. Private auditors are useful to a private company, maybe to review a prospective deal. But when the client is the public interest, a free market offers no mechanism to bring hidden truths to light … not before innocents are harmed. Profit is too tempting a mistress. If the private auditor is being paid by the very entity it's supposed to investigate, it becomes a situation where a negative finding might mean they don't get hired again. The incentives are flawed. The whole truth has to be forced out by law, without concern for profit, and with sanctions to give it teeth. Perhaps a nation of angels wouldn't be so concerned. But for us, it takes a nonprofit entity, like a proper government, to get the information we deserve.

Sam, you agree, don't you, that government only needs to be where the market doesn't work, nowhere else?

"Yes."

Do you agree that accounting, being akin to policing, is a natural function of the state?

"I can't say that."

Even if only businesses that make long-term promises to the public, like offers of insurance policies or warranties, need be subject to audits? Others don't need the accounting police. A free market is able handle transactions without help when the seller's financial soundness isn't pertinent.

"So no one else is audited?"

No. Only companies that require long-term trust from customers. It's not necessary to have government look anywhere else.

"Now you're talking!"

I knew you'd like at least some of what I'm saying.

"Why couldn't the market handle long-term promises?"

A long-term promise implies an ability to deliver, so a company's finances must be sound enough to back it. But it's wasteful for buying a product to require a degree in forensic accounting just to see if that promise is a good one. It's too much community effort. And it burdens a company to be subject to numerous investigations. So let the state do the work of getting all the facts out. We'll just interpret them.

"If a private company did it, we'd save on tax money."

Government would pay for it either way. But it must be government that does it, with the power to compel a full accounting. Because "off the books" is not an accounting principle. Anything "off the books" is, by definition, not being accounted for. A government must ensure that all the financial facts are in public view, so that we, as potential customers, or the private company that we hire, can interpret them. Once the facts are available, a free market can take care of itself.

"A company can still try to hide things."

Of course. But everything hidden has a path to finding it. With so many private eyes reviewing a company's books, the clue to what's hidden is likely to be seen. And remember—a big reason to hide things goes away when there are no taxes on capital.

"If that were real, I'm sure of it. A lot of people make a living by hiding money from the government. I'm glad at least you think the private sector can handle analyzing an audit."

There's a lot of curiosity and expertise among us, don't you think? If we didn't want to do it ourselves, we could just read a consumer website. I'm sure companies and entrepreneurs would sprout up, all happy to be paid for performing financial analyses. The need for financial industry regulation would almost disappear.

"Regulation? Disappear? As in none?"

Just about. I mean, sales practices warrant regulation because of the honesty required. But if a bank's internal operations, or any finance company's business, were operating fully in the light of public view, what financial regulation would be required? If the public saw things as too complicated or too risky, that company would begin to lose public confidence and customers and hurt its bottom line.

"Businesses should be compelled to give up competitive secrets?"

Businesses with proprietary secrets—special formulas for a soft drink, for example—can keep their secrets. But finance companies that market to the public cannot have secrets. If there is intellectual property they wish to protect, they can try to patent it. But every last asset and liability needs to be visible, to let the public see if their trust is warranted.

"How does public scrutiny mean regulations aren't necessary?"

Financial regulation is already a reflection of the public's taste for risk, but it stems from politics. Why not let the public judge directly? Remember too, with no taxes on capital, all the convoluted transactions conducted to avoid them go away.

"But integrity can be bought, Jorge. Even if the government could get all the facts out, wouldn't the free market's analysis still be subject to our human nature? A bad opinion is easier to buy than a full investigation."

But with a free-market competition in interpreting audits, somewhere truth would be out there. But you're right. Maybe it's a good place for a law to make sure that opinion payola could be punished.

"Oh? Your free market needs a law against payola?"

Remember—the market's not wonderful at sifting out lies. Bought opinions are lies. And lies hinder productivity. Since some people will sell their integrity instead of doing honest work, we need to make sure that's an unprofitable option in order to keep the market efficient.

"Like not allowing teams to pay referees directly helps maintain the integrity of the sport."

Exactly. That's why leagues pay them.

"What if the audit companies had to rotate clients every so often? They're not all going to be corruptible. That would deter dishonesty."

First, if the law mandates rotation in the private sector, we're not operating a free market.

"Ah."

Second, it keeps an auditor from knowing the regular practices of their client, which makes ongoing auditing more inefficient and irregular practices harder to detect.

"You think government employees are going to hang around long enough to make a difference? The same guy is not going to be auditing XYZ Company twenty years in a row."

No. Nor should he. Your idea of rotating auditors is a good one, so long as it's within the government. That way, when a new auditor gets the case of XYZ, there are prior XYZ audits that she can review. There's an institutional memory there—or at least the potential for one—that can be very helpful.

But look, most businesses won't need government audits anyway, because most don't make those implicit long-term promises. If their product claims don't extend beyond the point of purchase, there's no need for auditing. Even if there's a warranty on a small item like a video screen or a chair, the government doesn't need to be involved. These are easily handled by a free market or small claims courts. If a rubber ball I bought cracked on the first bounce, I'd probably just ask for my money back and maybe tell some friends if they were bored enough to hear about it.

"You're not making a good case now, Jorge. Government has to check our math, and we consumers are only able to take care of ourselves if we're buying a rubber ball? Come on. Are we children? It sounds like you don't have any faith in a free market at all."

Well, maybe a rubber ball wasn't the best example. Make it a toaster, or a painting, or groceries—anything where a durable promise isn't a major reason for the purchase.

"Or the vacuum cleaner I'm going to buy when we're done."

Yes. Oh? How late are they open?

"How late were you planning on talking?"

I wasn't. No. Do whatever you need to do.

"I will. Sorry. Family first."

I understand. Always. When are you leaving?

"Around five. Go on, Jorge. Plenty of time for you to keep talking."

Okay. Well ... if the manufacturer of your vacuum lied about it, you could end up in small claims court. But the market would be more efficient if the false claim was never made. And so the second avenue for our honesty police is to investigate the veracity of product claims.

"The store told me my vacuum will suck ... actually really hard. I trust they meant it in a good way."

Sam, do you ever quit?

"Nope."

So some people will say anything to make a sale. They always want you to feel special. Old and gone generations used to hear how every liquid was an elixir, and every shiny stone had a story. And people bought it. Sellers have seemingly lied and exaggerated about their products since the invention of business. This is why statements impacting our health or our finances require oversight by the state. Too much harm can be done before the market figures it out. But in other product fields, government wouldn't get involved unless the market deemed it necessary.

"When would that be, that the market deems it necessary?"

When marketing lies are the cause of suffering, that's when we demand that government do something about it.

"You mean write my congressperson?"

I meant personal stories and reviews of product claims that grab government attention. But if something slipped through the cracks, sure, a few messages left for a representative might get him or her to notice.

"I think it depends. If it's from you or me writing, I doubt they'd listen. But if it's someone famous or someone with a big wallet, they'd probably get heard."

No argument here. But that kind of tattling can be between companies too. I mean, if one company claimed their product was better than another's, the second company would want to have that claim tested. If either side found false statements, the issue could be elevated to the courts—the government—for a hearing. If a company claimed its vacuum cleaner was more powerful than another, but the competing company, or maybe even a consumer reviewer, finds that not to be the case, the claiming company would either fight in court or adjust their claim and would still be subject to government review and penalties.

"Parties can already go to court."

Yes, for a civil determination. But justice means criminal penalties can be imposed as well. That'd be determined by the community. Lying and cheating are not to be taken lightly within a proper free market.

"Honesty seems to be a big deal with you."

Isn't it with you?

"Sure. Especially with Ada, Marga, and me. But when shopping, honestly, Jorge, I expect lies."

That's probably prudent. But free markets without honesty can't be efficient.

"People and companies finagle the rules and truths all the time. Take income tax. I'm sure most cash businesses, like that guy with the best pizza in town, don't pay taxes on everything that comes in."

That advantage of a cash business goes away in a true free market.

"How? More police?"

No. There's no income tax. With no income tax, cash has no advantage.

"No income tax sounds good! It also sounds impossible. But it sounds good."

I understand. But for now, have we gotten to where we can understand each other about the requirements for fairness and freedom?

"Not yet. There can't be no taxes at all. And you haven't said who gets taxed. And your free land thing is hanging out there."

But we know that we need an unfettered no. And we are on the same page about honesty and how to enforce it. We needed to establish these ideas. Now we're ready for the rest. Or do you need to go?

"Do you think Ada will think talking into overtime with you is a good excuse for me to be late? We're going out tonight with friends. And I do have to get the vacuum first. But I have a few minutes.

"And by the way, Jorge, don't feel you need to bring a date when Ada and I make a plan with you. We can always go as three. Ada likes you, even divorced."

That's probably because you don't come home sweaty after seeing me, like you do when you play tennis or hoops.

CHAPTER 4

Taxing Issues

"So then tell me, where is government funding supposed to come from?"

Our communities are created by three elements that happen to be economically valued: land, labor, and capital. But land, of course, exists first. It's the quality of land that attracts people to stay. When people do, they work to sustain themselves. They labor to secure sources of food and the ways to trade with others. They build shelter and make clothes. All these items, by the way, and anything else a person can make or improve that is valued, is capital. If people are paid to work, they are paid in capital. Wages are capital too. So capital is the result of all individual efforts within the community. It's the product of an economy. Increasing trade in capital is what makes an economy grow. But capital and labor are only born from our drive to work. Land is here regardless.

"Okay. So where's the funding?"

Economic law has a dual purpose—to define the market within the community and to enforce the fairness of its operations. Taxes are primary definers of the market. They're really part of the playing field. Their presence alters the way we strategize the game. Taxes on the values of labor or capital alter their worth relative to any labor or capital that doesn't pay the same tax. The problem, Sam, is that finding relative value is what a free market does. Taxes that alter relative values must have a distorting effect.

So, if we want our economy to grow, why would we tax work or its products? Such ill-conceived taxes create these distortions and fundamentally cause feedback loops, sending normal balances out of whack. Like any tax on capital, income taxes turn economies from calm to qualm.

"You're not going to make your case with cute turns of phrase, Jorge."

Point taken. But still, income taxes go against free-market principles.

"Why? Death and taxes are the two things no one can avoid. They've been around forever. Well, at least death has been around forever."

Let me explain. It's easy to see the imbalance income taxes bring.

"My wait is over?"

Just about. A free market finds a job's worth through supply and demand. This is normally the lowest price at which an employee will take the job, or at which existing employees won't be looking to quit. The price, in effect, is the lifestyle that can be bought in exchange for doing the work. It's the total compensation someone receives in all its forms: salary, retirement funding, bonuses, and insurance plans that combine to buy a certain lifestyle. But ask for too much, and the employer will look for someone cheaper. In a true free market, the labor negotiation is about the work and its perceived value to both the employer and the employee, nothing else.

But when this negotiation is given an extra role, like funding the community's needs … then there is a distortion in the value of salaries. The market calculates income tax as an increase in the salary needed to buy that required lifestyle. A $40,000 lifestyle demands $50,000 in compensation when income tax is 20 percent. An $80,000 lifestyle requires $133,000 when income tax is 40 percent. This distortion of labor's value pushes through the entire economy, across all jobs and every compensation scheme.

You can see how income taxes that workers pay become part of the cost of every raw material and every tool and service. And why salaries for more valued workers must go up over time if income taxes for them rise.

For the entrepreneur, it's the same. Her lifestyle comes from the acceptance of her wares by customers. If she is able to sell to them at profitable prices, her revenue will include a portion targeted for taxes. Her lifestyle, like that of any capital-taxed person, is bought by what she keeps after taxes. And every business she buys products from will have the same need. Her pricing must rise, by the amount of tax, to give each owner and worker along the product chain their required lifestyle.

So income tax snowballs throughout the competitive market. It's built into the cost of goods as parts move from one level of production to the next. From the miner to the shipper, to the manufacturer, to another shipper, and to the warehouse, income tax is added to costs at every step. The distortion grows with every stage that goods are sold. Everyone expects a certain lifestyle from their work. And they're not going to sacrifice that lifestyle to a change in taxes, not without at some point looking for higher pay. Which itself leads to higher prices in order to maintain profit levels. So distortion builds upon distortion. The average lifestyle inevitably begins to wither, if only because the number of poor grows. And the only resolution is to have an expansion in government services. Unless … the country is willing to sacrifice its average lifestyle.

"What? How'd you get to expanding government?"

The poor are in the market too. If income is being taxed, the lives of people who are unemployed or retired are made more expensive, because whatever they buy is priced to support the lifestyles of those paid to make it. Pricing distortions are built into prices for everyone, working or not. Even what government buys for its needs isn't immune. These price distortions caused by capital taxes make both the cry and the cost for poverty programs ever greater.

"What? The cost of income tax is transferred to nonworking people?"

They cover part of it. And the more poor there are, the more of it they cover.

"And you're saying that doesn't have to be?"

I am. The irony is that these distortions from the tax, like exacerbating poverty by raising the prices that poor people pay, actually create needs that government must then try to fix. Ergo, antipoverty programs.

"I get it. You're talking about price effects in products and services."

But the problem is not just in pricing products. It's in valuing labor itself.

"So you said."

It's important to think of it in terms of lifestyle. Lifestyle is what's prominent in one's mind when applying for a job; it doesn't matter if it's a rudimentary one or one requiring great skill. The lifestyle a job provides is the crux of the value calculation and the crux of capitalism. Some people look more to a level of enjoyment from the work itself, but even then, the associated lifestyle still has to be acceptable, at a minimum. Or else, if the system allows, we're going to say no to it.

"You're repeating."

Sorry, but this means that those without jobs, unemployed or retired, are paying prices to subsidize the taxes paid by people with jobs, because everything bought—every single item—includes the cost of income tax. So the inevitable result of income taxes is more poverty.

"Wait. What?"

The cost of income tax is baked into the price of everything, whether the buyer has a job or not. That leaves the jobless at where the buck of that burden stops.

"The jobless are paying prices that cover the cost of income tax for the working."

Yes. Through paying market prices distorted by taxes, they fund workers' income tax bills.

"So they're poorer for paying the higher prices. And without income taxes, you're saying, that's not a problem."

Exactly right. Wages are given by an employer in exchange for labor. If the employer is going to profit, the capital labor creates has to be worth the wage, plus profit. That's a free-market result, plain and simple. It means that capital shouldn't be taxed at all; not the wage, the profit, or any of it, or prices will distort. And if the value of work is distorted, economic problems arise for everyone.

"If capital taxes distort value, what tax doesn't?"

Let's finish income tax first; there's another issue caused by it. A worker who is paid more for being a better worker ends up contributing more to the community. But why should a better or harder worker pay more to support the community, as income tax demands? It's a question that only raises eyebrows in a capital-taxed economy, because the taxes are then needed to counter the poverty problem. It's another distortion we've given our politics to sort through.

Of course, this mostly affects those who work, or who are poor, or who are working poor. People born into fortunes have the unfettered no and never need to seek out their value in the marketplace. They have won at life's roulette table, although not in life's competition.

"You do, I hope, believe that's fair?"

It's fair, so long as the accumulation of the wealth was fair. We're not naturally of equal ability or desire, so human nature demands that there's a disparity of wealth among us. As a society, we'll even tolerate a fairly large disparity. Good work deserves good rewards. Poor work deserves far less. So long as it is fairly achieved, disparity doesn't mean that ones with more must support the ones with less. We don't even seem to mind a little luck in the mix. The children of these good workers and the otherwise lucky will naturally benefit from this. But a truly free market demands that fairness be defined as equality of opportunity. We become so focused on money that we don't see that fairness is really about having opportunity, not money. Money results from economic actions. But it's our ability to act on if or how we make money that actually needs to be fair.

"This is about the unfettered no, again?"

Yes. Exactly. This is what it's for—to provide fairness of opportunity. Without a widely held sense of equal opportunity, the system starts to feel unfair. It's for each community to decide the point at which that happens. If the collective weight of inherited luck begins to warp the feel of a level playing field, it will threaten the integrity of the game.

"So, there's inheritance tax?"

I didn't say that. When opportunity is universal, when everyone can always say no in an unfettered way, inheritance taxes aren't needed. But if the community perceives unfairness, and politicians are forced to respond, inheritance taxes would be the least economically damaging way to address it. At least it's not taking earnings from the people who earned it.

"Who did the work, if not the person who built the estate?"

The deceased did the work to build up the wealth, true. But estate tax isn't taking from the deceased. Estate tax is paid from what the family survivors didn't themselves earn, to address concerns in the community they're still enjoying. If or when they establish their own paths, they'll have significant advantage over those without an estate to inherit.

The dead can only possess capital through artificial surrogates like trusts. But if capital taxes disappeared, so too would estate-warping trusts.

"How large an estate would this affect?"

You mean, if estate tax is even needed at all. It's up to each community. If the system were perceived as fair, estate tax wouldn't be needed.

"Then ... so far, government funds don't come from anywhere."

Obviously they come from somewhere. However, let's stay on point for now. We'll come back to the government's revenues.

"Why can't you talk about something when I bring it up?"

Because I know when you're going to leave, and I asked you here. I'm trying to say this with as few words as I can.

"I hadn't noticed. Go on."

Since valuing labor is an economy's most significant transaction, an efficient economy needs the agreement between employer and employee to be without distortion. We know it must be without income taxes. But it must also be in a market where both parties can easily walk away.

"Walking away … ladies and gentlemen, things are starting to connect. The unfettered no is in the building!"

Well, we're outside, in Central Park. But yes, it's in the building.

"Jorge, I was making an Elvis reference."

Oh. Ah. Didn't mean to step on your blue suede shoes …

So, Sam? Here's the scenario: a job applicant expects a secure lifestyle, while the company seeks improved productivity. The two sides have a good reason to meet. But, in a true free market, even if the applicant is jobless, he has a tolerable life. Anyone can walk away from a job offer if it doesn't offer enough. No one even needs to have a job, because there is a still viable lifestyle available to community members. Having the choice of a viable jobless life is the only way to never feel desperate to take a job. This is the basis for the unfettered no.

"How is not working, and let's say with kids to support, an unfettered choice? And you promised you're not taking from the rich to do it."

The first thing man ever learned in all of history is how to live off the land. If arable land were available to everyone, anyone could say no to anyone else. It doesn't mean self-sufficiency is an easy life. One still has to work. The responsibility to take care of yourself and your family doesn't go away.

"Is this why you want to give free land to the jobless?"

Not willy-nilly giving it to them. It's more like making land available to anyone who chooses not to work for another.

"I should start the clock again. You're crazy."

We're almost at the point where it all makes sense.

54

"One minute. Understand? I've only got one life here, Jorge."

I'm not wasting your time.

"I'll judge that."

In our economy today—what we call a free market, although it's not—some people have to take the next job they find, at any price, just to feed their family or put a roof over their heads. That kind of desperation is what gives employers leverage to move the price of labor down from true free-market levels, especially where work is for the unskilled, or seen as a commodity. Salaries are simply cheaper when employees have no alternative. The advantage is tremendous when someone who can easily say no is negotiating with someone who can't. This means the financially stressed earn less than they otherwise would. And because the amount of a satisfactory profit remains the same, the company owners can take what's levered away from their lower employees and earn more for themselves. It's man-made law that causes desperation in low-paid workers and perpetuates a whole class of needy people.

"If the government stopped trying to fix it, it would sort itself out."

If the government stopped trying to fix a system like ours—that taxes capital and lets all land be claimed—the poor wouldn't stand a chance. Their lifestyle would degrade into perpetual starvation.

"That's why we have welfare programs, to address that."

I thought you wanted government to be as small as possible. I'm describing a way to shrink all those welfare and fix-it programs without leaving anyone without a chance for a decent life.

"That's the only reason I'm still listening to you."

I'll take it.

"I don't blame you, really. This free-market thing is tricky."

What's tricky is trying to maintain the unstable market we have. You may not agree with the solution, but you can see why some people fear our current market. The problem is that we don't have a truly free market. The leverage that employers have to push salaries down is unrelenting. In a true free market, that leverage would evaporate. Gone.

"What about minimum wage laws? Not that I'm a fan, but for people with a job, wouldn't they counter that desperation? Of course, I realize many more will end up unemployed."

I'm not a fan either. So I agree with you, but for different reasons. If there's a minimum wage, and a company wants to grow, they'll hire regardless of wage laws. The problem is really the distortion—the tendency for anyone not on a salary, including the poorest of the poor, to pay the higher prices that begin circulating through the economy to account for the legislated increase in wages.

When self-sufficiency is an option, an always attainable, practical option, there is no desperation that others can take advantage of. The leverage that one person can have over another drains out of the system. Capitalism is opened up to maximize freedom when every transaction is structurally fair like that.

"What do you mean by opened up?"

Opened up means there's a way to leave it—to leave the competitive system altogether. That's the unfettered no. It relieves the pressure that comes from forcing everyone to be economically competitive. A closed economy is like that cage with too many mice inside; they turn against each other, and only the stronger or nastier mice win. Capitalism needn't be a cage where the economically stronger can take undue advantage of the weaker. They'll have advantages, sure, but they won't be able to use them in unfair ways. If we just put a doorway on the cage wall, let the mice freely come and go, then the stresses and villainy sparked by our mis-legislated system never need to happen. Even weak mice aren't kept from having a mouse's life. Open up capitalism, and the competitive will battle it out with each other. The rest can live without combat, sustaining themselves on free land. When I explain how that happens, you'll see.

Opening an economy restores economic power to the unskilled worker. He's no longer seen as a dime a dozen, taking anything to provide some semblance of a paycheck. Employers will need to pay a full, fair market value for their hires in order to attract them over a viable jobless life.

"And why would employers go for this, Jorge, if their employment costs go up?"

Because total costs wouldn't go up. Only lower-end workers would be paid more. Higher-end workers, who are currently paying income tax, could have lower salaries after those taxes go away and still have their lifestyles. Then too, there would be no taxes on income or profits, none at all. And the costs of supplies will shrink when capital taxes aren't embedded in prices.

"Well ... maybe ..."

We can't be freed from the problem of poverty until capital is freed from taxes. Besides, why should a capitalist accept laws that make capital more expensive in the first place?

I'm not saying it's our fault, Sam. Mankind has been doing this for over a thousand years. That's a lot of acceptance to overcome. It's felt normal for a long time. There's an old joke about two young fish happily swimming together. And coming toward them is an old fish. As they pass each other, the old fish asks, "How's the water, boys?" The young fish swim on, until one stops and asks the other, "What's water?" The tax system is our water. But, unlike fish, we're capable of changing it. Taxes can be changed to reflect the value of economic opportunities instead of reflecting the value of lobbying and favors, as they do today. Our bitter politics is from our swimming in stale water.

"Hold on. Salaries are a deductible expense for businesses. So that washes out your theory."

Not exactly. Companies don't have lifestyles. People have lifestyles. It's always people who ultimately pay income taxes—be they the company's employees or anyone who buys their products. So long as some people in a community, whether working or not, are paying a tax while others don't, the distortions will occur.

So, yes, we have a complicated system, Sam. But changing it to align with fundamental forces will make a far simpler one. The lowest paid will naturally have a living wage, without any aid from government. So the numbers of working poor—people who have a job and still live in poverty—will shrink to almost nothing. And the unemployed poor won't need any extra help to get by. That's what true equality of opportunity means to all of us, and all government has to do to achieve it is to pass the right laws.

"How can it be? What unemployed person can say no to a job offer without being concerned about it? Who ever heard of that? Jorge, in fact, the opposite is true. The world is filled with desperation. And unless someone already has enough money, there's no such thing as a tolerable jobless lifestyle. It's either have money or depend on government help.

And you want to give them land? It's wrong, I'm telling you, to ask me or any employed person to give enough to make someone else's jobless life tolerable."

I would never ask you to part with a single dime or a single acre of what you've earned ... unless it was for charity. But that's the same choice a true competitive market is founded upon; it's the ability to give or not, to do or not, or to join or not, without being faced with desperation, homelessness, or hunger. Only when that freedom is fact can there be minimal government involvement and minimal government expense.

"That sounds so counterintuitive. Where does this other lifestyle come from?"

It comes naturally when we're not distorting things. So we need to understand where laws should and shouldn't be, and where taxes should and shouldn't be. Much of our political rancor stems from ignorance about this. And ignorance is even worse than favoritism when it comes to distorting an economy. Economic forces are as natural as light. But poor understanding is like a lightbulb put in the wrong place to illuminate a painting; the glare can blind us to what we should be seeing. In economics, those moments of blindness can inadvertently affect millions of people.

Sorry. I think I've strayed ...

"No sweat. Hey, some people dream about sex. But you ... you dream of a better tax code!"

I dream just fine. You'd be jealous of my dreams.

Anyway, people won't easily shrink their lifestyle for something like taxes. They'll look for ways to offset the cost, and if they have the leverage to do it, raising prices or lowering salaries are logical places to start. It doesn't matter if you're giving speeches or making car parts. As long as some people pay and some don't, taxes on capital push the disparity between rich and poor ever wider.

"That's what causes income disparity?"

That's what causes the exaggeration of it. There are naturally higher and lower salaries, of course, but the incredibly wide difference between high and low is because of our water. Taxes on capital make the poor poorer, while at the same time the closed economy enables value to be pried from low-end labor. This one-two punch forces most workers to give up part of their true worth to those who benefit from their labor, upper management and owners. Wealth ends up concentrated in the pockets of a relative few.

"Umm … I'm telling myself, 'He doesn't hate the rich. He doesn't hate the rich.'"

Sam, you know I don't. But there are three classes to consider: poor, rich, and middle class. Poor and rich we've talked about, but not the middle class. Our economic design is devastating to them when there aren't government programs to aid them. And it's not their fault. Look, here are two statements: one, supply and demand determines the price at which there is a will to trade; and two, income taxes make the cost of goods and services higher than they would otherwise be. Can we accept that they're both true?

"Supply and demand definitely sets the price. And taxes are factored into prices. So yes."

Good. Now let's imagine the market for staples—not staples for a staple gun but the universally consumed things we need, like fruits and grains. Sellers of basic items like these have little room to absorb increased costs because profit margins are already thin. So when costs go up, and the seller's lifestyle becomes threatened, then the price must follow—up. Because at some point she'll either raise prices on her goods, or she'll lose money.

"The market's not as unified as you're claiming. In the city, I can go to four different stores and get four different prices on the same basic thing."

I'm not claiming it's unified. I'm only talking about tendencies. There is always the general tendency for an owner to raise prices to offset higher capital taxes. It follows that by taxing some of us, we are creating disparities that hurt all of us.

"You can't simply raise prices because you want to. That's not how markets work. There has to be enough demand so that your industry can raise prices too, or the price won't stick. I don't mean collusion. It's just the way of competition. If your competitors don't raise prices too, you'll be undercut and lose sales."

Exactly right. And that's the industry-wide tendency when any tax on capital is raised. Whether or not the higher prices stick in every instance is something else.

"Fair enough."

And so, as the poor grow poorer and the rich get richer, taxing capital puts pressure on the middle class—enough that over time it'll shrink as a percentage of the population.

"Where did that come from?"

It's another warping tendency from taxing capital. Like finding different prices for the same thing, the effect won't be uniform. But it works like this: The poor basically have to buy what they buy in order to get through each day. Their shopping lists typically don't have unnecessary items on them. Or, another way to put it, there's little elasticity in their budgets. So when prices rise, from increased taxes or otherwise, it's likely that an item or two will fall off their list. The unwelcome result is that their lifestyle is correspondingly shrinking, ever toward mere subsistence, toward desperation. Because the poor in a flawed economy, without laws or programs to aid them, don't get to add things to their lists.

The rich, on the other hand, can generally absorb a tax increase without any alteration of their lifestyle. Perhaps they'll shift assets to minimize a new tax on capital, but the rich won't need to curtail purchases of daily items to deal with it. And being forced to buy a smaller yacht due to higher taxes doesn't count. Not while a poor person, due to the same tax, might have to choose between buying apples and buying bread.

"The rich change their state of residence to avoid estate taxes. That's a change in lifestyle."

Yes, but that's a change in location, not a change in consumption. And keep in mind that in a truly fair economy, estate taxes, whether state or federal, would likely not exist. If they did, it would be to satisfy the community's psychology of fairness. But I see your point. The difference between estate tax and other taxes is that they aren't applied to daily living. They don't affect daily lifestyle choices, per se, the way other taxes do. Someone who needs to change residency status to avoid state estate taxes isn't likely to have to stop buying fine foods or fine cars.

So here we are. If capital taxes push the poor to become poorer while the wealthy are still able to function in rarified air, we can start to see what happens to the middle class. They're more budget constrained than the rich, but unlike the poor, they buy more than just basic necessities. All else being equal, they'll quickly adjust their spending to accommodate a rise in prices or taxes, most likely by dropping more luxurious items. In other words, the middle class can choose to cut back on their spending, while the poorest really cannot, and the rich don't need to. When it comes to daily spending, middle-class workers are the most price-sensitive.

"How does this shrink them?"

Successful business owners are usually in the middle or upper classes, not the poor, right? So when a rise in capital taxes hits the population, what happens to profits? With all else being the same, they go down. You rightly pointed out that a seller couldn't just raise prices willy-nilly, because there's competition. Owners of average wealth are often competing against much wealthier owners. When taxes rise on capital, the middle-class owners will feel pressure to protect their lifestyle sooner, and so they will try to raise their prices first. But if they do raise them, and the wealthy owners don't follow, they'll lose sales. The middle-class owners will either have to accept less profit and less of a lifestyle or be pushed out of business.

Again, it's not that it happens in every case, but it is a tendency in a capital-taxed economy. We all know stories, for example, of how large stores have forced smaller stores out of business. And when combined with wage pressures, due to our missing unfettered no, the shrinking of the middle class is only exacerbated.

"I see why you say it's natural for the middle class to shrink."

And if it's shrinking in a capital-taxed system, it means there's a far smaller number of far richer people who are getting richer still. It won't be shrinking because they're getting rich. It'll be shrinking because more of them are becoming poor. And the poverty in our system is very difficult to rise out of.

You might think a progressive income tax system, where the poor don't pay income tax and the wealthy pay a lot, could fix the problem, but it can't because it's still a tax on capital. So when taxes are raised to fund fix-it programs, even if the tax falls directly on the rich, the pricing pressure on staples grows. It's an inflationary pressure that can eventually drive those who are merely poor down to levels of bare subsistence or worse, and itself cause the middle class to shrink. Welfare programs end up fighting their own effects.

It's an ongoing, never-ending, economic force; people with no flexibility in their financial lives can find themselves at the mercy of those who have that flexibility. It's not that people are evil. It's that we don't see the problem, the way poor young children don't know they're poor, and rich young children don't realize they're rich: it's our water. Laws that pressure the poor are just what we've grown up with. Taxation on capital is all we've ever known.

So, combine this with no unfettered no, and the leverage of owners over others becomes unbeatable. Their power to keep salaries low pushes ever more people toward poverty. Even the employed can see their compensation cut the next time they're up for a review.

"Salaries aren't so easy to cut."

Not for individual workers, no. But without government intervention, cuts work like boiling a frog by first putting it cold water. Over time, as new workers are hired, older ones leave, benefits change, and slowly, overall labor costs for a company can shrink.

Even a whiff of economic desperation allows companies to be more profitable than they would otherwise be, and allows company owners to be richer. Artificially low salaries paid to workers allow those unseen savings to become artificially high incomes for company owners and company leaders. And people who leverage their capital ownership through finance or investing can amass even more. A good part of the concentrated wealth and widespread poverty we have comes from recapturing the wages of labor—and redistributing them up, because of the structure of our economy. This is the cause of the cartoonishly wide disparity in incomes we live with.

"My salary's not so low. In fact, I've been getting a raise each year. Only a little, but still …"

The general downward pressure on salaries doesn't apply when there's demand for certain skills in the workforce. Obviously, you're one of those skilled people, Sam. And you were never one of the lowest paid.

Even so, you'd have to consider yourself somewhat lucky to have your job. Had you been desperate at the time you were looking to get away from your old boss, you would have had to take the first job you could find. And there's a good chance it would have been well beneath your abilities.

"Maybe so."

Can we see how a poorly designed capitalism creates large and growing numbers of desperate people? And slower-growing numbers of rich people who are able to leverage that desperation? Our own laws are what cause this splintering—a growing poverty of the masses against the growing wealth of what will always be the few.

This is why widespread economic freedom begins with the unfettered no. It allows economic forces to dissipate throughout the community instead of clumping around one group or another. Desperation can't persist in the face of no. A true free market allows a man the economic burden of his own doing, but not an economic burden from his own birth.

"Sounds noble, Jorge."

Our world is without true free markets. People holding onto the lower and middle rungs of economic success deal with a pressure that persists generation after generation. Our market design forces them, every so often, to accept a lesser lifestyle and grow slowly poorer as a class. And that becomes ever more difficult to accept as others in society, richer, clearly thrive. So, if not helped enough by government, they are forced to make a choice: accept it or band together. Only a collective effort gives them negotiating power, enough to have the clout to protect, and even enhance, their lifestyle.

"Unions?"

Labor unions are a natural outgrowth of a market that isn't truly free. The need for them only comes from the desire to not be impoverished.

"You're saying unions are the answer?"

No. They're an answer for a poorly structured economy. A true free market empowers individuals to not need collective bargaining to maintain their lifestyles. Look, one might not like unions. One might even resent unions. But they're only a sign of a flawed marketplace. Erasing unions from a flawed marketplace means there will be more poor people. Those who want to degrade unions would be better served by looking deeper—to eliminate the flaws in the economic marketplace that cause their need in the first place. Whenever people are willing and able in body and mind to care for themselves and their loved ones but can't see how to accomplish it without help from others, the community has a clear sign—a real clue—that it has not engineered a truly free market.

"Unions already have too much power. They're destructive. They've brought companies down. And they threaten government solvency. It's like we're held hostage to their demands."

Sometimes union requests are overdone, Sam. No question. A strike can bring a company to its knees. I suppose, as they say, power corrupts. But it works both ways. Both corporate leaders and union leaders are corruptible. And while it's not exactly corruption, politicians dealing with unions often promise far too much, simply because it's easier than a tough negotiation that might cost them votes later. It's not a pretty situation, to be sure. It's certainly not economically efficient. But in a true free market, unions wouldn't be fueled by the very palpable pressure of falling wages. Individual workers would have the power to price their skills and ability on their own, without needing the power of a group. The incentive to unionize would practically vanish.

Workers need to band together when the economy is closed. When an economy is open, with an unfettered no at play, all labor is empowered to stand as individuals.

But that's not the world we're in right now. We're forced to regularly decide if, for those at the lower economic rungs, some corrective assistance is warranted. Allowing for unions is only one form of it. Minimum wage laws, antipoverty programs, and unemployment programs are others. These programs exist because it's prudent for the wealthy to give constant attention to people near desperation, to reduce the likelihood that they will turn to crime or rebel. Or, we could possibly see it as basic morality, as an attempt to keep vast numbers of people from falling into abject poverty.

But however they're viewed, these soothing initiatives inject distortion into the system. Government payments to the poor make taxes higher than what a more efficient economy would require. And because corrective actions inspire corrective taxes that are themselves taxing income, imbalances in the economy are exacerbated over time and never fixed. This, too, is how self-imploding markets are of our own mistaken making. A tower built by placing problems on top of mistakes is bound to crumble. Yet such payments are clearly legitimate and necessary when the market itself isn't truly free. So we're stuck in our capital-taxed economy. And stuck with a corollary politics that aggressively debates and redebates what the numbers and percentages should be. But it would be far better and far simpler to design a market that doesn't create its own need for fixing.

"If only ..."

In a true free market, welfare is only required for those who are unable to care for themselves—the mentally or physically infirm. The rest of us, of able body and mind, don't need government help and won't need government help. We'll need only our own effort. We'd have means to support ourselves, whether working for another or not.

Of course, at times there will be a natural tragedy. Lives and homes will be lost to nature's destructive outbursts. A moral nation will help communities reeling from those events. But, along with help for the infirm, that's all that's needed from government in the way of handouts. There isn't much placating required when government runs a truly free market. Multigenerational persistence of economic desperation is our best clue that ignorant law is afoot.

"Sometimes it's not ignorance. Sometimes it's politics."

Sometimes? It almost always comes back to politics. Economics is about how communities meet their needs. Politics is about how their beliefs are empowered. These are not the same. While overlapping influences exist between the two, unfortunately for us, gains in political power are often strategized by the economically ignorant.

"We're human. We're always going to be making mistakes. Your version of a market sounds good as an ideal. But it also sounds pretty easy to mess up."

I'll admit that, Sam. It could be messed up during our trying to get there, by powerful people wanting to hold on to power. But it's only ignorance that allows faulty arguments to gain traction. Ignorance might be natural, but it's not necessary for it to win the day. Avoiding ignorance requires that only some of us vigilantly and diligently question the systems and institutions around us, while others follow their inquiries. Not everyone has to engage like that. It's not a Herculean task. But it behooves a community to encourage and protect such lines of inquiry, lest ignorance becomes ossified.

"Honestly, Jorge ... all this idealism? I think you're dreaming. It's interesting to hear about. But you're dreaming."

Our choices got us to where we are. Why can't they take us somewhere else?

"Because people in power aren't going to give it up."

I didn't say they'd have to give it up. I said they'd be afraid of giving it up.

"But it's true. If power's going to pass to people who've never had it, it's got to come from somewhere."

Those with political power would still be in power. Those with land holdings or accumulated capital would still have what they have. The only thing they would lose is an unearned leverage over the less fortunate. They would still have great wealth and power.

"I don't know … I don't believe you. No, that's not true. It's not that I don't believe you. It's that I don't see how all this happens. It seems unrealistic. A fantasy … really."

Time will tell. But as long as this conversation can happen, I'll be happy about our chances.

"Why? You do know it's a dream, don't you?"

But that's fine. Dreams are where everything starts. Hope needs direction. I believe the more this is talked about, the better it's going to sound. And after that, who knows?

"Well, conversation I can give you. We're friends, after all. And I'm sorry, Jorge. I have to say I lied before about when I had to go. I just wasn't sure I wanted to have this conversation."

I can understand that. So you really do have time?

"We're eating at eight, not seven."

Thank you for explaining. I might have done the same.

"I should have realized I wouldn't hurt your feelings anyway."

Sometimes a thick skin is a good thing.

"No question."

So I'll go on?

"Please."

Can you see that if, if we were living in a true free market, even the poor could feel contentment in their lifestyle?

"Contentment? You mean spiritually, like a monk or something? No, I can't. And I don't see it as a practicality either."

Sam, economic freedom is a hope right now, but it's not pie-in-the sky optimism. When the unfettered no is recognized and protected, economic desperation and the imbalances that come from payments to correct it won't happen. Government can be as small and pure as possible.

"Great, really. I'll keep my fingers crossed."

But what we have is unsustainable. Government is always using morality to justify what it does. And much of politics today is debating the morality of fixing our own problems. But today, no matter which side wins, the nation loses. Either the poor get poorer, or capitalism becomes more distorted. Isn't the argument best conducted in a way that doesn't perpetuate the problem? Even cynically, if you believe political power for its own sake is the truer goal of politicians, wouldn't getting credit for solving a big problem help them to that power? The best solutions are foundational, close to basic forces. They leave government with as small a role as is fairly possible. No welfare state is required when there's no systemic desperation to fix. You like that, don't you?

"Who wouldn't? Look, I just don't see how all this works. It sounds great on the one hand but impossible on the other."

It's not impossible. It just doesn't exist yet. Being able to hold the contents of the Library of Congress in your palm seemed impossible until the understanding of how to do it existed. Self-driving cars seemed impossible too, not long ago. Anywhere we've been, and wherever we are now, came from decisions made along the way. Anywhere we go in the future begins with decisions we make today. A better economic system is absolutely possible.

"Okay. Maybe … maybe it's not impossible. But I sure don't see how it happens. You must think I'm a blind man being shown the *Mona Lisa*."

But you're not blind. And soon I'll be ready to show you her smile. Believe me when I say I wish I could fit this concept into a frame as small as hers, or better, onto a bumper sticker. But this is a big picture. It requires a certain amount of patience to absorb it.

* * *

Think of all the creativity and effort we've devoted to skirting taxes. At least three industries—legal, software, and accounting—have formed companies, large and small, around the need to collect and report them.

Yet when people avoid taxes, it doesn't grow the economy, it just shifts the burden to those who comply. How many better, more productive uses could all these paid avoiders find if income taxes and other capital taxes were not here?

And here's another one. You actually alluded to this before; cash businesses have an inherent advantage over noncash businesses under an income tax. They have the ability to report something less than their real income and pay less tax without leaving a trail that proves otherwise. A $50,000 income can yield much closer to a $50,000 lifestyle for a cash business than it can for a noncash business. Governments can trace noncash money but not cash. When society adopts a true free market, cash businesses will have no such advantage.

"Even though you're dreaming, you do sometimes make sense. Still, how does government get funded? A sales tax?"

No, not a sales tax either. A sales tax is another form of capital tax. It's the flip side of the coin from income tax. Instead of taxing what money comes into a family, it taxes what money goes out. It's really a lifestyle tax, a form of consumption tax. Consumption taxes impose pressures on an economy along the same fault lines as income taxes. They make a lifestyle more expensive. And by pushing prices upward, they have that same pernicious, regressive effect of pushing the classes apart.

This happens because while everyone pays a sales tax as they purchase goods and services, the rich don't need to spend all of their income to have their lifestyle. Many can even save most of it. But poor people must spend it all just to live poor. So a consumption tax affects 100 percent of the income of a poor person while affecting only a fraction of the income of the wealthy. The more one makes relative to their annual spending, the less a consumption tax is felt. So it directly makes the plight of the less fortunate worse and grows their numbers, just like an income tax.

And, just like income tax, even if a consumption tax is made progressive so that the poor don't pay them, as long as prices are, in part, determined by those who do pay it, there will be an effect on prices that the poor will have to bear. Producers of basic goods have some pricing power simply because food and warm clothing are not optional. In the face of higher taxes, producers of basic goods will test that pricing power to preserve their profits, to maintain their own lifestyles. And so the poor will pay more, or live worse by going without.

"You've said this before."

Sorry. It's just a basic economic force; prices will rise to accommodate taxes on capital. It always puts downward pressure on the lifestyles of most people, and it inevitably gives government the need to tax more, to fund a rising demand for support payments. While the wealthy seem to be targets for these taxes, they end up hurting most everyone else.

Over time, generations, the instabilities that capital taxes create feed on themselves, like Jenga bricks that are slowly redistributed in our economic tower. In the long run, nothing is solved except to see how high we can get before the tower collapses again. Ignorance can create a very believable, although illusory, need for more ignorance.

"So if it's not sales tax or income tax, what's left? Property tax?"

No, not property tax either. Buildings are capital. They're part of what we make and trade. It's never good to distort the value of capital.

"I can't believe this is such a mystery."

It's not. Remember the three economic categories that we value: capital, labor, and land? Only one of them existed prior to us. And it is our playing field.

"Land?"

Yes, Sam. Land. We didn't make it. But we sure need it for what we do make; all our goods and services require it. Everything draws from it. Whether we're working during the day or resting at night, land is where we do it. It only gains value because of our activity on and around it, from our community. No one can point to raw land and say, "I created this." And only the ongoing availability of land allows for the unfettered no that defines a free market.

"So why should it be taxed? Sounds like it would wreck the heart of your true free market, just like capital taxes do. Why would anyone want land to be more expensive?"

Since land existed before us, the only thing we have given it is value. And that value doesn't come from one man, not without many others standing with him. Land's value comes from the community that forms on and around it. Whether a farmer uses land to harvest corn, or a developer uses it to build a skyscraper, the value of that land comes solely from other people's desire to use it. So if it's only the desires of a community that give land value, then doesn't it make sense that land value is the natural source for community funds?

"You're talking about a property tax?"

No, not property tax. A property tax includes buildings. Just land value, nothing else.

"But if a guy builds a skyscraper, doesn't that add value to the land?"

So long as what's built attracts other people to live or work in it or near it, then yes, his actions have added value. And because there are no other taxes, he'll reap the full profit from the capital he's used and created. And the land's value will grow too. Land developers can reap quite a healthy reward with no taxes on income or profit.

But my point at the moment is that the land itself isn't built by anyone. Land is already under our feet before we do anything. Sure, someone with a magnetic idea for development has created value. But the vast majority of that value is in the structure, not in the land itself. And if by chance the project was a boondoggle, because no one showed up to use it, the structure might only be worth its raw materials in scrap while the land's value would remain substantially unchanged. Fundamentally, land value grows as people see potential in locating on or near it as the community grows.

Two acres in the middle of Manhattan are always going to be more valuable than two acres in the middle of Montana ... that is, barring any new discoveries in Montana's mountains or plains. If one could lift two acres out of the middle of Montana and magically place them in Manhattan, the value of that land would surge as soon as the trick was completed. And the value of Manhattan's land sent to Montana would shrink. It's the same exact parcel of land, but the change in its value is due to the economic strength of its location.

Another way to look at it is through the development a community can support. If identical sixty-story skyscrapers were built—one in the middle of Manhattan and one on an equivalent plot in the middle of Montana—we could easily imagine the Manhattan tower surrounded by competitive people and the tower being fully occupied and busy. The Montana tower, surrounded by a relatively sparse population, would attract some tenants but perhaps stand mostly unlit at night, with whole floors fallow as a field. The difference is in the economic potential of the surrounding community. As a rule, an increase in people brings more value to land. A developer will pay more for Manhattan property because he can do more, profitably, with it.

So, if community is supplying the value, it's natural for community to use the value. And because it doesn't distort the relative value of capital, a tax on land value doesn't distort a free market. Land-value taxes are economically neutral. They don't exaggerate the qualities of a life being rich or poor. And they don't exaggerate the normal ebbs and flows of an economy into headline-making booms and busts.

"How is it neutral?"

For one thing, since nobody made the land, taxes on it aren't altering the value of labor's efforts. And for another, everybody needs to use it. What land offers is materials or location, and that's the same for rich and poor alike. The need for access to land is universal. So a land-value tax doesn't inadvertently target any group of people over any other. The value that gets taxed comes from the people who use it, which happens to be everybody.

"But you're making land more costly. By your own calculus, that's a distortion. What happens to farms? And the prices of food? How will poor people afford food?"

Since land is the economic playing field, think of specific locations as points of economic opportunity. The opportunity in Manhattan should cost more than the opportunity in Montana. There's more demand for it. The potential is greater. And by the way, that's reflected in our current system, so values wouldn't change much. The question is only who should be collecting that value in order to have the most efficient economy; private hands or public hands?

As for food, farmland might well drop in price. What today are cheap lands could well get somewhat cheaper.

"Land value is taxed. But nothing else?"

Nothing else.

"No matter what I build or don't build, I only pay tax on the land I own?"

Yes. But it's more like a lease. Tax is for the land you use.

"I don't own my land?"

You'd be free to use it as you like.

71

"You mean the government owns it?"

Land-value tax is the admission price to the community's economy. Community creates the value for it. It's also the community's to collect.

"So, we're all renting? From the government? I could own my house but not my backyard?"

It would—

"Why would I ever do this, Jorge? Why would anyone? It flies in the face of human nature. Until now, you've been so careful to explain yourself in terms of human nature. That's how I could listen to you. But the whole history of humanity is how people took land or looked for land, to control land. And you know why? People want to feel safe. Owning land does that."

I do agree with you, Sam. Much of our past is, and much of our future will be, about how groups try to control land. When past leaders wanted more power, they sought land. They used diplomacy, arranged a marriage, or went to war, but they sought it. Kings rewarded military heroes and powerful loyalists with plots of land. Even the ancients knew having land was the key to accumulating wealth and control. However ...

"Do you hear yourself?"

The ownership coin has a flip side too. Every historic conquest of land has meant disenfranchisement for the losers; large groups of people had their land taken, riches stolen, and power upended. So remember that. The feeling of safety you get from owning land ... is really only as strong as the government that protects you.

"So?"

Economic forces in this wireless age are no different. It makes sense to want an economy that makes government as stable as possible. It's legitimate to ask: is the wealth and power that comes from owning land best held in the private desires of land owners or in the bedrock of community itself?

"It's a loaded question. And it sounds like it's leading to socialism."

It's the foundation of a truly free, very capitalist market.

"Not when government takes people's land, it's not! Private property is the bedrock of community!"

But I'm not ... I'm not suggesting taking people's land. People need control over a property. That's an absolute premise for our freedom. Control of property is what allows us our economic dreams. You're right; it is the bedrock. It's the key to growth for our markets and our communities. By all means, use your backyard as you see fit. Build a deck, a barbeque pit, or a pool. Your use of it, your private desires, will be secure. I'm just saying that land must be taxed for its full value, and all other taxes must disappear.

"Along with ownership!"

What's the practical difference between owning land and having full use of it for as long as you'd like? And everything ever made by you or anyone can be owned or traded tax-free. Look, human aspiration seems to move along a continuum of seeking risk or seeking safety. One's chosen life might embrace attaining great wealth or just creating something to cherish. Or it might be a generous path that endears gratitude and admiration from those it touches. Or it might be a quiet path that maintains anonymity. Whatever it is, Sam, for anybody, just choose. Gamblers will choose risk. Others will choose safety. The goal is for everyone to have a choice for the life they want, unimpeded.

"Not if I have to pay for it."

In total, if you add up all the different taxes you pay, you'd probably end up paying less. Yes, people with assets fear losing them. And owning land has always seemed a source of stability. It is, after all, what kings went to war for. But land is only as safe in ownership as the government is secure and honest.

And still, if property taxes aren't paid, the government will take its land back anyway. Isn't that effectively a lease already? Ownership might have an indefinite term, but it still requires annual tax payments to keep it, so the reality is, land and property taxes are already rent. Omnipotent ownership by individuals is just an illusion.

"It's still cheaper to own."

For your home alone, yes, it's cheaper. But only because land tax is such a small part of the total taxes you pay. The math changes when all the other taxes go away.

Sam, what we call land ownership is actually an exclusivity of use given by the government in exchange for paying taxes. That's your feeling of security. If it's knowing that we can come and go and use our land as we see fit that makes us feel secure, do you really want that feeling—that bedrock feeling—based on an illusion?

So what if that secure feeling officially came not from the ownership we pretend to have but transparently from the guaranteed, secured usage of a property? It wouldn't feel any different. The same government that lets you pretend to own it today would be the one offering it. But it would be called what it is, a lease of secured use. You could still come and go as you please and build whatever in the backyard.

There would be no illusion. A lease of secure use would give the holder the same rights as ownership and could last five, twenty-five, or fifty years, or as long as the community and user decided. And, just like now, so long as the tax is paid, land leases would be enforced and defended by the community.

"But twenty-five or fifty years isn't forever. Why would I accept that?"

Well, you could renew the lease when it's over and stay as long as you'd like. And overall, taxing land while not taxing capital allows government to be as small as possible. The economy would be undistorted and efficient. And the total tax burden required to run things would shrink. So many landowners, including you, would pay less tax overall. But it's true; a few landowners would never accept it because they'll pay more in that tax. It comes down to my question from a few moments ago: is the value a community creates best held by that community or in private hands? The great majority of our community would have to want a land-value-taxed economy for it to actually happen.

"What happens in a sale? How would it work?"

Whatever you're selling, a house or a skyscraper, you'd get the full value of your building, tax-free. If the market sees value in the remaining time on the land lease, you'd get that value too. And the government begins receiving lease payments from the new secured user.

"And what happens when my lease is up, and I want to stay?"

The government gives you a new lease, which will require a payment matching current market values for your land. It wouldn't matter how you've expanded the house in the interim. And Ada will kiss you because she loves the house.

"How is it a free market if the government is deciding the rent?"

The government doesn't decide. Values come from the free market. The government would just put a fair market value on the lease. And you'd have the choice to accept it or not. If you didn't like the number, you could request a public auction to more directly find the right value. At auction, anyone can bid. But, as the current leaseholder, you would have the right to match the highest one. In a true free market, the market determines values. Government can't pick numbers out of thin air.

And by the way, any lease—your lease and every other—would be public knowledge. If anyone thought your lease was below market levels, they could request an auction for it too.

"And take it from under me?"

No, no. You always have your tenancy rights. Making lease values public keeps lease values fair. It also limits the chance for the process to be corrupted. It would be hard to make sweetheart deals, for example. No government worker could give a bargain lease to a cousin, because the public would always be informed and could call for a new auction on the property.

"What do you mean?"

If every land lease and lease payment is public knowledge, and every lease is subject to public auction by anyone in the community, then the free market controls all land values.

"That sounds scary. Someone will want to screw with me."

They couldn't screw with you, Sam. Land values couldn't stray from free-market levels. A winning bidder will be obliged to take the lease, so there's no incentive to jack up the price to screw you. Not unless someone was willing to screw themselves with an overpriced lease just to screw you.

"Stranger things have happened."

If someone is willing to hurt himself, there's not much we can do about it. At least the community would benefit by getting higher-than-market revenues. And if they tried to welsh on their high bid, they'd become an issue for the legal system, facing jail and penalties. We can't allow games with the very crux of an economy. The community must get its due or get justice.

"Someone could go to jail for that?"

If someone manipulated or attempted to manipulate the auction process ... absolutely. Both the government's interest in the land value and the seller's interest in whatever structure is built there are at stake.

"How is someone in jail supposed to pay rent?"

75

They may not be able to. Justice is served case by case. But the message of justice has to be that an economic obligation to the community is a serious one.

"And so, my 'I'm not a socialist' friend … why must the government own all land?"

Two … no … three reasons. The first is that if government is going to collect rent from land's value, it must act as the landlord.

"That's semantics."

I'd prefer to think of it as a mind-set. Government is always the ultimate landlord, no matter what economy is in place. It's how rules for land usage are enforced. We create parks to prevent development on some lands, and we create laws to prevent chemical spills on others. Those are governmental doings.

The second reason is that, to avoid economic distortions, taxes must only fall on what people don't make. And the only thing people don't make is land. If we're going to let people own what they don't create, we might as well let someone own the air. And that's like the plot for some fictional mega-villain.

"I suppose. But do us all a favor and don't write the script."

And the third reason is that proper land usage allows for the unfettered no. Only a nonprofit land manager, like a government, can fairly tend the gates of opportunity.

"You make a land-value tax seem like an economic panacea."

Well, it would go a long way in eliminating many current problems, not least of which would be providing a fair playing field for the economy.

But there is no economic panacea, Sam. Any economic system is going to require the belief and fortitude of the community to make it work. History shows that even with popular backing, most economies, even major ones, haven't lasted a hundred years without some major revamping or engaging in war to expand economic horizons. It's a sign that something's off when a community can't go five generations without engaging some crisis to reignite its future. And since income tax began, we haven't gone more than a dozen years without significantly changing our tax code.[i]

"Not in my lifetime, we haven't. I think I've only seen eight years without a change. It's depressing, really."

And so unnecessary. Land-value tax allows for consistency. The whole economy would be stabilized. It wouldn't need so much tweaking.

"That would be great. Still … you're going to have to really sell me on this."

That's what I've been doing ever since this conversation began.

"Oh?"

Of course.

"Selling me how?"

How? Well, it's either the kind of selling that tries to convince you with a quick, confident answer. Or it's the kind that is patient, taking the time for you to discover for yourself what suits you.

"Ah …"

I hope you feel we're going the second way?

"I wasn't even thinking that I was being sold, up until now. It's just interesting conversation. I've had this dissatisfaction with the way things are, as you know, for a long time. So I'm open to this sort of talk. And I like that you don't seem to be railing from a political point of view. It's kind of refreshing. But honestly, Jorge, I can't judge it. Not yet. I don't really understand it."

How could you? You're just hearing it for the first time.

"Then let's keep going. What's the worst that could happen? I end up disagreeing with you? Been there, done that. But soon, I'm going … to buy a vacuum. It will make Ada and me happy for an hour, watching it learn our layout. Then we'll go out to dinner and see how good a job it did. And in the morning, I'll still feel a nebulous dissatisfaction with the way the world works. But maybe—and I'm being blatantly optimistic here—you'll have had some decent idea that distracts me."

I hope so, Sam. I truly hope it's only your vacuum that sucks.

CHAPTER 5

Where Taxes Land

"At least it's easy to see the bill going to landowners ... sorry, 'secured users' ... every year. A one-line tax form, call it rent or whatever, is almost righteous. Of course, I'd rather pay nothing."

That's it. One and done. But, Sam, paying nothing isn't going to happen for you.

"But some people will have free land. Why not me? How is that fair?"

Land is always valued for its perceived economic opportunity. The market knows that access to it is access to the economy. So, in a true free market, everyone pays admission in proportion to the opportunity they claim. If someone like you wants to be in the competitive market, with your job and your house, then the value of the land you secure for them is your price of admission to the competitive market. Living and competing in the New York City area is going to cost more than competing in Bozeman. But if someone chooses not to be in the competitive market, then they are choosing to not use competitively valued land. Since they're not claiming any opportunity the market values, there's no need for them to pay admission.

"I get a salary, Jorge. I don't pay to claim the use of my office."

Not directly, no. But your employer does. That cost is accounted for in your salary.

"Okay. Hmm. Wait a second. You said problems arise when not everyone pays a tax."

I did. Because a closed economy offers no ability to opt out. Its structure permits capital taxes, like income and profit taxes, to spread into everyone's prices whether or not they live on wages. An open economy though, as established by land-value tax, provides an opt-out mechanism. There is a noncompetitive economy created, separate from the competitive one. People living in those areas aren't shopping in competitive markets. There aren't even permanent stores in their communities. They're living off their land directly, trading with neighbors. Tax costs don't leak into their barter prices. Only people in the competitive economy pay competitive prices. People in the noncompetitive economy are mostly unaffected by taxes.

"It sounds like a class system."

Every economic system has classes. But it's a free system if it's your choice to live that way or not, and it's a choice every day.

"I think my imagination stalled. I'm lost. I understand what you're saying, but I don't see it working."

The competitive market sets the value for land, right?

"Right."

That value is assessing the economic potential at that location. If the free market is saying it doesn't value the land, then there's no competitive opportunity there. It's almost a paraphrase of what Neil Armstrong said on the moon. A land claim is the small step of a man; land value is from giant leaps of mankind. If there's gold in the ground, its value comes from demand in the community, not from the individual discoverer. Everyone uses land, and in fairness, everyone pays for the quality of opportunity they use. It doesn't matter if they're highly competitive locations that cost a lot or noncompetitive locations that cost nothing. And the value of land is large enough, more than enough, to satisfy the whole community in its needs and ambitions.

"How do you know that?"

Because the total value of all land is the full economic potential of the community, and a naturally growing community can't have needs that exceed its potential. But there are two exceptions to this: one is when a community is overwhelmed, as could happen with, say, an influx of refugees from a bordering war; the other is if a community allows its natural resources, including the inventiveness of its own people, to be squandered. Aside from those situations, if we were to just tax land value alone we could meet all our needs, start paying down our national debt, and have change leftover, all without distorting our economy.[ii]

"I didn't realize …"

Even more than enough land value, for government to tax, if it needed it.

"And it won't distort the economy because …"

It doesn't alter the relative values of the work we individually do.

Deciding where taxes fall is a way of sealing our fate. An empty lot in the middle of town is valued only by demand from the surrounding community, regardless of who has claimed it. If the claimant decides to build something, and it attracts people, then she has created value. In a true free market, that value is hers to keep. None of it need be shared with the community. But merely staking a claim creates nothing and returns nothing, not even as time passes. A claim on land is an even swap with the community: the claimant gets secured usage, and the community gets rent.

"Jorge?"

What?

"I get it. When property's sold, the government takes the land value, and the secured user keeps the value of the structure. And when the lease is up, the secured user gets a choice: to accept the government's offer for a new lease or to put it up for auction."

Well, Sam, I'm glad to think I've been making sense.

"Just because I've been listening doesn't mean it makes sense. I'm willing to hear you out. But it seems what you're saying is that you can add to land value by building something attractive. But then you end up paying a higher rent for having built it when the lease renews. What's appealing about that?"

Actually, if you built successfully, you'd not only keep the profits tax-free but if the community grew, you'd be able to collect some of that rising land value through charges to whomever used your property. Only when the lease renewed would you pay a newly market-valued rent. But because it's the free market that determines the rent, it will always allow room for profitability. So what's wrong? If it's a successful endeavor, the secured user will reap the benefits of the project's profits, plus some ability to collect accrued land value for the term of her lease. And profit beyond, if she renews it.

But generally in cities and towns, unless yours is a domineering project, it's neighbors' projects that will have more impact on the value of your land lot than what you do. Just as your improvements contribute to the value of neighboring lots. This is what makes land value the natural source of a community's revenues; it's community-created.

"Landowners already pay taxes. It may not be federal, but it's tax."

True. But that's different than the notion of a land-value tax.

"Why? It's property tax. Land is part of it."

That's the problem. It's only a part. Property taxes fall mostly on the assessed value of structures, not on land. In rural areas, sure, property taxes more reflect land value, because structures there are small relative to the acreage. But those are generally areas where land values are cheapest. In urban and suburban areas, where land value is concentrated, land value is only a very small percentage of the bill. The way we levy property tax, if you improve your structure, your tax goes up. That's a perverse incentive.

"I hate those assessments. But, Jorge, what we already do sounds just like your plan; land is reassessed anyway whenever the lease renews. What's the difference?"

No, I'm talking about only the raw land getting revalued, not the structure. And only when the lease ends. And leases can be pretty long. That's not tax assessments going up within a year or so after an improvement. Assessments on capital are taking directly and promptly from the creativity and effort of the owner. They shift personal profits to community use. They really are hateful; any tax on capital is.

What passes for property tax today is barely sticking a toe in the right pool. To the extent the bills include land value, that's great. The problem is that, nationwide, it's too small a number. A true free-market tax bill would be the value of land alone. One righteous number on a single page—local, state, and federal combined.

"I've never really understood that assessment thing, especially when someone is just adding a deck in the backyard."

You're referring to last summer?

"They raised my taxes 6 percent!"

I know. You told me the other day.

"But still, I can sort of understand it. Isn't the argument that when someone's adding a whole new room to their house, or adding ten stories to a building in the city, they're also signing up to use more services from the community from then on? More water? More electricity?"

Those are paid for separately in utility bills.

"Okay. But also fire and police. There's more to protect and inspect."

There is a certain logic to it, yes, a proportionality that seems to be fair. However, it misses a larger principle at play. If a true free market is designed to nurture our economic ambitions, then taxing improvements on a property flies in the face of what we're trying to accomplish. How can a community claim to provide economic freedom if it charges people directly for the expression of their economic desires?

"Ada and I designed that deck together. And we'll be paying forever with that assessment."

It is a very nice deck.

"Jorge ... I don't mean to be flip, but what will all this accomplish? I mean, how would my life be different with a land tax, in a nutshell? Not some poor guy. Middle-class me. You think I'd save money?"

If there's land-value tax, and an unfettered no is enforced?

"Yes. All of it. What would it do for me?"

What government needs to spend will shrink, so the total taxes we pay will shrink. And you won't need to pay for tax preparation either, because it will be simple. Big economic swings between good times and bad go away, so you'll feel more secure about your future. You wouldn't worry about Marga getting a job when she graduates—the particulars, maybe, but not whether she gets one or not. The university itself would cost less too. There wouldn't be as many government regulations to distract you at your job. Homeless people would stop appearing on that street near your office because there wouldn't be homeless people ... at least not because of finances. And that blighted area you pass on your commute would be rejuvenated. Sounds like it might be worth a try, no?

"It might. But my total taxes would be less?"

Yes. Compared to the federal, state, local, sales taxes and the rest combined, that you pay today, yes.

"But that's it? I mean, it's really nothing major for me; I'd have a little more money. Right?"

You're fairly comfortable, Sam. Your particular life wouldn't change much, except that you'd notice a better world around you. And people way richer than you would stay way richer than you. But you'd all have less stress about money and less concern about the government's desire to use what's yours.

A typical financial life would be much better though, especially for the poor, without the rest of us being hurt by the change. Their shackling to cycles of extreme poverty would be gone. The fear of destitution from a failed endeavor would be gone. Imagine not fearing poverty. It frees every dream, every thought, to a reasonable chance. Aspirations, however great or small, in every neighborhood would feel possible, except when they conflict with the rules of fairness. You want it personal, Sam? How would you like to feel freer to start your own business instead of staying where you are, because the risk would be less scary?

Even the day's news might be different, with less financial fraud going on, and governments no longer stumbling on basic economic issues like debt.

"All that? Wow. And from a little misguided property tax?"

I know you think I'm overreaching. But your sarcasm reflects the problem. We've been using a magnifying glass to zero in on issues while losing sight of larger principles.

"Jorge, I didn't mean to sound sarcastic."

No?

"It just seems like a butterfly effect to me. That whole storm of words from you came out of a simple misconception about property tax."

I don't think I said it was all from property tax, but there absolutely is a butterfly effect in economics. All structural decisions cascade through the system. I'll give you an example: states compete with each other to attract jobs by giving tax breaks to employers.

"Or by keeping labor costs down."

That's true, but since we've already talked about unions, let's talk about tax breaks. If ten thousand jobs are shifted from California to Tennessee because of a tax break, does that help the country?

"Just a straight shift? I suppose not. But it helps Tennessee."

Exactly. Nationally, it's a worthless endeavor, a zero-sum competition. And it may or may not help Tennessee. There are good reasons for companies to move, such as consolidating operations or improving proximity to supplies, that effectively help all of us because they attempt to improve a product or service. Profitability matters that way. But taking advantage of a tax break doesn't do that.

And even if it does help Tennessee, it'll be temporary. The cost of targeted tax breaks is ultimately, over longer periods, paid by other workers in the state through their tax bills, and the rest of Tennessee's population through theirs. Plus the playing field in that industry is altered to benefit the new company at the expense of competitors.

"Why is the burden shifted to other workers?"

This will be a bit of a roundabout, but I'll get there. Can we assume that taxes are at the level they are because certain community needs need to be met?

"Well, people differ on what needs need to be met. Need is a matter of opinion."

Of course. But in a democracy, tax levels mostly reflect the view of the majority. So we can use that as a view of what the community's needs are.

"Then, for the sake of argument, yes."

So if taxes are cut, we can presume that either needs have diminished or that there is hope that following the cut, needs will diminish. But the likely scenario is that over time, the burden of needs won't change much at all, except to grow.

"Why not?"

Because the economic structure that exacerbates community needs isn't changing. The economy is still closed. Capital is still taxed. The burden will slide from those who got the tax cut to those who pay taxes but didn't get the cut, to those who don't pay taxes. It's inevitable that the tax cut for some will end up hurting others. Need will move up or down along with booms and busts, but overall, over long periods, community needs won't change much, except to slowly get worse.

Any municipality that attracts business by putting its tax base on sale is either courting political opportunity or trading the short-term need for jobs for a number of longer-term needs, like increasing demand for schools, health care, and infrastructure. Those things come from attracting ten thousand new residents and the ancillary growth they'll bring; and it's everyone who didn't receive the tax break who will end up paying, including competing businesses, as soon as taxes rise.

Plus, from a national view, nothing has changed. The job growth in one state is offset by the jobs lost elsewhere. States today compete by distorting their own economies and with no incentive to help the nation overall. It's a dual downward spiral of lesser lifestyles or future higher taxes for most of the nation.

Wouldn't it be better if states competed by building better infrastructures? Instead of a misguided effort to help a few, infrastructure helps all of us. Businesses need efficient infrastructure. By building it, states don't create economic distortions. And by helping their locale, they're helping the nation too. That's what is incented by land-value tax.

"Couldn't states make deals over land-value tax as easily as with income tax?"

They could. But why would they? First, the unfettered no makes the labor market efficient. With full employment, the pretense for offering tax breaks goes away. Second, it would be very risky politically. Remember—if land value were the state's only source of revenue, the deal could backfire before any benefits, suspect as they are, were seen. Either way, shifting tax burdens among employers and citizens, which is what tax deals do, doesn't create lasting economic stability.

Sam, great suffering has come from what you called "a little misguided property tax." Years of focusing on economic minutiae instead of the larger view have gradually vanquished the unfettered no from all but the richest, and it has helped them get richer still as the middle class shrinks, and the number of poor grows. Little mistakes can have large consequences.

"Okay, but 'great suffering'? From property tax?"

It makes the poor unnecessarily poorer.

"You said income tax did that."

I did. And it does. But so does property tax. Have you ever seen a property sit empty for years, or be drastically underused, maybe like an outdoor parking lot that's surrounded by ten-, twenty-, or thirty-story buildings?

"Here comes another story ..."

Does it strike you as a little weird when an outdoor market or a pavement lot is in the shadow of giant buildings? The skyscrapers clearly speak to that lot's potential. But to see it remain year after year, obviously underdeveloped, is just economically odd. There might be legal wrangling going on. But it's also likely that the potential of that lot is on hold by the lot's owner, off limits to anyone else who'd wish to use it. Have you ever wondered why that happens? How it's economical?

It happens because we tax improvements while leaving land itself all but ignored. We make it affordable for one person to hold land for years, unused, keeping an opportunity away from the rest of us. It's a problem because communities will always strive to meet their needs. It doesn't matter if the economy is growing or not.

"How's that a problem?"

A thriving community needs land for its people to do what they do. Let's call that area of competitive activity the community's economic footprint. In it is an underused lot with a fruit stand on it. If entrepreneurs can't secure that lot at a market rate, they'll take their plan to a lesser lot. Ambition won't fade just because a single property is unavailable. Ambition will look to be sated. So the acreage used by the community grows as participants are forced to take less desirable properties. A persistence of vacant or nearly vacant lots causes the economic footprint to expand.

This incremental demand for land pushes prices for those once less desirable lots higher than they would be otherwise. The more underused acreage there is, the greater the effect. And the closer to the economic center it is, the greater the effect. It's a real problem, the result of which is another economic stress shouldered by the less-than-wealthy. And it gets worse as the community grows bigger. An excessive footprint causes prices to destabilize, kind of the way when you've held sticks by one end, the longer ones wobble more at the tip. But in economics, that wobbling goes everywhere. During upswings, underdevelopment makes the price of land—the price of opportunity—grow unaffordable unnecessarily. And downswings have the converse effect, also to an unnecessary degree.

"The community takes more land than it needs, and that hurts the poor?"

The poor and the rest of us. Anytime valued land is allowed to remain undeveloped or under-developed, it hurts.

"But isn't the guy with the vacant lot allowed to keep it and not sell it?"

Nothing is wrong with his not selling the land. What's wrong are rules that let him hold it without compensating the community for the value of that opportunity.

"Jorge, I need an example. Say a community has the population to sustain a billion dollars in economic activity. You're saying they're going to do that billion dollars of activity, regardless of how much land it takes to do it?"

Yes. But with one caveat; the more spread out a population is, the less economically efficient it's going to be. So at some point, potential starts to shrink. But for your illustration, yes—they're going to do a billion dollars regardless.

"So, let's assume, if the land is efficiently used, they would need a thousand acres to do it. You're saying that if 10 percent of the land is unused, or inefficiently used, that same billion dollars of activity might require 1,100 acres?"

Yes. And at 10 percent, that's a reasonable degree of inefficiency that we see nowadays. At least according to government statistics totaling unused properties.[iii]

"So there's a squeeze against neighboring communities by a hundred acres."

Yes. And the neighboring communities are almost certainly as inefficient, because they operate under the same flawed rules, so they, too, are using more land than they would otherwise need. Supply and demand ensures that property values, especially in the areas of those extra needed acres, are pushed up—not as high as prime properties but far higher than they would be otherwise. So the effect when laws allow land to be held out of use or underdeveloped—

"Like a paved parking lot in the middle of Manhattan."

Like that. It not only cheats the community of its economic potential but it also distorts the value of other community properties. And the closer that wasting land is to the economic center of town, the more people will suffer the impact.

Places that could otherwise allow for an unfettered no end up getting pushed further away from economic centers. Our overall freedom as a people is decreased when the amount of underused property is increased. We not only make the prices of goods and services higher for the poor, but their access to land is made more costly. Capital taxes go up. And it's all unnecessary. Inefficient land use swells their ranks.

The bottom line for you, Sam, is that poor land usage creates more demand for government help. Our laws are quite effective at creating needy people. See how "a little misguided" decision can have a huge impact?

"Maybe."

And there are more effects from this ignorance. That neighborhood you pass on your commute—it's severely underdeveloped relative to neighboring areas. And it's been that way for years.

"Underdeveloped? Understatement. It's downright seedy."

Well, under our current law, some deep-pocketed developer can create that seediness. She can buy property there and just let it decay to drive down neighboring prices even more. And then buy more, slowly and cheaply, waiting years if need be to consolidate a large parcel. Then, one day she'll announce a development plan, and the investment community will flock, driving land prices—now her land—up again. Her wealth will come from whipsawing the neighborhood from hardship to hope. This could never happen in community structured by land-value tax. There wouldn't even be the underdeveloped neighborhoods to trigger it.

"If you say so."

No. Not if I say so. This has to make sense to you.

"It does. You're being logical. I'm just trying to absorb it."

I hope so.

"But how can one guy control the fate of a neighborhood? I mean, if neighbors control the value of his land, like you said, then how does he control a whole neighborhood?"

In our economy? It's the way our land-tenancy laws work, the result of emphasizing the value of structures over the value of land. So the larger the development plans, with land-value staying in his pocket, the greater the impact will be. A deep-pocketed speculator can easily come to control a neighborhood. But smaller developers—no. They can't unless they band together. The fundamental forces have to play. Laws can only channel their path. If laws allow something to happen, for better or worse, it will happen. Under a land-value tax, it would be far more expensive to manipulate neighboring values.

We'd all be so much better off. Why we still think it's a good idea to tie government revenues to capital is a mystery to me. Whether it's income, property, or profit, it almost never makes sense. If you're the government, why would you hitch your revenue wagon to the most jittery horse in the economic stable? Not that there's anything that doesn't fluctuate in value, but capital fluctuates the most because it's what we make. Capital is exactly the stuff we overdo or underdo from time to time.

And that's the biggest reason that property tax is inefficient. Unless it's a political project, buildings are always constructed in anticipation of their use. And big buildings or big developments take time to get built. Since predicting the future is a guessing game, it's natural that every so often, too many buildings will be built. Overbuilding leads to slowing, or even halting, further development until the oversupply gets used up. And because construction involves many different industries, economic stagnation spreads to all of us.

"That's a recession."

Exactly. Building values can change enormously through booms and busts. And property taxes are based on those values. Municipalities that depend on structural assessments can find budgeting difficult as these cycles take their course.

During an economic downturn, not only asset values, but profits and incomes all shrink too, so there is less capital generating taxes at exactly the time when human needs placed on government are expanding—the time ranks of jobless, homeless, and hungry all grow. Then, when times are good, the community tax base grows as needs shrink. This mismatch makes economic cyclicality more intense than it needs to be, and not least because there are more needy people than there should be, even in good times. Capital-taxed economies … our economy … place the government's revenue pool in opposition to our community needs.

"Liberals say the government should be spending more when times are tough and less when times are good."

If needs are defined by a basic national lifestyle, some maximal amount of suffering that anyone should have to endure, they're not wrong. It's because the government's revenue is from capital that we suffer economic stress to the degree we do. What some see as excessive government spending is really a symptom of problems, not the cause. Those who would rather free the market than have government fix it need to understand what that freedom entails. A true free market doesn't develop a needy population. But with ill-conceived laws, neediness arises. Even on the face of it, Sam, you would think capital is the last thing a capitalist would want made more expensive by government.

"Jorge, I have to say, I hear you."

Land, on the other hand, isn't created to anticipate demand. It's just here. So of land, labor, and capital, it is easily the most stable. Unless its prices are leveraged by inefficient usages allowed by government rules, land values grow or shrink, mostly, in accord with the surrounding population. Population levels don't boom or bust so quickly, so its value isn't as susceptible to cycles. Land doesn't become overbuilt or underbuilt. And it doesn't get laid off.

"But it's not immune to economic cycles. Even in your dream, land value is going to rise or fall depending on the strength of the economy."

It will. But we've only experienced a capital-taxed economy that exaggerates the effect. When government revenues aren't based upon capital, economic cyclicality will be a much weaker force, particularly on raw land value, far weaker than population size.

People don't move out of town at the first sign of economic stress. After the local potentials are seen as limited or exhausted, but not before. Someone not working still represents economic potential, though, and is still part of the population that drives land values. So land value tends to be stickier than that of structure value, which depends more on actual activity. Land value isn't as leveraged by faulty predictions of the future as are buildings. And acreage is constant. Yes, land values will change, but not to the extent building values will. Land values tend to grow as a population grows and shrink as a population shrinks.

By using property tax, governments are tapping what is relatively more variable. If they used land value, governments could budget from a more stable revenue source.

So land-value tax makes a desirable building far more likely and an underused lot more rare. Excessive pressure on the poor is eliminated. And secured users get to keep the profit from all investment on their land, tax-free.

"Wait. So who's paying this land-value tax? Only secured land users?"

Directly? Yes.

"Not everyone in the competitive market?"

Directly? No.

"So leaseholders pay tax for everybody else? How's that fair? Maybe it doesn't distort the economics, but it sure sounds unjust."

Everyone in the competitive market pays. Secured users, those who control the opportunity land represents, pay directly. The rest pay too, just indirectly.

"Indirectly? I thought everyone pays in proportion to the land's value."

They do. Just like your office building costs are factored, to some degree, into your salary. The cost of tax for secured users is passed through to their land's tenants and workers. If you had a farm but couldn't work all the acreage yourself, what would you do?

"I'm not a farmer. But I guess I'd hire someone to work it for me. Or I'd lease it out."

If you lease it out, won't you pass through your costs on the property, or try to, so that the rent you receive won't be at a loss to you? At least a proportionate amount of your expenses, including your cost for the land, is going to drive your negotiation. You're going to try to charge your tenant a fair portion for the tax on those acres. And if you hire someone, what you offer for a wage will incorporate the tax you pay too. So, no matter if you're hiring or leasing, the calculation accounts for your taxes.

"Okay. I see. That's normal economics."

Of course. Either way, both the worker and the lessee are sharing in the cost for taxes due. Any access to land, in any free market, bears the price of its opportunity. Whether it's a home rental, a car rental, or a movie rental, owners are always passing their costs along. That's how they profit.

"Really? A movie rental?"

When you ask that, are you implying that some of us never use land?

"Well … no. Of course everybody uses the land."

It is pretty hard to avoid, even for movie distributors. Even the Internet needs land for server farms and antennas. How do you live on Earth yet avoid the earth? People on boats are even on a structure that came from land.

"Then it's the same as income tax!"

In what way?

"Income tax raises people's salaries so they can have their lifestyle, right? You made that point. Then so does land-value tax."

I see. It's a good thought, but there's a big difference. When goods and services are priced to account for income taxes, not all consumers are working for their spending money. But when goods and services are priced to include land value, everyone, no matter their circumstance, is using land. You can't be disenfranchised from land like you can be from labor.

I think we're trained by what we know. Pick a tax today, and there are many people who don't pay it. So it's reasonable, at first blush, to think the effects of land-value tax would be the same. But no one in the competitive economy can escape it. The future doesn't have to be beholden to the present.

If economic fairness means fair opportunity, then we have to deal, structurally, with access to land. The income generated from work or wealth is irrelevant to a community's management of opportunity. If government's role is to oversee a fair playing field, then we need to be more mindful of how we do it. A land-value tax at least recognizes and values the economic nature of opportunity.

"Landowners are going to hate you."

Land speculators may well be angry. They're used to their privileged low cost, low risk situation. But most landowners interested in currently using their property might appreciate not paying tax on profits or income.

Remember—someone who puts a fruit stand on a lot next to twenty-story buildings will not generate sufficient revenue to pay land-value tax. However, should she build a multistory structure, as her neighbors have done, she'd be able to profit. It's in the nature of land-value tax to promote efficient use of spaces.

"Then what about parks? With land so valuable, wouldn't parks begin to disappear? Ada and I enjoy the park on a nice day. Our dog too, for that matter ..."

Parks won't disappear. I don't know of any thriving town or city that doesn't enjoy the benefit of a park. I know I enjoy the respite. That's why I asked you to meet me here.

A now orange sun took an illusory perch atop a silhouetted building that lorded over the west side of the park.

People need their parks. It doesn't matter if the government is capitalist, socialist, or communist. The human value for parks will be recognized and protected, just as now. Besides, parks attract people. And giving people reasons to move nearby keeps those land values rising.

"Those people on boats? They're not living on land."

As long as they're using land-based products or services, they'll pay tax. When they dock, to use electricity or the community's drinking water, there's a fee charged by the manager of the dock. The fee will include a portion of the dock's land-value tax, passed through.

"And if the boat people weren't docked? Not using community water?"

If they were truly self-sufficient, for their health care and everything else, then no—they wouldn't pay taxes. But then, like a free land user, they're not part of the competitive economy, anyway. Although their boat would have had some land-value tax built into. The boat was built from land, after all.

"What about a space station? You mentioned the first man on the moon. So ..."

Sam, we're not ready to discuss that yet. But I can tell you the same principles apply. The same principles always apply.

"I was kidding, Jorge. But really, I'm not ready for economics in space? Why not? Do I need a pressurized bank account first? A radiation shield on my wallet?"

Please ...

"Before, you said acreage doesn't change. But there is landfill out there. That changes the acreage. And since man builds it, how do you tax it?"

Man-made land is only a very small percentage of all land. And since we did build it, it requires a transition period for taxes—a transition from capital to land in the eyes of the community.

"A transition? Why?"

Land created by private development is clearly capital, as you suggested. However, it's not purely a free-market project. It requires government to partner because it will require resources from the community. For example, any basic landfill project will change, displace, or redirect water usage. Infrastructure will need to be expanded—energy usage, transportation systems, garbage disposal, and the like. So the community has a rightful say in how, or even if, the project progresses. It's only prudent. So the creation of new land, primarily and fundamentally, requires the permission and partnering of the community.

Over time, though, it becomes as integral an addition to the map as would an earthquake's creation of new coastline. So, over time, it's fair for there to be a transition in the collection of the new land's value.

"How long a transition?"

That would result from a negotiation between the developer and the community. But there's no reason for more than half a lifetime—fifty years or so. Of course, if the community funded the development, then tax could be collected from the get-go, in proportion to the contribution. But however it was negotiated, the secured user would keep, in full, any profit he could procure from structures on that property. That alone is ample incentive for an ambitious soul to embark on such a project.

"What about community boards? Or zoning rules? Don't they contradict your principles?"

Everything is a balance. Zoning is what manages a community's character. And that character can be a significant part of a community's attraction. After all, who wants to find out that their longtime neighbors moved out of town and their quaint, old house, where the children played, is being torn down to make way for a chemical plant?

"A nightmare ... that could be a movie."

Local governments or community boards make all kinds of decisions to prevent nightmares. So sometimes, local concerns will carry more weight than these principles. Like if the fire department can only work to a certain height, then a community board would be justified to limit the height of buildings or insist upon specific construction for buildings above that height. Communities in earthquake zones or flood zones might come up with similar sorts of restrictions. Or sometimes, it's just about aesthetics. If a town has always had orange on its roofs or a certain architectural style, the community board might deem to keep it that way.

Zoning and local rules can be a kind of glue keeping communities prideful. But economic forces will always exert themselves. Like I said, it's a balance.

"Speaking of which, I'm running out of time. I have, um, twelve minutes left. So why hasn't this happened already? If it's so good, why isn't there a land-value tax now?"

That's a good question. I can't say I know. But it's human nature to think what's known is more comfortable than what's new. So what did the first Europeans see here? American Indians owned land communally. They didn't claim land for individuals. And their wood or mud constructions didn't have the grandeur of cathedrals and castles back in Europe. It's likely that Indian models for engineering didn't win a second thought from the settlers. And so their economics didn't warrant a second thought either. I'd guess the settlers applied feudal methods, simply because that was what they knew. I can imagine them seeing land to the horizon and claiming all they could defend. And the next to arrive would do the same. As Europeans continued to arrive, communities grew around what they knew—individually owned land like the kings and lords back home. New community leaders were, again, the ones who owned the most. The old patterns were repeated. Claiming land, owning land, was everything. Even our original Constitution allowed states to limit voting to landowners.

The old European ways were of rulers using land to gain favor and secure power. Kings gifted parcels to those who could aid them. But if land is used like that, taxing it becomes impossible. Even as king, you can't charge tax on a gift you just gave.

"That's just bad form."

This could be why the taxation of land value never became a serious economic notion. Because the king needed landowners' loyalty, common sense guided him to promote advantages for them over everyone else. A land-value tax would have forced them to be productive, and forced work is not a gift cherished by the powerful.

Also, Sam, since land-value tax offers independence to the poor, it's conceivable that the very prospect was frightening to a king. It's plausible to believe that taxes were levied the way they were to secure control over populations.

In those days, unpaid debts were a cause for death or enslavement to the lender. At least one king must have seen how taxes could create debts and, therefore, slaves. Like magic, a king could have a subject's strong son build for him, or have a peasant's beautiful daughter or wife at his beck and call; just tax them into debt. Most of a king's subjects were peasants, so devious tax levels could be set in accord with the worth of a good growing season—a level that left the peasants with just enough for a tolerable life.

But when the inevitable bad growing season arrived, the shortfall of harvest would become an intolerable problem. It put peasants into debt for taxes due. And future harvests would only rarely be good enough to let him catch up, not while the king's tax was in place. Debt incurred like that could be forever. Monarchal control became as relentless as time's passing.

The peasant, made responsible for having turned his family into slaves and helpless to save them, would then find that only devout loyalty to the king would protect his loved ones—who were always chained or guarded and rather dispensable to the realm.

"Sounds like the basis of another movie."

If only the technology were around, it could have been made centuries ago. The creation of poor people, to have them be dependent upon the rich, has been a perverse but persistent impulse in history. It even crossed cultures, with variations around the globe—Asia, Europe, Africa, and South and North America. Almost everywhere has had slaves. The impulse to control others seems to stem from the beginning of mankind.

"'Creation of poor people?' Are you saying poverty isn't natural?"

No. Poverty is natural. It can reflect a lack of ambition or a preference for less remunerative pursuits. But what isn't natural is the large number of needy poor and for the poor to have no say over their lives.

I believe that early on, after debt was seen as an effective cudgel to control people, the methodology of debt was institutionalized. An entrepreneur lending to a needy person could say, "Pay me back in full plus interest, or I will take your home, your wife, or your life," and have the backing of the state in saying it. The thing is, remnants of this path are still with us, although today it is not so blatant. But taxing capital ineluctably creates a desperate class of people.

"Wouldn't land-value tax also create debt for the peasant after a bad growing season?"

If land-value is set according to a true free market, it will account for occasional poor growing seasons. Therefore, the value will be some price that allows a peasant a decent lifestyle and that anticipates risk in the weather. If the auction value began to exceed the attendant risk, wiser people wouldn't bid. The auction would soon end.

So, sure, falling into debt simply because a land-value tax is instituted could still happen, if several poor growing seasons occurred in a row, and the timing of the lease were unlucky. But a free-market valuation means the debt incurred from an unfortunate season or two is accounted for. The price wouldn't be so onerous that the farmer couldn't catch up and be cash positive after normal weather returned.

CHAPTER 6

Land Lauds

Do you want to stop now?

"Let's use the minutes I have. Just talk fast."

I'll try.

The remaining sun became a blood-orange sliver between two silhouetted towers, heaving long shadows over Central Park's trees, a field, a lake, and a castle.

"Suppose I discover gold ... a lot of it. Or diamonds. Or gas. The point is ... I'm taking stuff out of the land. How would the tax work then?"

Congratulations on your gold strike!

"Yeah, thanks. Come on ... the time."

If you can pretend to strike gold, can't I pretend to be happy for you?

"This is you talking fast?"

Okay. Okay. Like any free market, a true free market will assess your discovery and assign a value to it, as it is, in the land. But that doesn't mean you're instantly rich. Getting rich depends on what you do.

"I can't just sell the land and retire?"

No. The community is due its value for the land, including what's in it.

"You're taking all the fun out of having land. What happens to 'striking it rich'?"

Nothing. You can still get rich, but it won't be because you've simply pocketed the value of a discovery. That value in the land belongs to the community. If you want to depend on luck, go to a casino. It's not a solid principle for building an economy.

"So how do I get rich?"

How long before you have to go?

"About nine minutes. Try to speed it up, Jorge."

The difference between the new land value and the old land value is that of the discovery. As it lies in the ground, it has static value—the gold or whatever. But the old rent was only for what was known about the property, its surface potential. So, by rights, add the static value to the original surface value, and a new land value is established. And a new rent.

"Wait. If all the static value belongs to the community, why would anyone mine anything? Where's the incentive?"

Clearly, in a land-value economy, mere discovery is not enough to line your pockets. Only work on land creates wealth, which is what allows for profit. So when the material is mined or drilled or somehow removed from the earth, it then becomes capital. That's how you become rich. What was in the ground has been given added value; it's now a product, out of the land and ready for trade. The new value, resulting from work, is the active value. The difference between the static value and the active value is the province of profit. And it's not subject to tax.

"So tax is only on the value of what's in the ground?"

Yes. Valued by a free-market assessment. After that, it's yours free and clear.

"How quickly are leases revalued after a discovery? What if the secured user can't afford it?"

It depends.

"Depends on what? If someone signs a lease for twenty-five years on Monday, and Tuesday gold is discovered, does that person get a free ride for the next twenty-five years? You said the value belongs to the community."

Revaluing a lease after a discovery can only be the secured user's choice. He doesn't have to use the discovery. And his original lease will remain intact. But if he chooses to mine the gold, then the process for a new lease will begin. And if it goes to auction, he'll have the right of first refusal.

"What happens to the gold value if he doesn't mine it? How does the community get it?"

The community will have to wait. A lease is a serious arrangement, a contract. And liberty is always about being able to say no. So, if the lease didn't anticipate the discovery, the community will benefit when the secured user chooses or when the lease expires. But the value will be had. Asking capitalists to ignore value is like asking the straight men at a singles party to ignore the most beautiful woman there.

"Okay. Say he goes for the gold. He gets a new lease. But what if he has a cousin in that department of government? Or if he bribes somebody? To get a break on the reassessment?"

All land values and tax payments are public knowledge. The whole population can see if it likes the valuation or not.

"Ah ... and they can request an auction. Okay. Maybe I'm getting it. I think."

The public's ability to oversee and participate in any auction goes a long way to preventing favoritism or bribery with government officials, just as the threat of jail incents people to make honest bids. But a true free market can always be trusted as the final arbiter of value. Government gains credibility by abiding by the market's wisdom and, consequently, keeps cheaters at bay.

"Not all cheaters. What if it's stolen?"

Stolen? The gold?

"Yes. Technology today means that just because a hole is made on one property doesn't mean what comes out can't be from another property. How does land-value tax address that?"

The market has its expertise. Drilling and mining companies have long experience in protecting their underground interests from competitors. There's no reason a government can't tap that same expertise. If they could detect it as it happened, justice could be swift. But if it was found only after your lease expired, or after you passed away, the thief would be liable to the community for the full static value of what was taken. And you, or your estate, would be due the active value. And I'm sure the legal system could figure out ways to occupy the thief's time too.

"But why am I, or my family a victim, if I chose not to mine in the first place? Especially if the community owns what's in the land."

The theft is also against your authority as secured user and your rightful claim on a potential profit.

"What if a lease expired for some elderly woman? You said a new lease triggers a reevaluation of the property. Could she be forced to move?"

If the new lease made it unaffordable for her?

"Yes."

There's no reason why we couldn't give the elderly a little extra respect. If it were up to me, her lease would simply be extended until her passing. But it would be up to each community to decide. Sometimes the cold laws of economics can yield to the warmth of community values. Since land-value tax makes communities financially stable, forgoing a few years of collecting full land value to accommodate elderly citizens would be affordable. But again, it's for each community to do what suits them.

This is just my personal view, Sam, but once people reach a certain age, there is nothing to stop communities from offering lifetime leases on home properties. Maybe their land leases could incorporate life expectancy, in addition to the regular factors. So instead of applying free-market rents to ten- or twenty-year leases, rents could be set by actuarial tables, sort of the way insurance companies charge premiums. An elderly person could just live out life at home, without worry.

"That's not a bad idea. But why was it personal? Hasn't everything you've said been your take on things?"

That would be like claiming "two plus two equals four" as your own idea. I've been talking about the laws of economics as they work at the roots. They have always been here. And they always will. The only thing that changes is the degree to which we recognize them.

"Have these ideas you're talking about been written about or spoken about before?"

The idea that man doesn't own the land goes back thousands of years. It's even mentioned by all the world's major religions. But the significance of land value to economics was first singled out in the eighteenth century. François Quesnay brought it to the world's attention in 1758 when his *Tableau Economique*,[iv] which was really more of a chart than a book, illustrated the importance of agricultural land to the economy. Many have written about it since, including David Ricardo and Adam Smith, but they didn't emphasize taxing land value. Henry George put the emphasis on taxing it and tried to popularize the idea here in America. It caught on enough for him to make a decent run for mayor of New York. He came in second but beat Teddy Roosevelt, the future president, who took third. This was late in the nineteenth century.

But even after I found all that work about it, the nuts and bolts of how land-value tax could work in real life were not immediately apparent to me. So I chose to think about it (a long time, as it turned out) before deciding I was ready to speak about it—to you, Sam.

"Why me?"

Because you're strong willed, but I also knew you'd be open to the conversation. It's conversation that I'm after.

"Huh. Thanks."

You also ask questions that make me think. Like your question of creating new land from landfill.

"What happens if the mine is emptied before the lease expires? Does the lease get revalued again?"

See? That's what I'm talking about. That's another good question.

No, the lease wouldn't get revalued because it was valued, in part, for the static value in the first place, for the duration of the lease. If a miner can get the value out quicker, that might help their profits, but it wouldn't change the lease. What happens when the lease ends is the real issue.

Then, what is there for the future of the community, is the surface of the land. Remember—there is a static value component and a surface value component to that lease. So if the surface is left in the same condition as before the mining occurred, the community can enjoy the fact that, economically speaking, the property was well tended. The act of mining did not cause harm.

But if the surface is left uninhabitable after the mining is done, or even in some way worse than before, then the community is not whole. The community has to be compensated for whatever value is taken from it. So users are always responsible for maintaining their property either by restoring its surface enough to attract a new user or by compensating the community through a new lease for the original surface value.

"You're going to kill the mining industry!"

It's not so onerous if you consider that mines are often in areas where habitability is low to begin with, so restoring the surface to an equivalent value is not necessarily an untenable burden. But it must be done or be accounted for. We can't have habitable land being turned to rubble without the community being compensated.

"So what then? When the mining company is done with it, they have to restore the land to where people can live there again?"

Yes. And then their obligation is over.

"What if people don't want to live there?"

Then the mining company is on the hook for what that rent would have been. By law, they would have to sign a new lease at the value of the land's pre-mined surface condition.

"So I see that land-value tax comes with built-in incentive to maintain the surface value. And why won't that kill industry?"

It's community responsibility. And, like I said, mining is usually on land with low surface value.

"What if the land was never habitable, like a mountain? And a strip mine knocks it down?"

Strip mines are mining's version of low-hanging fruit. Less work is needed to get the product ready for market, so static values are greater there than for identical stuff buried deep down. What remains the same, regardless, is the active value. Once it's loaded onto a train, the value of a ton of whatever is the value of a ton of whatever.

"So?"

So ... because the market is going to value them that way, the community receives more static value from surface deposits than from deeper deposits. It may turn out that surface mining is not significantly cheaper for mining companies. But if a profit can be made, rest easy, Sam, it will still be done.

"You're not talking fast, Jorge. And I have to go. And you didn't answer my question."

I'm sorry. You're right about the mountain. There's a beauty lost to strip mining that cannot be replaced. That's a shame, but it's also realistic. I have heard of people trying to replace mountains, and if it can be reasonably done, it should be done. But at least the community is compensated for the material that is taken.

"From the static value. I get that. But the beauty's gone. What happens to the guy who had a view?"

Unfortunately, land-value measures potential use, not natural beauty. Rent isn't collected for a property being something to see. Rent is collected for being where people want to stand when they look. But it can sometimes happen that views get blocked or lost. If something to see is valued enough by a person, let that person bid to secure it. If it's valued enough by the community overall, then it's the role of government to protect it, maybe make it a park. In any case, when the mine is depleted or abandoned, a new lease will value that land at its potential for industrial or residential use. The free market will determine this by saying which use has greater value. The mining company's incentive is to bring its land up to market potential. Either it does, or no one else will want to take the property off its hands. If need be, the mining company will have a brand-new lease based on a hypothetical restored potential.

"Even if no one lived there before?"

Yes.

"That'll kill business! How is that fair? They could end up paying forever."

The incentive is to take care of the community, not pillage the community. The company will get a fair profit on what they take, but it has to leave a property the community can use. It's not fair either to take both the static value and the surface value.

"Making them pay forever sounds more like extortion than taking care of the community."

Sam, you're saying it would be forever. But I'm not. It's not like mining is going to happen there again. The land needs to be available for residential use or industrial use. That's not a task that will take forever to complete. And especially not when it's known to be a leasing condition in the first place.

"Still, wouldn't that make land-value tax onerously expensive?"

Well, it's also a cost to the community if the land is left unusable. It could be a big cost to its future growth. So you tell me: who should bear that cost—the company or the community?

"Well, I know enough to know you're going to say the company should bear it."

Shouldn't it?

"If it doesn't kill business."

Then let's look at economic efficiency. The value lost from a community's future can far exceed the cost to a company's profits. It's businesslike to let the money talk, right?

And why would it kill business anyway? If you're going to dig a hole in the land, just save your dirt, keep it clean, and refill the hole when you're done. Nobody expects things to be exactly as they were before, just economically useable. If it's arable, it could even become free land.

"The private company is going to be more efficient with the money than will the government."

If government funds are going to meet community needs that the free market failed to meet, then who's to say?

"So land users really have to be mindful of potential land values. One company could see higher value if they tried to reconstruct the way it was. But another could decide to prepare the property for another use altogether. This could change the way some businesses think."

It could, and it should. We all must respect land, especially in that it doesn't belong to us. It's only when land's surface value is ruined that there's a problem. No one has the right to cause land to fall out of use from the community … not without paying for it, whether it's intentional or not. A chemical spill, for example.

"Ah, pollution. That's got to get complicated."

If spoiled land can't be restored to its original state, then economic potential is forever lost. It's not complicated. The spoiler must pay rent as though it wasn't spoiled.

"In a free market, wait, or what I thought was a free market—okay, let me restart. Jorge, you know I don't want government in my business. But those who pollute and try to hide from their responsibility are repulsive. I mean, if they actually harm other people, poison them, or warp the gene pool or whatever, and they try to sweep it under the rug, well … that's just evil. I root for industry and business wholeheartedly, but I draw the line when profit is more important than life. It's … just disgusting."

Economics can't do everything. Some actions are criminal and beyond what is available to economic principles. But a land-value-based economy does have incentives to help avoid such behavior, be it intentional, accidental, or somewhere in between.

"It's never the place of economics to punish, is it."

Was that a question?

"It started to be, but then I realized it wasn't. You've said it's not up to the free market to punish. A market punishment is financial loss. That's all. I'm glad you think so. I like the market to be agnostic."

The market's morality is held in the rules that define it. If the goal is to provide human aspiration with an equality of opportunity, it's best when the rules show no favor and are drawn from simple principles of justice and fairness. It's only when they try to steer relative results that things get out of whack.

"But those polluters—what can an agnostic market do about it when it's not just their property that's ruined but the neighbors'?"

The market tells us the value that's lost. Land values move in tides of technological change or population drifts. So neighboring plots are not going to vary dramatically from each other unless something special is found buried in one. Barring that, if it's seen that the value of one plot is newly and dramatically lower than those of adjacent plots, the economic harm is clear. Desecrated land causes the community to lose economic potential, and polluted property can remain both harmful and underutilized for a long time. Still, with land-value tax, there's a lease. A secured user is responsible for the duration of it. With ruined land, she'll find it quite hard or impossible to earn her rent.

The community is due the value of land, as if in unsoiled condition, regardless. So when that lease expires, if no other person steps up to bid a new lease, she'll be obligated to continue paying the community that original value ... not the diminished, spoiled value. This obligation could continue for generations, through a company's life or a family's legacy, even a hundred years ... but not forever. Forever, as you say, is a very long time.

Probably the biggest difference between miners and polluters is that miners tend their own land while polluters can wreck neighboring plots too ... unless the miner is also a polluter.

"That's rich."

Either way, if there's a measurable drop in value, the offender becomes responsible for that diminishment. The amount of lost value on any land affected becomes part of the polluter's obligation. She will be made to pay rent for what she cost the community, on her property and her neighbors' too.

But the secured users with damaged plots would still have responsibility for whatever economic value remained of their properties. Only the value lost to pollution would be borne by the offending neighbor.

"What if the victim can't use their land at all?"

Then it has lost all economic value. The polluter is responsible for paying the lost value, every year, until the land is useable again. Whatever harms are born by the victim, from lost capital and lost opportunity, is for the courts to decide.

"Just economically, that's a lot of incentive for anyone to take good care of the land."

And it's just.

"Seems like it would kill business."

Why do you keep thinking land-value tax will kill business? You said yourself there would be an adjustment in the way businesses think. The new thinking is: In exchange for using a community's land, take responsibility to tend that land. And the community, in return, won't charge tax on anything created or earned. If this is known before any lease is signed, why is it too onerous for business?

"It sounds like a real burden ... the potential liability, anyway."

The destruction of the opportunity that land represents shouldn't come without a proportionate cost to those who destroy it. Lost land affects everyone.

"So what if free land is ruined by pollution? Then there's no value to begin with."

It's not very likely to happen. Land is free because there's so little economic activity on it in the first place.

"Don't dodge it, Jorge. You've heard of dumping? Trucks have been known to leave things behind in the dark of night ..."

Been watching a lot of mysteries lately?

"Or maybe even in broad daylight. It happens."

Then ... assuming the dumper can be found ... because it's a business, it must lease competitively valued property, and the amount of free land ruined is compensated for at the level of the business's most expensive lease.

"Huh?"

Free land is still economic opportunity. It provides for economic freedom. If a business dumped pollutants and ruined some acreage of free land, then it should pay the community back by giving up equivalent acreage of its own land, or pay double rent until that ruined land is restored. The community can decide, so long as the punishment is taken seriously.

"How would giving acreage back restore the balance? If my property's in the middle of town, it's not like we just ship two acres over to where the free land is."

Yes, that's well seen. But if your actions cause two acres to be lost to economic use, it's just to give up two of your own. You're right, Sam, that the economics isn't really restored. It can't be, unless the ruined land is restored. The point is that the penalty for a deliberate or even a negligent polluter needs to be severe. Jail wouldn't be out of the question either.

"The government would just take my land, my two acres?"

If you've shown no regard and ruined someone else's land or the community's land, why not? Wouldn't it be fair?

"Well, I suppose an eye for an eye; an acre for an acre. But then, it's not just land. It's the water. It's the air."

I was just going to say … a more appropriate term than land might be Earth. Soiling the natural purity of water has a negative effect on the land it quenches. If air becomes less breathable, that, too, hurts the value of the land it blankets. All of Earth counts—land, water, and air. It's Earth, in its combination of resources, that we're giving economic value. Polluting it can ruin the potential of an entire community.

But the reasons to care about pollution aren't just economic, or the notion of caring for Mother Earth; it's ultimately about freedom. If clean land, clean water, and clean air were at the very beginning of our economic development, then they are the original conditions of freedom. And they must stay that way. All three must be kept clean for man to have his true freedom. Unless there are accessible places where air, land, and water are free to use, man cannot be free.

People need the choice to act competitively or not, or there's not freedom. This is why the unfettered no must exist. If you must pay for what nature originally provided, be it the land, water, or air, then it's impossible for you to be free.

* * *

"I really need to go. I'm late. But, Jorge, consider me sold."

You are not sold.

"I'm not?"

No.

"Why not?"

Because there is more to understand before you can believe it deeply. I'm glad you don't think I've wasted your time. But without delving further, your good feeling can be swayed. Sam, I want you to carry this in your bones. I want this economics to be akin to your knowing the sun will rise and set, akin to your knowing that gravity pulls things down. Even if it's never implemented, the forces of a true free market will always exist. Understanding them can only help you.

"I'm late. I really have to go."

That's too bad. Is our whole conversation over? Or just for now?

"We can continue. But I'll have to meet you tomorrow. My place, and we'll go from there."

Okay, we'll stay out of parks. You tell me what works for you. And I'll make it work for me. Please say hi to Ada for me. And Marga. Home safe, Mr. Rueul.

"You too, Mr. Olduvai."

CHAPTER 7

Free Land Ho!

Jorge saw Sam on a cement sidewalk, watching him as he exited the cushioned commuter train.

Hey there, Mr. Rueul! Did you get the vacuum?

"One of those robot hockey pucks. We watched it work while we had wine on the couch. Moves like a drunk genius."

Such domestic bliss!

"Right. Here, this way, Mr. Olduvai."

The town's Main Street was a walk uphill from the tracks that paralleled the wide, shimmering Hudson River.

"And while I was sitting there, I was thinking, Jorge. There isn't any free land anymore."

No, unfortunately, there isn't.

"You can't just will it into existence. So in your plan, how does it come to be?"

Yesterday we talked about the competitive footprint of a community. Once the business people are doing business and the residents are residing, the competitive market is satisfied. It doesn't need to use any more land. Land that's leftover is the free land, managed by the community to maintain the unfettered no.

"People aren't going to leave land sitting there, Jorge. If it's not spoken for, someone is going to claim it. There won't be any free land."

But the competitive market requires only so much land. We agree on that. Claims on what's left, by definition, can only be speculative in nature.

I understand, Sam, that this might be hard to imagine. We've never seen a land-value-based economy. It has been tried but not properly. A town called Free Acres, New Jersey, tried. And Pittsburg, Pennsylvania, less than fifty years ago, gave the idea a small piece of their tax code. But of course, the true effects were lost to being overwhelmed by the larger surrounding economies. So we're left with imagining it. Imagining something that's never existed isn't easy.

"Yeah, yeah. Fine. But what's the logic? How does it happen?"

Is it clear that our economy is structured inefficiently?

"Our current one? Very inefficiently. I'll give you that."

Well, according to government statistics, as we speak, about 10 percent[v] of all the acreage in the country, not including parks, is not being used. Some of that unused land is in our cities, some is in our suburbs, and some is in rural areas. It's sitting somewhere, and it's almost everywhere, with nothing productive about it. So it's reasonable to say that our current market economy doesn't need 10 percent of the land it claims. Otherwise it would be in productive use now or soon. So, if 10 percent of usable land isn't being used under our current inefficient scheme, how much land would be unused if land use was more efficient?

"Ten percent?"

Yes, at least! And that, Sam, would be the minimum. With smarter laws in place, the percentage of free land would likely rise even higher because once city center plots are fully developed, they will be absorbing economic activity that now uses land in outer areas.

All this is saying that land-value tax shifts land vacancies from random places, like we see it today, to concentrate them in the least economically desirable areas. Over time, inner-city vacancies will fill with productive uses. Suburban vacancies will be replaced with homes, apartments, office buildings, and stores. The holes in land use will fill in.

"So rural areas get all the vacancy?"

Yes. But we're not talking about dumping abandoned buildings on ranches. We're talking about seeing the availability of unused land becoming concentrated and obvious, in big sky–type areas or wooded ones.

What I'm saying is that when the competitive market has digested all the land it needs, the remaining unclaimed land around it will be left with little or no value assigned. That's where the noncompetitive part of society can thrive, where anyone not driven by competition can make a home.

"Where might these free lands end up being? I mean specifically … in reality."

Well, the island of Manhattan won't have marginal land. There's far too much economic activity there for land value to be low or free. But in the state of Montana, which is large and sparsely populated, there will be many, many acres of land with little or no demand available for this use.

"Really? So in a true free market, if a poor New Yorker doesn't want to work for someone else, he has to move to Montana?"

No. Certainly not. I was just using our old example. Because New York City is so densely populated, it would take some distance from Times Square for land value to decline to free. But, as one travels out from the center, places will be found with only sparse economic activity, perhaps in upstate New York, Pennsylvania, or Connecticut. But within the picture I'm drawing, since current land use is inefficient, those cheap or free lots will be closer than you might think. They could be 10 or even 20 percent closer when under a land-value tax.

"There are no free lots today."

But there will be if capital taxes are replaced by a land-value tax. The efficiency of a true free market might surprise you.

"Since I'm not imagining it, it would definitely surprise me."

Competition is straightforward, Sam. Its attractions and limits aren't complicated. Places are finite, right? Competition sorts out who uses what. It is reasonable and fair to expect Fifth Avenue to be efficiently used by hard workers, or those who saved enough and used to be hard workers. And it's reasonable and fair to think that anyone who aspires to live or work there would have the opportunity to achieve it through legitimate competition, by working in a fair market. Cities are for people who want to engage in the free market, or who have already done so and can afford the lifestyle. Cities are the epitome of economic competition. Cities are not for those who would rather minimize competition.

"So the poor have to go upstate?"

They would have the choice to live in multifamily housing as they mostly do now, or they could move to live on free land and support themselves that way. It's not that in a true free market the poor suddenly find their lives to be great in an aspirational sense, but they will have lives that are dignified and truly free in an economic sense.

"What happens with welfare?"

No welfare ... not for the able-bodied. It's not needed. Welfare only helps the incapacitated or the infirm.

"As you were saying it, I already knew you'd say it."

Good.

"Maybe, Jorge."

Maybe? That's something.

"So what's to stop speculators from speculating, especially if land is free? I'd be a land speculator too if it was free! Who wouldn't?"

The rules of a free market work as a mechanism to prevent it.

"What rules? You mean the government takes it?"

No, the free market takes land. It has dibs. Government has only the leftovers to manage. In very rare cases, if the economy needs more free land, the government can reclaim some, what would be low-value land, and make it free. But this isn't likely to happen, because a true free market is stable. If it ever did have to happen, well, the unfettered no must be ever-present and work for all, after all, and is the priority. Democratic government's operating principle is to ensure opportunity and freedom for everyone.

"But if the market values it, even cheaply, why is it okay for the government to take it? How, in any case, do you expect people to just give up their land? There'd be a civil war over that."

For one, land is leased, so no one is going to ask anyone to give up his or her land.

"Yes, you are! And in two ways. One, you just said if more free land is needed, the government could take it. And two, to issue land leases in the first place, to start your whole economy, you're taking people's land. It's land we bought. Right now, as we speak, we own it."

Again, the free market determines all this. By setting the rules for fair competition, it's freedom that's being served. We're accustomed to being on rolling economic seas with a certain power structure guiding us. Some are bound to wobble with their first steps on land value, as the power structure shifts.

But once a land-value-taxed economy is established, there'll be economic equilibrium. There'll be city centers with high local land values. Moving outward from them, land value will gradually decline, down and down, until land with little or no value appears at the rural edges, at the margins.

"Like rings on a target ... but the point values are prices."

Yes, Sam. I like that! So any change in demand for free land is then slow and predictable. Only in extremely rare cases would government take land—very, very rare. So, in the extraordinary case that additional free land was needed because of something like a population explosion or a huge shift in technology, low-value land could be procured by eminent domain, which is just what we have today, written into our Constitution. Government today is allowed to remove people from their property and compensate them. The difference is that, in a true free market, leases wouldn't be renewed. And government would buy any structures or improvements on the property. With users being given years of notice, land could move into community control fairly painlessly. Because of the economic efficiencies in place, this would only happen on already cheap land. And it would happen less often that it already does today.

Jorge labored with the long uphill walk to the town's center, accustomed as he was to the relative flatness of the city. Sam didn't seem to feel it at all.

"Remember I had asked about speculation? If land's so cheap or free at the margins, what's to stop a speculator?"

Are you comfortable that on competitive land, land-value tax takes care of the problem?

"Yes. We went through that."

So where land is very cheap or free, it's easy to think that speculators, as you point out, have no real cost to making their bets. This is why there are rules. Rules define the economic playing field for competitors and noncompetitors alike.

"How can a rule tell the difference between a speculator and anyone else?"

A rule can't tell. But with no leases available, speculators will stay away. They can't speculate when they have no claim on a property.

"So there are no secured users on free land?"

No.

"Really? No one will do anything without having a stake, Jorge. Who would go there?"

Anyone who wants to live outside the competitive market.

"But who would want to? When you don't have a stake in your home … your own home?"

People will have homes and their own bed to sleep in every night. The government will be assigning plots to people as they apply for free land.

"So there's a record of who lives where … an official record?"

A record of who has the right to live where. Yes. But government would retain discretion over free land. So if it did acquire a competitive value, government could decide to auction it, depending on the general availability of free land. But since free land users will have no favored standing in those auctions, speculators will have no incentive to speculate. Also, a free land assignment means you actually have to live there.

"Second homes?"

No. Free land is only for people who choose to not be in the competitive market.

"Then you can't speculate from a distance."

You can't speculate at all.

"What about the big ranches with acres and acres?"

What about them?

"How can you tell if they're using the acres to speculate or to ranch?"

There just needs to be enough ranching done on them to justify paying land-value tax. Ranching is a competitive activity. That's what would distinguish it from speculation. Ranchers will use land and pay for its use. Speculators won't have that option, not on free land. The community's power to protect accessibility to free land lies in not offering leases. Or if the bids are very low, it might not be leased. The government will decide if that cutoff is needed, based on the demand for free land.

"I don't know. It doesn't sound as free as the rest of what you're saying."

The ability to say no is the crux of economic freedom. True economic freedom has to start with preserving free access to land.

"Doesn't mean land owners won't be pissed to lose their land."

I'm sure you're right. Change is always hard for some. But if people are willing to die for freedom, it should be relatively painless to give over control of a little unused land for the same cause.

"Isn't the guy who owns it entitled to freedom?"

Of course! He just has to compensate the community for its value. It's his choice to live competitively or not. If there's no value, and his choice is to compete, it's hard to say there's much of a threat to his individual freedom. Although there is a large threat to the rest of us, in keeping freedom from others. A plot with no development, no tax revenue, and no opportunity for others is an economic drag on the community. But it can be turned into a positive if it's used to ensure the presence of the unfettered no and keeps the government as small as possible. Maybe that newly reclaimed land becomes a school or a hospital. Or ten or fifty new households will homestead on it.

Look, you could interpret the fact that we can't yell "fire" in a crowded theater as infringing on our rights. But you don't, do you?

"No."

That's because of the obvious harm that can be caused to other people. Occasionally taking properties out of private circulation amounts to the same understanding. It's not infringing on someone's rights if the effect of not limiting him will harm others—just like saying to someone, "You can't yell 'fire' right now." That's exactly what freedom is—the right to say or do whatever you want so long as it doesn't harm or threaten others' rights.

Because here's the point—once the competitive market has made its choices, and free land is available, economic freedom can begin. Poverty is no longer a problem. Earth is better tended. Economic cyclicality is moderated. A meritocracy of skill and ambition replaces the lottery of birth. And the compensation for our work is only our own.

Land leases are crucial to get right. They are how people put down roots, raise families, and start businesses. Leases will be appropriate lengths for our lives, as the free market determines it. With that resulting economic stability and this simple, transparent land-tenancy system, a shift in land use won't cause local panics.

"Sounds like there are insecure users in your dream, not secured ones. Not comforting."

We're now harping on extremely rare cases. All land values are public knowledge, so the lowest-value land will always be clear for all to see. None of it would be capricious.

"Rare or not, it sounds wrong. And it sounds ripe for government corruption, with people asking for special favors all the time."

They can ask, but they won't get—not in a true free market. Transfers can only be made from the private market to the government or vice versa. Government doesn't get involved in what a free market does, other than to establish its basic rules or to ensure the defense of the nation. Open auctions make any transfer fair. Auctions effectively disallow any prearranged deals. And if the government ever did reclaim land, it could only happen through lease expiration and fair value paid for structures. With sufficient notice, there'd be little surprise or harm. Besides, any land government "takes" could only be for government use, like a school or hospital, or perhaps a park or a military base, or, yes, free land.

"Government can only take land out of the free market for its own use? Nothing private?"

Correct. And by the way, again, only from what lands the free market refuses to significantly value. So we, collectively, decide that.

"So basically you're going to piss off landholders, and they're just going to roll over and take it?"

A few will be angry, of course, and they will fight these ideas. But, as land value is recognized and seen as benefitting all of us, they won't have a lasting argument. Landowners who are efficient with their properties have little to fear, profiting as they do from their land through the capital they employ. And remember—because all other taxes disappear, the cost of development will shrink. The price of labor and materials won't be tax-inflated. So if landowners won't develop enough to make a go of it, then perhaps they won't even bid for their lot. Economies don't guarantee everyone's success.

But truly free economies do guarantee everyone's opportunity. It's just that if you are going to claim an opportunity, you need to be ready to use it ... and pay the value at something close to its best use. Owners who are now just holding land, waiting for a highway to be built or a law to be passed, or for city growth to bring value to the property, are the ones who won't like it. Land-value tax makes it expensive to hold an undeveloped plot for years on end, simply to see what happens. I'm sorry about the angry people. But the cost of lost freedom and opportunity is born by all of us, so I'm not sure what rational arguments they could find. Are they going to argue that the rest of us should pay for their hopes? If you're going to claim land, use it. Or let it go for someone else to work.

"Come on, Jorge. They'll find a way to hold the land for speculation, anyway. They'll blame the bureaucracy for being slow with a permit or an inspection or something. Or the property will be tied up in a lawsuit. It won't be hard for them to come up with a reason."

If you're talking about competitive lands, yes, rich people can afford to be uneconomical for far longer than the rest of us. At least land-value tax makes sure the community is fully compensated for their wait. But, regardless, we can't allow land use to be controlled by manipulating courts. The rules in place when the lease is signed are the legal conditions for that lease. If a secured user tries to change those rules, full rent would still be due throughout the process.

"What if a new law changed the value of the property in the middle of a lease?"

If the change made a property more valuable, presumably there wouldn't be an issue. But if the new law decreased a property's value and could be shown to be capricious, then the court could make an adjustment in rent, retroactive to the start of the law.

They passed a quaint store with two old-fashioned neon signs glowing behind its window.

"We'll be at the restaurant in a few minutes. But I can get bottles of water here, if you'd like."

Thanks, Sam. I'm fine.

"So, what's the difference between a lease on competitive land and being assigned free land? It doesn't sound much different."

A lease is a commitment to working or living in the competitive market. One is then actively trading for a salary or a profit, or is retired and living off of those competitively earned savings. When land is assigned, the commitment is to working that land, with minimal trading. On free land, one is not allowed to work for a salary, and one is not allowed to hire others for chores.

"Then what do you do?"

You grow your own food. Maybe arrange with your neighbors to take care of each other.

"What? It's like a barter economy?"

Barter would be the bulk of it. On free land, sustenance has to come from what you do with the land, so barter might include swapping excess food for furniture that neighbors built. So free land plots have to be arable. Because if they don't offer self-support, they don't offer an unfettered no.

"What about money?"

It could be used, but only for light trade. Money could buy you transportation if you wanted, but it couldn't buy your daily food. That has to come from your effort on the land you're given.

"But how do you define it? At what point is light trade crossing into the competitive market?"

If you're using money, you're in the competitive market. To maintain the free-land lifestyle, money use has to be limited. For example, everyone on free land will have a home that reflects our community generosity. And if you're living there, you've committed to the lifestyle. You'll be able to use your money to decorate it to your liking, but you won't be allowed to expand it. No decks or pools out back. No additions up, down, or sideways. You could buy an expensive painting to put on your wall. But you won't be allowed to improve on the infrastructure by running special pipes or wires. The thrust of the life on free land is in living off the land. If you choose that lifestyle, your deal with the community is that you've been provided means to care for yourself and your family outside the competitive market, and in exchange, you must follow the rules about living there.

If you can't afford a starter set of seeds, the community can give it to you. But any help anyone on free land hires, at whatever cost, would be limited to occasional or one-off situations: to fix something in the house or to help remove or trim a tree. And there will be no stores around. Free lands are residential only. The main rule there is to tend the land yourself.

"What would they do, arrest you for hiring a gardener?"

They well might. But if you're living off the land, wouldn't you be better off hiring a farmer?

"Okay. Obviously, I wouldn't know the first thing about it."

I'm sure you'd figure it out if you needed to. How to grow food is one of the first things mankind ever learned. And it can't be that hard or we'd have starved ourselves into smallness as a species a long time ago.

"With my own hands?"

Yes. Or the hands of your immediate family.

"I don't know …"

I'd have faith in you, Sam.

"Could you do other things out of your home? Like an artist—could they sell art they painted in a free-land home?"

They could sell, sure. But they'd still have to get their hands dirty to grow their own food. No grocery shopping. It's about lifestyle. Free-landers actually have to live off the land they're using. If one is painting so often that they can't do that, or if they start buying their lifestyle, they won't be allowed to stay. It's time to move.

"To the competitive market."

Yes.

"And pay rent. Become a professional artist."

Yes. Or whatever.

"So how is there no ownership, or secured usership, there? I mean, why plant seeds if you're not sure that what grows is going to be yours in the morning?"

Lot assignments will be public record. The local police will enforce it.

"Then why not offer leases?"

It's the free market that has determined there's little or nothing that a lease would be worth. And the only way a community can be sure of a free-lander's commitment, and keep speculators at bay, is to make sure that they can't devote themselves to profit.

"Well, if they're not allowed to profit, then they're not free! And hasn't economic freedom been your whole point?"

But they are free, Sam. It's their choice to live that lifestyle in the first place. It's their choice to opt out of the competition. If competitive blood is in you, then you're free to earn a living through jobs or entrepreneurship. If not, the noncompetitive lifestyle is there for you. There's that choice. But in today's world, there's not that choice at all.

That choice makes all the difference. People who abuse the free-land pact will be ejected—even sent to jail for frauds against the lifestyle. That may sound harsh to you. But free land is the heart of everyone's true freedom. The bargain that their users make with the community can't be taken lightly. If you want the land, then you have to live from the land.

"But it's not like people can move to free land, and in the morning they suddenly have peas and carrots and tomatoes. It takes time to grow food. So the government would still have to tide them over, wouldn't it?"

That's true. People won't have homegrown things to eat right away. There can be a transition period established by the community, perhaps equal to a growing season, when edibles and seeds are supplied to those who need them. But the decent living wage a proper market affords means a person is able to save something for the future and take responsibility for their future. Ex-workers going to live off free land can have a last hurrah of sorts, buying what they want to bring to their modest new life. They're already getting a place for free. The government doesn't have to get further involved with those who can take care of themselves.

"What about water and electricity?"

This is what every community needs to decide. No able person in the nation is going to live a lifestyle less than that lived on free land. So the community's question is, do we want that lifestyle to be from arable land alone or something more? Competitively unneeded land isn't likely to have robust infrastructure. It's initially likely a place with well water and a septic area, rather than a water main and a sewage system. But, once these free areas are established, in the transition to land-value tax, the community has to choose how lacking poverty should be. Should it be given a sewage system or a reservoir? Should people have electricity or wireless networking? Anything that can be considered infrastructure is fair game to define the nation's standards.

We could reasonably expect a more luxurious lifestyle on free lands of wealthy nations than on free lands of poor ones. A wealthy nation ought to have better infrastructure.

"And the housing?"

That's where the difference between rich and poor nations would really show. A rich nation will find it affordable to seed free land with modest housing, including flushing toilets, as opposed to a poor nation's tin-roofed shacks or tents. But once established, the housing on free land would sustain itself, as with any market. People there would fix up and tweak their homes, and when they moved on, they'd leave them for others to occupy.

"What incentive would people have to take care of their home if they're not invested in it? People, some of them, would just trash it."

Don't you think people can care about their lifestyle? Especially when it's completely their choice? We're talking about a system with little economic frustration to vent. People who desired a more luxurious life would be elsewhere, but pride would be everywhere, not just in competitive places. Besides, if anyone did trash a home the community gave them, the community would have every right to claim an equivalent value from whatever assets they had. Or jail them.

"Of course, jail. I can't forget whom I'm talking to. Would they have a choice in where they live? Could they pick their home or plot?"

People could choose the general location. There'd be a public registry of where free land was available. But the government would assign the specific property.

"I don't know. It sounds expensive, like a big cost to government."

The only big cost is in the transition from a capital tax to a land-value tax. But that's a one-time expense, and the amount depends on what the community chooses to do for the infrastructure of free land. Afterward, savings would be felt throughout the economy. Significantly smaller food programs, welfare programs, and unemployment programs become the norm. Public housing programs will shrink, too, after the start-up cost. And then, between the emergence of the unfettered no and the public audits of financial and other promissory businesses, there will also be a shrinking need for employment regulation, financial regulation, and even environmental regulation. For other than the auditing, policing, and military, government can shrink dramatically. Savings will also appear from no longer having to understand, explain, or enforce thousands of pages of tax code.

"You're saying all that aligns?"

I am.

"It just seems so different. It's hard to grasp."

But it can be imagined.

"Sorry, Jorge, but it's bothering me. This sounds so ripe for corruption. You're really just depending upon the good will of politicians to administer it, right?"

As I said, no economic system is a de facto panacea. Every economy depends upon shared beliefs and the community's fortitude to make it work. Participants have to believe in the system and want it to succeed. What if a sport hired a referee who didn't care for the integrity of the game? He could easily make it an event to bet his own fortune or to give out favors without regard for players or fans. The quality of the game would suffer. Likewise, regulators and administrators have to believe in the economic system for it to work.

"We're not angels, Jorge. You can't depend on the kindness of politicians."

This might seem specious to you, I understand. But ultimately, after all the incentives and disincentives have been accounted for, a system can only be as clean as the people running it.

"Have you accounted for all the incentives and disincentives?"

In our conversation, not yet. When we do, this whole regimen will, I think, seem sounder to you.

Poorly designed free-market economies, like ours, suffer exuberant highs and depressive lows. A true free market is far more stable, its capital and economic energy more efficiently deployed. But for an economy to have that stability, free lands have to be available to absorb and release the flows of workers as competitive markets expand and contract, like economic ballast. This is another incentive for the community to manage free land well.

"Ballast?"

A true free market is a three-way balance. The balance is among people working competitively for a living, the small minority who instead choose to live off the land, and a government whose workers enforce the rules, protect us, and provide us with what the free market cannot.

"So where's the ballast?"

The ballast is in access to free land, in the openness of the economy, to accommodate changes in labor. I'll give an example: Sometimes technology will create shifts in the skill sets required for workers. Access to free land means that employees who are resistant to being retrained can drop out of the workforce, without any lasting dependence on community funds. And without being forced to look for new work, which only helps keep salaries down for all the equally unskilled. This is not to say that so many would make it their choice to opt out, but everyone would have the choice. Just having it available removes much of the pressure and leverage that exacerbates poverty, the way opening a window even a crack lets fresh air into a room. Once equilibrium between competitive and noncompetitive people is achieved, government expenditures to care for the needy won't appreciably rise or fall during economic cycles. Today's able-bodied needy become truly self-sufficient.

"Wouldn't government expenses rise in a downturn? Free land will fill up."

There might be a slight increase in demand for free land, but regular economic cyclicality wouldn't cause it to fill. Employers are the ones competing for workers, remember; it's not like today, where workers are competing for employers. After enticing good employees, there'd be a businesslike resistance to firing them as a way to maintain profitability, for fear of losing them. That means government unemployment costs wouldn't rise so fast. And because low-end wages wouldn't be dragged down by the desperation of some, there would be no working poor, nor their poverty-level dependence on government.

"But … I don't get it. Government expenditures rise when the economy tanks. That's basic. Unemployment goes up, so those government payments go up. Food stamps go up. Even government disability payments go up. I suppose people ache more when the economy's tough. But that's what happens … today. That doesn't happen with a true free market?"

It will happen, some. Cycles are natural. They just don't have to be so strong. Sam, capital-taxed cycles swing to where the wealth of affluent people is raised like mountains in good times, and poverty is spread like gravel in bad times, subject only to the government programs that mitigate it. Cycles will be muted with a land-value tax, because of that balance I mentioned. People who want to work for compensation will be working. And people who'd rather work for themselves will be working on the land they live on. So the notion of structural unemployment is effectively vanquished. There are only short, temporary displacements due to cycles in a true free market. Long-term unemployment is not an issue either. Even in a down economy, free land can absorb the few who might become newly unemployed, leaving government spending levels relatively unchanged.

"Wow."

Sam, I hope this is a reasonable plan to you, not just my fanciful hope.

"Well ... it's hard to adjust to your way of thinking. There's reasonableness to it, even if I don't get it all."

Here's the thing about today's economy: taxing capital results in politicians managing incentives and disincentives for economic behavior. That's always a concern, isn't it? But taxing land value is about letting the market work without manipulations and only charging for the price of the opportunity taken, like admission. It eliminates artificial pressures on poverty. It eliminates artificial downward pressures on wages. It leaves employers with only one way to improve profits: to make the land more productive. That means the whole economy experiences new breath in the ongoing need for capital investment, and employees, at every level, become inherently dear to employers.

In a land-value-taxed economy, free land acts as ballast, absorbing and releasing cyclical ebbs and flows that curve around an already more efficient employment base. Free land becomes a resource for the needy, a refuge for the tame, and a salvation from overreaching government. Government is no longer leveraging its revenues to capital, bringing exaggerated swings of value to the economy's capital base.

"I'm not sure I see it all clearly. But some individual things make sense, I'll admit. I just can't get over how simple it is, yet how big the effects would be."

I'd love to know where you find the holes. I want the opportunity to fill them in. If I can't, I'll say to you, "You're right, and it's not going to work." But at least I will have tried. We have so many problems today. If people just start thinking about it, how freedom is forged by economics, even if these ideas get torn apart, I'd be thrilled.

"Why would you be thrilled by people tearing your ideas apart?"

Because by having the conversation, no matter the result, we'll get a better economy for it. And I don't think I'd be wrong on every point.

"I at least like that you enforce the idea of personal responsibility. And since government responsibilities will shrink, what happens to Social Security? Gone too?"

A lifestyle earned from wages must include saving for one's future when wage earning ends. But under our schemes for taxing capital, many people don't do it. And not necessarily because they don't want to. Most simply don't have the wherewithal to save. When the government's role is outsized by the very system it chooses to support, people expect help from government. We have to insist that we learn, as a community, how to allow individual responsibilities to be owned individually. Not everything is predictable, but even a child can learn that life requires planning for the unknown. The least we can do is provide an economic structure that allows each of us to prepare for what is predictable—our aging. By eliminating desperation, a true free market allows all workers' salaries to be large enough to allow for saving. A land-value economy will allow personal responsibility to take root again.

"So Social Security disappears. I sure hope you're happy talking to angry people!"

Social Security needs to exist in our current economy because we tax capital in a closed economy. The issue is not the cost to government; the issue is our structural inability to allow for personal responsibility. Too many employers see employees as a cost instead of as a benefit. But we know that can be reversed. The economic attitude of the poor could shift from trying to survive to having hope and opportunity. Receiving a true wage instead of an artificially depressed wage would leave more room to save. And a more stable economy breeds more confidence in growing one's savings. The need for Social Security would evaporate, and the program could be comfortably phased out.

"Wow, Jorge. I never thought we'd see eye to eye on that."

If the need is no longer there, then there's no need for the program. The land-value economy is set, literally from the ground up, so that government doesn't have to do for people—like save for retirement—what they can do for themselves. A true free market allows every able-bodied person to have dignity and self-sufficiency.

"Jorge, I'm starting to get it."

Good.

CHAPTER 8

Some Things in the Air

Now I want to go back to your space question.

"Space question? Oh, paying tax from space? Really, Jorge, you don't have to answer that. I was joking. I mean … it's not really an issue … is it?"

If it's not an issue today, it will be. One day, communities will be in space. Children will be born there. Satellites are already there, by the thousands. We should talk about it.

"It's up to you."

Remember the family living on a boat? How land-value tax treated them?

"Yes. They got taxed through the fees from docking."

Well, space vehicles will be treated just like that. The materials used to build them will have come from land on Earth. The communities that hosted those mines will have been compensated with the material's static value. So, similar to the boat family, no tax is due simply because people are up there, at least initially. But docking fees will apply.

"That's one helluva long pier you're imagining."

Okay, I should have said landing fees, whenever they shuttle back. The economic difference between the family on the boat and families in space is, as more people and tools are sent into space, the growing demand will create value for specific locations of space.

"What locations are in space? You mean the moon and Mars?"

Perhaps, one day. But I'm also referring to orbits, geo-synchronous orbits. As ephemeral as it might seem, they're specific locations just like land, and they should be treated, economically, just like land.

"Orbits? Are land?"

As land is of limited supply, so too are orbits, especially geo-synchronous ones. Early pioneers found land for the taking. Early space-users have found orbits for the taking. Satellite owners are already claiming them. Just like land, they are in nature first, and then we claim them. And their available number is dwindling. As more orbits are claimed, their value will start to rise. And that value, like land value, comes from community demand and is due, like land-value tax, to the community. Economically, it's the same.

"What do you mean 'community'? In space? Who gets the tax?"

We do, here on the ground. Orbits are part of the planet's resources; they preceded us. But if countries claim orbits as property, secured users will begin to pay those countries rent as orbit values grow. It's just like land value, up there. Of course, if countries cooperated, all countries could share that value. It's hard to say exactly how the politics will play out.

"It's easy to guess that we won't play."

Ha! You're probably right. But you never know. Maybe it'll be a role for the United Nations; member nations could share in the orbit-value tax.

In any case, before orbits gain competitive value, space communities will be like families on a boat—only paying tax to the extent they depended on Earth-based communities.

"Depended on how? They're in space."

If they made regular trips to Earth, maybe to visit relatives or to get supplies, they'd need a place to land and take off again. The developer of that spaceport will be paying land-value tax. And he'll pass it along to users of his property.

"That's it? Costs get passed along to the space dwellers?"

That's it. Although a spaceport requires people to run it and maintain it. So people will be drawn to live nearby, to work there.

"Ah, you think a town will grow?"

Wouldn't it? New jobs will attract people.

"Go on."

But ultimate demand would come from the space station itself, with those thousands or tens of thousands of people on board.

"That spaceport land could be a steal. If a space population grew quickly, the spaceport could be a profit machine, collecting fees—huge fees—for every takeoff and landing."

Wouldn't that be great?

"But it seems like a case of one man creating land value, which is what you said couldn't happen. Look, I'm not opposed to someone getting rich, as you know. But with this spaceport, it seems like the exception to your rules. We have to be talking about remote land, right? Presumably, there's hardly a neighbor to give that land value. Yet a secured user can basically start a town and never pay much tax because the town grew after he signed the lease? Personally, I'd admire him. I'd want to be him. But couldn't that be a flaw in the system, in the context of what you've laid out?"

I see. It's true that land's value comes from those within a usable distance of it, but we're talking about an economic proximity. Installing elevators allows a property to generate more revenues because people can live or work above ground. Planes and trains allow people to use land in distant places. Land anywhere grows more valuable if people travel to be on it. And where they come from doesn't matter; it could be Rio, London, Shanghai, or outer space. When there are people who need the service, land takes on the value of that potential use. With travel or trade, it doesn't matter if it's a spaceport, an airport, or an ocean port. So it doesn't matter where people are coming from. It only matters that they arrive. Land value always comes from the needs of the population using it.

"But in your scheme, one guy doesn't create all that value."

But everyone can profit from the capital they employ. Our spaceport builder is merely anticipating the demand. The spaceport he builds is designed to channel the space dwellers' desires onto his site. Economically, it's no different than building an amusement park that attracts people from thousands of miles away. If he can make a development of that scale, and it works, and the land value grows under him, more power to him.

If someone has great foresight in anticipating our wants, the whole community is better for it. If his land lease seems undervalued after his success, we should congratulate him. It means others have been drawn to live and work nearby, and each of them has leased property at an ever-rising value. Our community should be grateful and happily wait for when his lease is renewed. The community coffers will grow anyway, along with the growing population he inspired.

It's exactly the sort of vigor from free capitalism that we'll always want to see.

There's something else in the air that operates the same way economically.

"So tell me."

Wavelength frequencies.

"What?"

The whole frequency spectrum. Radio. Cell phone. TV. Light. Anything that uses a frequency to communicate.

"How are they like land? At least someone can live in an orbit."

Economically speaking, they're the same as orbits. The principles are exactly the same. They're not man-made.

"Wavelength frequencies?"

Yes. They were here before we were, like land. They're of limited quantity, like land. And a platform for man's work, like land … and geo-synchronous orbits. So while we can't live in a frequency, our capital is employed on them. Their value certainly grows as demand grows. Our community is entitled to that value.

"How are frequencies not man-made? They wouldn't exist without radio and data networks."

Of course they would.

"Come on, Jorge. How can you say we didn't make them? It's not like dinosaurs had Wi-Fi."

They didn't have the transmitters or the receivers to use them, but the frequencies were certainly available. Man didn't invent frequencies. Wavelengths and vibrations were around before we discovered them. We only figured out how to use them.

"So you're saying there should be a frequency-value tax?"

It's operationally the same as a land-value tax or an orbit-value tax. The community, collectively, creates that value. And like land, frequencies can be securely used, so long as the public is fairly compensated for providing that secured use.

"I don't think we do it that way."

We don't. Spectrum is generally auctioned, but for ownership, not leasing. Consequently, much of the available spectrum in the frequency market overall is under-used, like the airwave equivalent of putting a paved parking lot in midtown. Certain segments may be fully used, but as a potential of what's available, it's not used very efficiently. It's clumpy, just like our current land usage. Airwaves would be efficiently used if they were leased at prices set by auction.

As last at a street traversing the top of the slope, the great river and train tracks shrunken below, they turned, away from a corner store selling state lottery tickets, toward the busier part of town.

"Jorge, I'm surprised you haven't mentioned income inequality. I mean … I don't have a problem with it, as long as the poor don't revolt. But you've talked about the poor being extra poor because of capital taxes."

And the rich being extra rich.

"The missing unfettered no, I know. But you haven't mentioned income inequality. That seems odd."

Income disparity is a problem when it's accompanied by a general sense of unfairness. If great wealth arises for a few while opportunity is limited for the lower classes, then society has a problem. In other words, if the only way out of poverty is by being unusually blessed with athleticism or intelligence or some other extraordinary luck, resentment will naturally grow. But if the system is resolutely fair, there can't be credible resentment toward the wealthy.

"Why not? Jealousy has nothing to do with fairness. It's just people wanting what they don't have."

If jealousy were the cause of class resentment, you'd have a point. But it's more likely that resentment is from a sense of unfairness, when someone else has gamed the system or was simply luckier at birth. People don't resent others for having what they've earned. They resent them for having what they haven't earned.

The real problem with financial inequality is where it wends its way into politics.

"Where's that?"

Politics is where the economy's rules are made. And people who have capital end up making the rules for those who don't. I'll get to that later.

To have a true free market, though, our ideas of ownership need to change. One fundamental rule of a true free market is: if a man didn't create it, a man cannot own it.

"That's simple."

It's universal. It applies to land, water, frequencies, geo-synchronous orbits, DNA, everything. We can claim them for long periods of secured usage that compensate the community. But we cannot own them.

Only what people create, by rearranging what existed before us, is ours to own. Like a tree gets turned into a chair and a table. Buildings, cars, jewelry, water pumps, windmills, art, media, medicines—these things are created, as opposed to discovered, and so are within the purview of ownership. They are capital and should not be taxed.

CHAPTER 9

Patent Tending

The confusion of what can be owned and what should never be owned creates stress fractures in an economy. But simply: only the result of work can be owned. To not allow that principle its full expression breeds inequality. Allowing ownership of anything else curdles fair opportunity.

"But owning genetic engineering? I heard you say DNA ..."

Yes.

"Really? DNA can have an owner—a secured user?"

Yes.

"Wow, Jorge. Now you're getting me a little scared."

Why be scared?

"Of genetic engineering? Are you kidding? Why wouldn't I be scared?"

Tell me why, Sam.

Across the otherwise peaceful street, a car honked at the slow backing-up of a loudly beeping truck.

"It's messing with the very nature of life, for one. And it's not like we don't make mistakes, for two. So how are you *not* afraid of genetic engineering? We could end up creating some Franken-creature that we can't control. God knows what harm we'd do. And you know we'd start redesigning ourselves. We'll end up losing touch with who we are. I'm not interested in the being without the human, if you know what I mean."

I do. I have those concerns too. But I'm not afraid of the science.

"How are you not? Instead of fear, you call it what, a healthy respect?"

Rather, if a true free market were in place, I wouldn't be afraid.

"Really? You're going to land-tax the fear away? Unfettered-no stupidity away? A Franken-thingy is a Franken-thingy; how could it matter where the taxes fall?"

But it does.

"Why? If all the wheat crops are eaten by some lab rat's mistake, taxes won't matter a whit."

No, not at the point the crops are devoured. But a true free market can make the fear of getting to that point matter a lot.

"To me? Or to the scientist?"

The scientist. Or whomever she works for.

"So you think financial incentives are going to protect us from a mistake? I think you've fallen off of Mount Rational, Jorge. It's called human error. You can't incent it away."

No. You're right. But we can incentivize precautions to prevent errors from getting too far.

"How, an error tax? Why am I not surprised? Actually, I am surprised."

May I? We just have to back up a bit.

"I'm sorry. Go ahead."

Well, all those things I've mentioned that existed before us: land, water, frequencies.

"Orbits."

Orbits too. They're about the distinction between legitimate and illegitimate ownership in a free and fair economy. They all require us to stake a claim in order to use them. And they are all finite. Access to them can run out. Therefore, the opportunity they represent is finite. Someone is likely to show up and want to use the exact same resource that is already in use: that very spot of land, that very water source, or that exact frequency. Without laws to sort it out, there would be chaos at best. We need a claim system, respected and secured by the community, or we wouldn't be able to create wealth or home with any reliability.

It's necessary that when a claim is granted to one, opportunity is lost for another. So it is just for the community to be compensated for securing a use for only one of us.

Take gold, for example. Anyone can own an amount of gold, but no one can own the rights to the element because gold is gold; it was here before we were.

"Gold is gold?"

It can't be changed. Elements are elementary. One could own the design if could be altered somehow. To be entitled to own whatever it became, it would have to be new to the universe to be patentable … a tricky challenge, at best.

"Can we back up some more? I need to get away from the periodic table. One thing you're saying is that the principles always apply. Or the forces, rather. The economic forces always apply."

Yes. They always apply.

"So in terms of ownership, after a gold deposit is discovered on someone's property, that person …"

Yes?

"… only owns whatever happens to it after it's out of the ground."

Exactly. It was their work that mined it.

"But what's this have to do with DNA? Why do you say we can own it at all, if it's already here like gold in the ground?"

Ah. We can't make more gold than what's already here, and we can't change its nature. But with DNA, while most of it, yes, preceded us, new forms of it will arrive after us. And some DNA is us, in our actual makeup. Gold has a single history; it got here and hasn't changed. But the variety of DNA has different histories; it might have been here for a million years, it might have more recently arrived, or it might be a new species we find in the future. But basic principles of economics give us a framework for how to treat each case.

Let's start with DNA that was, as you said, already here, those microorganisms—plants and animals—that have long been used by us for food and medicine. According to economic principles, none of these things in their original form can be owned, except by all of us beneficially through our community. They're like land in that way. Agreed?

"I don't know."

The question becomes: Can we stake a claim on these living things? Can a lease be struck so that the community is compensated in exchange for a biological code's exclusive use being given to a person or a company, for a fixed period of time?

"This is when I get a little scared about DNA."

Well, there's no reason to be afraid. Yet.

"Yet? Messing with the genetic code is no joke!"

Sorry, Sam. Let me be serious then. The question was the possibility of leasing living things.

Part of keeping a claim is the ability to control it and defend it. With land, we know a secured user can control it, and the community can defend it. A particular wavelength or frequency is the same; a secured user can control it, and the community can defend it. But for a preexisting microorganism, plant, or animal … who can control them or defend that claim? Seeds are windblown. Thriving animal populations can't be corralled. Microorganisms can't be seen. Any claim on the code for preexisting life is impossible. Even if some future technology made claiming a preexisting species doable, the price the market demanded for it would be huge. Imagine someone trying to say, "All cows are mine." All cows? Everywhere? A claim on all cows would be untenable … worthless, both impossible to defend and infinitely expensive to acquire. Not to mention what it would do to cow prices for the rest of us. Even if the claim was for just a tiny piece of every cow, like DNA, it wouldn't change these points. So for both moral and practical reasons, claims on forms of life that precede us cannot be valid.

"Is all preexisting life the same?"

I'm not sure what you mean.

"Beings were here a long, long time before we were. People might learn how to use them. Or clone them."

Are you asking about owning dinosaurs?

"Dinosaurs, plants, fish … all the prehistoric life that's gone."

Because someone was first to chip at a rock, can they claim to own millions of rocks? And if the rock has a bone in it, can they claim ownership of all relatives of that bone, not to mention millions of years of history?

"You tell me."

No, they can't. The first person to discover a trilobite fossil did not have a claim on all trilobite fossils. No one can justly claim that legacy. And whether the thing discovered was alive or not is irrelevant. The first person to discover that nitrates allow plants to grow didn't have a claim to all nitrates. No one can claim all instances of a natural building block of food as his own. And someone who discovers a chemical in someone else's body doesn't own that chemical in anyone else, not in your body or mine, or even in the body it came from. See the pattern? It's a rule: in a true free market, if someone didn't create it, it can't be owned.

"So you've said. It's a nifty little rule."

Only because it works. It's fundamental.

"So no one could own my DNA?"

No. Tiny as it is, it would be like granting a form of slavery. Ownership of even a piece of a person can lead to controlling the whole person, and there we are, in that same repugnant place. The DNA code that makes us human can never be owned or claimed. In terms of economics, like land, it wasn't created by anyone. It also violates the principle of the unfettered no. However, because slavery is profitable, it's not something the free market can police. That's government work.

"No slavery, fine. But it sounds like you're saying it's okay to create life forms with DNA. Like life forms would be a product ... a patentable product?"

If they were new life forms and not just man's version of old ones, yes.

"Really? Well, I have to tell you ... that scares the crap out of me. I can understand the principle of patent owning—why you say it's okay for new plants and even new animals. But principled is not the same as smart. There is the possibility of mistakes in engineering them. And the next step after that is engineering people. If you're saying newfangled human beings can become a product, through DNA rejiggering or whatever, I'm just absolutely disgusted. Maybe this is where your economics goes over the moral railing."

Human beings can't be owned, no matter the source of the DNA, because our template is already here. But I understand, Sam, that we're not always dealing with good scientific precision. Unintended consequences of biological manipulations are easy to imagine. Pestilence, horrific mutations, crops disappearing ... as you said, it's all scary. However, if our community wishes to ban it, well, we can. We make the rules, after all.

But the benefits are also easy to imagine—better health, greater food supplies, cleaner land, air, and water. They, too, would be lost to such a ban. The choice reflects our courage, understanding, discipline, and moral fiber, but not our economics. Economic laws accommodate our desires. They don't prescribe what must be done. For example, we didn't have to learn how to manufacture livers. But a lot of people are grateful for it. And while liver designs can't be owned, because they preexist us, the design of the machines that make them can be owned and protected with a patent.

"It's the thing we can't see that scares me, Jorge, not livers. What about them? Good intentions don't guarantee outcomes."

Releasing unwieldy organisms or creatures into the environment is the same, economically, as pollution.

"It wouldn't prevent the error! And it's not like money can even make up for that kind of damage."

Can human errors ever be prevented? But the right incentives, civil and criminal, can lead researchers and manufacturers to be extraordinarily careful before allowing anything into the world. If the penalties are severe financially, and if jail could be for life, then people will triple- and quadruple-check their methods.

"There are evil people out there, Jorge. And madmen."

Economics can't do anything about them, unfortunately. If they're mad or evil, rules don't really matter, anyway. The whole issue starts with the choices a community must make.

"Ugh. Maybe I've seen too many scary movies."

I don't blame you. I've seen my share too. Imagination can be a very wonderful or a very dangerous thing.

"Hah. No question!"

It's kind of crazy. A major benefit of an open economy is the unleashing of our collective imagination, letting people be rewarded for their inventions and creations without being crushed by bureaucracy. But that same imagination can scare us back to our reflexes. Imagination can be scary, but I don't see anyone asking to eliminate it.

"Maybe not eliminate it. But some countries do control their people by stomping on their imagination to limit it—communist and fascist ones."

And it's why they are doomed to fail as social systems. An enduring system is not going to be one that suppresses human nature. We have to be embraced in our range of personalities, on a systemic level, for any political economy to endure. Otherwise the state will always be in fear of revolution.

"Are we still talking about ownership and patents?"

Who owns what is what revolutions are usually about.

"You're not saying a poor patent scheme can spark a revolution, are you?"

No. But a fair system that allows community members the benefit of their own creations is fundamental to a people's satisfaction. We're not usually saints, willing to give the fruits of our efforts to strangers for nothing. Occasional charity, yes. But "from each according to his ability, to each according to his needs," flies in the face of human nature. It's forcing charity and disregards our differences in ambition or talent. A more humane system allows the inventor to enjoy the benefit of her invention while striking a balance in sharing the invention's value with what the community itself has contributed—the peace, security, and preserved knowledge of all that came before.

"The standing on the shoulders of giants idea?"

Yes. Or what I've been calling a tower of knowledge. But yes.

"You know, the fact that I even used that phrase, shoulders of giants, means I'm guilty. Some appreciation to Bernard of Chartres is due, and to everyone since who bothered to remember what he said."

Who? Didn't Isaac Newton say it?

"That's the popular notion. Newton said it, but he wasn't first to say it. Turns out Newton was paraphrasing Bernard of Chartres, whether or not he knew it."

I never heard of him.

"He wrote about how God and other big, eternal ideas present themselves in the material world."

You must have been a pretty good student of philosophy.

"In college, I was. I only remember because every time I hear that 'shoulders of giants' phrase attributed to Newton, I think, wrong. Four years of college. And that's all I remember."

That's funny.

"It's true."

Well, clearly his idea is true too. We only have time to invent today's sophisticated stuff because community works. The past contains the building blocks for the future. Our community curates the process.

Sam halted on the sidewalk in front of a large glass pane showcasing dark wood dining tables and dim lights glowing from inside.

"Let's go in here. It's going to get busy with brunchers."

Jorge found that even the weak air-conditioning inside was a welcome relief after their climb.

"Sit here?"

Take it. I don't think we have a choice, Sam. Haven't we been here before?

"You know what, Jorge, I think we have ... wow, years ago. Good memory."

Not every saloon has dried flowers hanging from the ceiling.

"Wow. We just made it. Look at the people coming now. It could be a while before the staff even knows we're here."

We were lucky to get this booth.

"So what about the people who discovered nitrates or dinosaur bones? Don't they deserve some compensation? I mean ... I'm glad a scientist can't claim parts of me. But at the same time, I want them to want to work. It's far beyond what I could ever do."

And beyond what I could do. But discovery can't translate into ownership, not if the goal is economic freedom. No one can own what is already here. Ownership comes when, through the application of work, it is changed; gold is taken out of the Earth, or DNA is coded anew. So no, no one can own nitrates or dinosaur DNA.

"But those are important discoveries. Shouldn't the discoverer benefit? Where's the incentive for the science?"

They get the joy of discovery. They gain understanding. And it all goes toward building our tower of knowledge.

"Seriously? I hope you're kidding. That's not compensation. Money is compensation. There's got to be something in it that's real, beyond sticking some imaginary brick into an analogy for learning."

Their joy, I'm sure, is real and motivating. They are also getting salaries that can provide them a very nice living. Companies value people adept at discovery. It can lead to patentable products.

But, to your point, Sam, discovery is of what's already here, so there's no claim to be made on that. But the new knowledge can be turned into products like books, or lectures, or videos. And with further work can come new medicines, or new modes of transportation, or a million other things. Knowledge can always be turned into a product.

"So if I find a dinosaur bone, I can't keep it?"

I didn't mean to say that. You can own the bone. You just can't own the DNA code that's part of it.

"Now you're contradicting yourself. If I'm a paleontologist, I can keep the bone. But if I'm a biochemist and find the same bone, I can't keep the DNA?"

DNA is a code, like a template. That's what can't be owned. A dinosaur bone is an artifact. It tells us something about nature's past in the same way ancient pottery tells us something about culture. It demands preservation exactly as it is, at least according to the scientific community. If it's altered, its value is diminished or even destroyed. As such, it is capital, like an old vase—whole and complete unto itself.

"Isn't dinosaur DNA an ancient artifact too?"

In a sense, in that it's a physical thing—a molecule. A bone can fulfill its potential by being displayed in a museum as a unique thing. But copies of DNA are just as valid as the original. Its code is what can't be owned, no more than could the species it came from.

"So why can't the DNA be owned? If someone figures out how to bring a species back to life, they've created something. Something awesome, actually. It's your rule, right, that something created by man can be owned by man?"

There's a big difference between creation and re-creation. If a man created a new species and could control its wanderings, he could claim to own it. But a species that preceded us cannot be owned. Only a man-made brand-new species can earn a patent.

The effort of digging and discovery gives the paleontologist a claim on the bones she finds. But only on the ones she finds. If she were the first to discover a new species of dinosaur, she would not hold a claim on all skeletons found of that species.

"I'm listening. Just looking for the waitress. Keep talking."

And if he took the dinosaur DNA and cloned that species—no matter how wondrous it might be—he could not make any economic claim for the whole species. It's an act of re-creation, not creation. The design of the machine that does the cloning can be owned and patented, but not the DNA code itself.

"Machine design I get. That's easy. But the animal, the woolly mammoth or saber-toothed tiger or whatever ... who owns that? And couldn't someone put it in a zoo and collect admissions?"

Yes. But someone else could clone another mammoth and put it in another zoo. You can't own a species that's already been here. Although if you've recreated a creature like that, poor thing, you are responsible for its well-being.

"But if the paleontologist sells the bone as an artifact what about the DNA in the bone? If you can't own it, you can't sell it."

As it's part of the bone, it can be sold. But no ownership can be had for the code it contains or the life it represents.

"Are you being helped?" *asked a waitress wearing an abundance of dark eyeliner.*

"We are now."

"I'll get you some menus." *She turned and instantly blended among customers passing between tables.*

"Would a land lease have to be revalued because a dinosaur bone was found?"

Not for a single bone. No.

"Why not? What's the difference? What if it's worth millions of dollars?"

The ongoing opportunity in land is in its potential usage. Mining, for gold or whatever, changes the usage. Finding a single dinosaur bone won't do that.

"But a whole digging operation would change the usage."

Correct. If a dig were started, then the land lease would be revalued.

"But doesn't the community lose the value of the million-dollar bone when it's removed and sent somewhere else? Why is that okay? How is it different from gold that way?"

It's a question of what is capital. And, honestly, a bit of luck.

"Luck? Sounds like this 'simple economics' is starting to get complicated."

Any transition can seem complicated. But this will stay pretty simple. You'll see. But there's clearly an element of luck involved.

"Yesterday, didn't you say having luck in the system was bad?"

I said too much luck was bad. There's always going to be some. Luck is bad when it overwhelms a sense of fairness in the system. It can't be allowed to become such a force that it's competitive with our collective skill or effort in influencing outcomes.

"Okay. Yes, I remember."

But otherwise, it's unavoidable. Luck is a natural part of things. Remember—equality at birth is about the opportunity for choices in life, not about our attributes as individual beings. Someone's always going to be faster. Someone's always going to be smarter. Someone's going to be more sensitive. Someone's going to be more courageous. And someone's going to be luckier.

Luck is finding a dinosaur bone on your property ... or finding a beautiful wildflower you'd like to pick or a rabbit you'd like to trap. The key to having luck is that, in the community's eyes, the usage of your property is not being altered. It's when the use of the land is dramatically changed that the community demands compensation for the change. So the community doesn't receive value for a single dinosaur bone; only the finder does. That's luck.

"What if a bone dig would make the land worth less?"

Then the secured user could choose not to allow the dig, or would likely demand compensation for the value lost, from the scientific group that persisted in pursuing it. It's always the user's decision to allow what happens on her property.

"Who would compensate her?"

Members of the scientific community, their institutions, or their benefactors could choose to compensate her if they felt the dig was worth it to them. Or the community itself could compensate her with a rent reduction, on behalf of the scientific interests. Community, via government, can choose to do what the true free market cannot.

"Why couldn't the free market do it?"

If pursuing dinosaur bones makes the land worth less, a profit-driven entity wouldn't make that choice.

"Ah. Of course. So it takes some beneficent group, like a scientific charity, to do it."

Yes. Or a government.

"Or the government ..."

Exactly.

"So who owns what's found?"

Whoever is paying the user for the use of her land. If it's the community, then the community owns what's found.

"Jorge, at this point, you should offer to buy me the drink."

Happily. I'll even buy the next one too.

"You're a pal. Do you think if I get drunk, this will make more sense?"

It's not making sense?

"I'm just playing with you."

And?

"Go on, Jorge. Please."

You sure?

"Please."

Let's say you're on public ground, like a park.

"Which park?"

Oh, so now you want this to take as long as possible?

"No, no. Go on."

If you're in a park and find some capital, something man-made on the ground, not built to be part of the park like a memorial plaque, but say, a coin—it's yours. Whether you keep it or try to find the previous owner, that's your choice. That coin becomes subject to whatever you decide.

"Understood."

On secured property, though, not public land, things are different. What you find is not yours. Unless you know who dropped it, that same coin belongs to the secured user. So would a dinosaur bone. Everything rightly belongs to the secured user of the land on which it's found.

"Okay. Basic property rights. Got it."

But claiming what's found in nature isn't so simple. Back on park land, every leaf and stone rightfully belongs to the community. There can even be zones that keep people out of certain parts to prevent people from interfering with the wildlife. Public protections can even extend to private property, concerning a rare species, for example. The ability to claim what occurs in nature can always be restricted by the community for economic, moral, or scientific reasons, because long-term concerns aren't compatible with the market's need for current profits.

"So like hunting seasons requiring a license? Or limiting fish to a minimum weight?"

Yes. Exactly. Or hunting for dinosaur bones. Restrictions don't mean that nature can't be used. It's just that the community can legitimately manage what's important for science, or demand compensation for what will change the community's economic potential.

"Like starting a gold mine requires compensation to the community."

Precisely.

"Some … some of this … sounds reasonable. But I am thirsty, and here's that waitress! Excuse me, miss? Stouts?"

"We only have Guinness." *The harried waitress hardly broke stride while two menus slapped the tabletop.*

"Two. Thank you."

I hope it sounds reasonable, Sam. Honestly, I'm just thrilled we've gone this far. Is the difference between discovery and knowledge clear?

"You can't own a discovery, the thing discovered, but you can own what you do to change it or mold it, or turn your knowledge of it into a product."

I guess it's clear.

"I have a good teacher."

So then does it make sense that ideas aren't patentable?

"I'm sure my idea to eat here isn't patentable. But no, it doesn't."

It's because useful ideas are really a discovery of what already exists.

"What?"

Ideas are a form of discovery.

"Either you're losing it, or you're losing me. How can ideas already exist? There was never a nuclear bomb until people designed one."

No. But the physics that allowed for it were already here. We just had to discover them, and figure out how to apply them.

"You could say the same for the airplane that dropped it."

Exactly!

"Oh, come on."

Let me try to explain by example. I'm going to warp history to do it, if you don't mind.

"Warp it. Why not? You're already warping the present and the future. Might as well be consistent."

Let's pretend the idea of the wheel has just come into being. Pretend there are no wheels in the world. And a woman named Paulina is the first to ever think of one.

"Go, Paulina!"

After she gets the idea, is it fair to give her a patent on the idea of "wheel," so that every form a wheel might take—be it used as a pulley or a gear, or shaped to roll on a track or a rocky field, be it made of wood, stone, or anything else—every use and iteration entitles her to compensation? Or is it right to publicly acknowledge her wondrous idea but grant her a patent on the specific wheel she comes up with, and not for every wheel imaginable?

"So you're saying it's overkill to compensate her for the very idea ..."

I am. A marketplace is about putting out products and living with the results. Products are patentable. Ideas are not.

"But isn't Paulina entitled to make a killing? She invented the wheel!"

Wouldn't she make a killing though? She would reap rewards from anyone who used her product designs. That's great for her but good for us too. The point is that economically sound ideas, ones that inspire good products, share a common trait. They recognize what already exists.

"I don't know if I'm being dense or what."

You're not being dense.

"You said Paulina was the first to have the idea for the wheel. But there were no wheels before her. How could she be recognizing what already exists?

The need or desire for a good product is always there. It's in the world. It's our desires. The proof arrives when the resulting products are successful.

"Maybe. I don't know ... no ... Sorry, Jorge. Actually, I'm lost."

At some point, Paulina must have felt a desire to move heavy objects more easily. Maybe she was inspired by the sweat or backaches she and her friends complained about. So while no one knew what they needed was a wheel, she realized it. Maybe she saw something in nature to spark her—a log roll down a hill, or stones tumbling in a rockslide. But her insight was to harness her desire to move heavy things more easily to what was evident around her.

And wheels were quickly and widely adopted. So it makes sense that people had desired them even before there were any.

"They desired what didn't exist. Okay ... If we were talking about soul mates, it would sound romantic."

Sam, you were a student of philosophy. If the starting point is a desire, and the end point is a product that fulfills it, then there is a concept to connect the two. That concept exists, whether or not we see it. It's here. We just haven't discovered it yet. For example, Leonardo da Vinci foresaw the concept of a flying machine long before an airplane was invented. Hope for pain to go away existed before the discovery of aspirin.

"I desire a transporter that will get me to places instantly. But that's never going to happen. It won't ever exist. Just desiring something doesn't make it real."

Of course not. There has to be a product that proves the concept. But if the product arrives, doesn't that mean the concept existed all along?

"Jorge, tautological reasoning isn't going to work any better than my transporter."

Hmm … Have you ever experienced a new product that inspired your pride? Like some inventive genius is taking care of us?

"My new amazing wrist-phone."

Could that be how the first wheels were experienced? You know, could that sensation, that satisfaction you feel when you know in an instant that your life is being made easier, be an indication that the idea for the product always existed, like gold in the ground, until someone had the wherewithal to discover it? Ideas are a form of discovery.

"Then the idea for my wrist-phone has always existed?"

No. Not as that particular product. But the desires to communicate better, to get answers to questions right away, to never get lost, and to not drop or lose the thing while you use it have always been in us, haven't they?

"I suppose."

That's why those ideas can't be patented. Only the devices that satisfy them for you can be. Ideas are the only spark capable of driving economic growth beyond the rate of population growth, so it's critical that ideas be appreciated for what they are and flourish.

"I'm going to need that stout."

So … all patents, all inventions, are built upon past work.

"The shoulders of giants."

Right. So to allow our tower of knowledge to grow strong, patents must expire at some point.

"You're going to tell me how long that should take?"

No. It's hard to say.

"Hard to say?"

Yes.

"Why?"

Because every industry has its own rate of change. I mean, try napping for ten years ...

"My wife would never let me."

When you wake up, your amazing phone might seem ancient compared to what else is around. But your dining table wouldn't seem out of place at all.

"Ah. Got it. There're different rates of change, different rates of innovation, in different fields."

Exactly. Some new table joint design could easily seem new and fresh for twenty years. But in the world of technology, twenty years can be a dozen generations of a product; hundreds, if not thousands of new tools and processes are coded, etched, printed, or stamped every year. And many become building blocks for more generations of product.

So here's a question: why should a patent term last for one product generation in one field but a dozen generations in another?

"On the other hand, if patent terms are uniform in years, why isn't that fair?"

A patent system is an attempt to deliver a just form of ownership. If a patent lasts too long, through many generations of product, it becomes a windfall for the patent holder and costs us all further development. Inventors and product designers are pushed into awkward or expensive work-arounds, which, several generations down the developmental road, will seem to be an unnecessary waste of effort.

"How do you define a product generation?"

I don't know.

"You don't?"

All I know is that different businesses experience different rates of evolution in their products. And faster-moving industries could reasonably turn patents over to the public domain sooner than those in slower-moving industries.

"How are you supposed to create a law to accommodate that?"

It only takes some judgment and expertise. But there's no reason to expect government to be the expert. Patent committees could be drawn from people in the field, and they could figure out the appropriate terms. What company wouldn't want to have input into the laws of its industry?

"They do now. That's what lobbying is about."

But it wouldn't be lobbying. Representatives of customers, companies, and competitors would look to each other for a consensus on the merits. For a patent to be granted, a competitor would have to agree. And so would customers. Even a global company would find it difficult to buy off both its competition and its customers.

Lobbyists aren't negotiating with each other like that. Their words rattle in the minds of politicians and regulators. It's then those people who have the so-called debate. But they don't necessarily balance all points of view, because a well-funded lobbyist can make only one point of view matter. A check cashing is all a politician might be willing to hear.

"Well, the free market pays people to do their jobs."

It does. But as government doesn't have omnipotent expertise, why not let a committee, mandated to comprise the product's consumers, producers, inventors, and competitors, hash it out? Combined, they'd offer a great deal of wisdom. And everyone would have to play by the same rules that they impose on others.

"Maybe. What happens when a patent is violated?"

Good question. Especially since the value of a patent is only as good as its enforceability. So obviously there's a criminal aspect to it, potentially. But the violation of a patent could be judged through the same committee that granted it so that those with significant financial resources won't hold great advantage over those without those resources. The committee would just apply its own original rational to the situation.

"There's no trial?"

The patent committee would act like an arbiter. Both sides could make statements, but the determination would be based on the committee's intentions in granting the patent. Much of the debate and interpretation that happens in trials is eliminated because, presumably, if you can assign a patent, you can also tell when it's being violated.

"One would think."

So there would be a simple decree of patent violation or not. Then a court case would follow for the damages.

"Even if a little guy wins damages, companies on the losing side can delay and delay until the little guy gives up or dies. I've seen my own company do that."

That is sadly true. But it's not a problem economics can solve. Maybe the law wouldn't allow undue delays … especially if a violation has already been established at that point. I said the true free market would greatly level the playing field, but I didn't say it would be completely leveled. Shenanigans will happen. The saving grace at this point is that the violation would not be in question. Damages would flow to the violated in a matter of time. So even a person with small pockets could hire a lawyer based on the contingency.

"What about countries that don't care about our patent system? Our police don't have authority overseas."

It's a local responsibility. But as long as we had diplomatic relations, our government could assist if a patent holder requested it. I'm sure you've noticed that large companies often ask for the government's help in protecting their patents internationally. Sometimes it takes a government to deal with a government. If the request is made, we, the homebound community, are entitled to compensation for providing that effort—a percentage of revenue generated by the internationally protected patent.

"Wait! What? Do my ears deceive me? A tax? Another tax? I thought you had a one-tax system?"

It is a one-tax system … one mandatory tax. I'm talking about a fee to compensate our government for conducting industry-specific or company-specific international work that's done by request. It would be completely voluntary.

"If you don't want the service, you don't pay?"

Yes. We need to charge for this service because we can't charge land-value tax in a place where it's not our land. And compensation to our government doing good things beyond its borders is reasonable. There are out-of-pocket expenses. The patent holder should reimburse those expenses over time, as a percentage of the product's sales, since our country's help was given by their request. After all, they're always free to handle the situation on their own.

"I like that the patent thing is voluntary. But why not apply it to everyone with a patent?"

If you're working in a foreign country and paying taxes there, you're already buying that government's services. If that works for you, so be it. If you're happy on your own, fine, keep all the revenue you can get. But if our community help is needed, then pay for it with some modest percentage of your success.

"But government's work in foreign countries goes way beyond patents. Should companies be paying for trade agreements and the like?"

No, because trade agreements, like immigration issues, security, and general diplomacy, are not expenses generated by for-profit economics. They're the basic work of building our economic playing field. It's the natural work of good government, not anything extra.

"I've got to tell you ... after all you've said, I'm flabbergasted that there's a second tax."

Well, that's your term for it. It's really a fee for a service.

"Toe-may-toe, toe-mah-toe, Jorge. Semantics."

CHAPTER 10

Disparities and Distributions

Understanding what situations are and are not suitable for a free market isn't semantics, Sam. Understanding where government needs to be involved in economics and where it needn't is the only way to minimize its involvement. Okay?

"Okay as long as I've got a beer to sip on ..."

Our government deals its own hand by choosing to tax capital. People inevitably start to demand that certain economic results get corrected. But because our economic pretense is capitalism, redistribution of capital is the only way to satisfy them. And, Sam, have you noticed that not even conservatives are willing to get rid of redistributive policies? They'll shrink them but not completely eliminate them.

"That's how I feel."

The programs are too popular to eliminate. The perception of need for them is too strong. Funding them though, even somewhat, causes problems. Using the capital-tax system to take from those who have created or collected wealth and giving it to those who seem to need it is a bighearted idea, but it necessitates more taxes on capital. And we know this causes more unintended hardships. However noble it feels to want to equalize results, it's an economically misplaced solution. So think about this: what if proper taxes are levied not on wealth but on opportunity?

"Hmmm ... and land is opportunity. Of course."

Isn't opportunity what true capitalism is about? Letting people compete on a level playing field to find their own level of satisfaction, or not? Isn't that the idea of economic freedom? We've seen how there is a fundamental injustice in a community that taxes the wrong things. And our tax coders and politicians have been trying ever since to come up with a way to fix it. But they insist on working with capital to do it. Do you know our tax code has never lasted even close to two generations without being changed?[vi] Typically, it's changed within five years. This is not the mark of a confident and wise tax scheme.

Imagine if it we knew, in our bones, that all our economic opportunities are absolutely fair, that luck has only a minimal impact, that no one is forced into taking a job he or she doesn't want, but that each able-bodied person is responsible for his or her own financial situation. No one collects unearned gains by owning land or holds it out of use for long, keeping the opportunity from others. No one has the leverage to suppress the wages of another.

"So you're saying that with only one mandatory tax on land value and a voluntary tax on government's international services, our economy can be completely fair?"

Yes.

"Jorge, that's bold. So ... no income tax."

No.

"No capital-gains tax."

No.

"No estate tax."

No.

"No sales tax."

No.

"No tax on interest."

No. It's not necessary.

"Or dividends."

It's the same as interest.

"How about tolls?"

No. Communities with a bridge or highway are going to see that benefit reflected in land values, so the community will be compensated without them.

"User fees or inspection fees? Or anything like that?"

No.

"And no property taxes."

Not on structures.

"Just on land."

Yes.

"Hmmm."

Sam, on the face of it, doesn't it seem woefully inefficient to tax so many different things?

"Yes, well … I don't see how this scheme can possibly be fair."

Eliminating all those taxes isn't fair? Why not?

"The wealthy could make out like bandits, if they wanted. They could live on some cheap, big-sky land and barely pay for what the government does for them. I know this is weird coming from me. But having a free market doesn't mean that some get rich, don't contribute anything back, and everyone else eats cake, does it?"

If the wealthy have made their money without having leverage over others, people who either don't own land or have to work for another, then they have earned it. And with land-value tax, they will have paid the community fair value for the opportunity. It's only a closed economy that makes inequality a problem.

"It's not that they make the money. I don't have a problem with that. But they do owe something, just something, back to the community that allowed for their success. At least now they pay income tax. You're saying someone born into a billion-dollar family could live on free or cheap land, and barely pay a nickel back to the community."

That's true.

"You agree?"

Yes.

"So? Isn't that unfair?"

No. Why is it unfair?

"Why? It … I don't know. It just feels unfair. I need to think about it."

We can even move your billionaire from cheap land to some of the most expensive land, like on Fifth Avenue across from Central Park. And he still wouldn't have to work a single day, ever. And it would still be fair.

"But at least there he'd be paying taxes. Okay … here's why it's unfair. It's because no wealthy person got that way alone. It's like the shoulders-of-giants thing. Even the wealthy built on what came before them. And they had people work with them and solve problems for them. The community

154

protected them from thieves and extorters, and their customers were protected too, to make the whole enterprise possible. Even if someone got rich by winning the lottery, the state lottery system was behind it; that's infrastructure. So everyone contributes to everyone, to some degree. Jorge, you were even saying this yesterday. It's unfair to pay nothing or almost nothing. Taxes should be low. But society itself does have value; paying nothing while being rich is absurd. A single tax just enables that.

"Without the society we have, no one could be as rich, no company as profitable. And much of that's a direct result of our infrastructure. Police, firefighters, paved roads, water, and sanitation are part of it, if only so we can go shopping. We all—no matter our wealth—we all need that infrastructure. We all drink out of that trough. Hey ... what's so funny?"

Sam, I could have said almost everything you just said.

"You agree? That's a little bit scary."

Well, yes and no. I agree with your premise but not your conclusion.

"Why don't you think it's unfair that a rich person can pay almost nothing?"

Fairness is about fair opportunity. If you're using good land, you're using what could be someone else's opportunity. So pay for the privilege. It's like paying more for a better seat at the stadium. That's the principle. If land doesn't have competitive market value, that's the community's judgment. You're going to tell me the free market's judgment of value is unfair? Why should the fact that we all—rich or poor—use infrastructure make a land-value tax unfair?

"Because in eliminating those taxes on capital gains and dividends and, well ... those are rich people's concerns. Poor people don't have capital gains or dividends. And if they do, it doesn't amount to much. I'm not saying capital-gains tax rates should be high, but they shouldn't be nothing. Some tax should reflect a person's wealth, shouldn't it?"

Dividends and capital-gains taxes are no different than any other tax on capital; they create economic distortions.

"Okay ... yes, I remember. But it still seems you're giving them a gift."

I suppose it does. Eliminating capital-gains taxes can feel like giving a billionaire a 10-percent-off coupon for groceries. He certainly doesn't need it. It won't change the quality of his life. And yet, because our community has needs to be met, it feels ridiculous to allow a billionaire tax-free capital gains and dividends.

But if the economy were fair, the government had ample revenue to meet community needs, and wealth came only from hard work and not enhanced by the desperation of others, would it then seem unfair to you that there was no tax on dividends?

"If everything was just flat fair, of course not. But it's still not right, Jorge. You said no tolls. But poor people, if they can, avoid toll roads, or they don't have cars. Eliminating tolls is allowing wealthier people to get away with not paying for the infrastructure that helped them get wealthy. So I'm starting to think your tax code doesn't equalize anything."

I see what you're saying.

"They rightfully should be giving something back. There will be riots if we try this system of yours."

I agree that the wealthy should contribute to our community. All of us, rich or poor, are obliged like that. Land-value tax is no different.

"It sure sounds different!"

Do you agree that land value arises solely because of the economic vitality of the surrounding community?

"Yes."

Do you agree that infrastructure feeds that vitality?

"Yes, of course. I was just saying it does."

Then someone who never crosses a bridge still benefits from that bridge. It's not that they possibly benefit. They benefit. Perhaps they'll eat strawberries that were shipped on a truck that crossed the bridge. Or their boss's customer, or the company's supplier, will use the bridge. Adding infrastructure grows land value, so long as it reflects a community's economic activity. I mean, building an eight-lane bridge isn't going to help a two-lane town; it could even hurt it with unneeded expenses. But barring something boneheaded like that, land-value tax will capture the commensurate amount of value gained from infrastructure. The community is already compensated through land value, without the use of tolls. So why have them?

"So ... everyone benefits, but nobody pays."

If infrastructure adds to land value, everyone benefits, and everyone pays. Economic flows are always the same. If the companies that build that infrastructure helped grow the community and helped land value grow, why should their profits be taxed by the community they helped? The community revenues will rise anyway.

Every operating business contributes to the economy. In fact, every commercial activity, from those of an individual up to multinational conglomerates, helps to grow the value of land. That's why no other tax is necessary.

Land-value tax does equalize the experience of an economy, by equalizing opportunity. But the tax code should not be equalizing results.

"Whatever we give the needy, food or whatever, is paid for by taxes and is equalizing results."

Not if the price of opportunity is where those revenues come from. How can results be distributed if results aren't being collected? Land-value taxes and capital taxes could not be more different that way.

"You're really describing a completely different world, where taxes fall on land value instead of capital."

And I'll give you that taxes on dividends and capital gains can be seen as you see them. They could certainly help to fund community needs. But it's only because we focus so much on income and capital that our society has so many needs. We've lost sight of the opportunity, literally and figuratively, beneath our feet.

"This is so hypothetical."

Our entire conversation has been hypothetical. The land-value economy doesn't exist yet. But it's also quite hypothetical to think that if we don't look at the cause of a problem, its symptoms can be made to go away.

And it's not hypothetical to say society isn't free when growing numbers of people live in economic fear. Most of us live with a daily stress that we don't even recognize, because we've never lived without it. It's just a part of every day. Have you ever imagined freedom to be a stressful situation for a healthy adult? No, of course not. Well, stress is what describes most of us. Wealth can certainly buy playthings and luxuries, and indulge one's whims, but freedom? That's what we've got—the unsettling, illogical fact that freedom is for sale.

"I thought we agreed that it's natural for the wealthy to have advantages."

We did. And they do. And always will. But something's amiss if basic freedom is one of those advantages. Sam, if freedom were everywhere, it would have little economic value. That's supply and demand, right? But if freedom can be bought, and only by the wealthy at that, then by definition it exists in limited amounts. If you believe freedom is a basic right, then you must also believe it shouldn't be for sale. Only in a flawed system would anyone need to buy it. We like to call ourselves a free people. So it would be nice if freedom were held universally and always, by all of us.

"But the wealthy are always going to able to buy more of everything, including freedom."

That's true for material freedoms, like having more choices for vacations or easier modes of transportation. But the fundamental freedoms, like an unfettered no, can be held by all. Everyone can have the rich child's ability to say no to the marketplace without fear of homelessness or starvation. If the ability to pursue happiness is a fundamental right, then it can't be preordained by birth. If everyone could freely say yes or no in any market situation, it seems to me that life on the whole would be much fairer, not less.

"This unfettered no is huge, isn't it?"

It is.

"There's still a big difference, though, between saying no and living as a billionaire, and saying no and having to grow your own food."

Of course there is. I never said wealth won't have advantages. But with an unfettered no available for everyone, economic desperation is practically eliminated, allowing confident, unforced decision making by everyone. It will mean there's fairness to competitiveness, to success and failure, that far exceeds what exists today. And the tax code, when it's so simple, will leave politicians with little to fix. All of us, rich or poor, can have the same certainty of enduring a cyclical downturn.

"Come on, Jorge. How many maladies is this going to cure?"

Just the economic ones.

"I'm toasting you, Jorge. Here's to open economies. And thank you for the drinks."

Thanks for listening. Basically, a capital-tax policy ensures that government will always be larger than it needs to be.

"Forgive me, but the cycles would be more survivable because …?"

Because the creation of capital occurs with the anticipation of demand. Overall capital investment is a collective guess about the degree of economic activity in the future. Remember that we talked about this yesterday? When the guess is wrong, capital is oversupplied or undersupplied. This is what causes the economic cycle. It's totally normal.

The problem today is that almost all of our community's funding is based on those guesses. Most taxes fall on capital. Therefore, government revenues are based upon this huge, collective bet. Aside from our basic community services, like the military and police, which are necessary expenses regardless, capital taxes add to and even create the need for government programs to fix things: food programs, income programs, housing programs. These needs only grow when the cycle turns down, when capital creation is shrinking, which is precisely the same time government revenues are dropping. So we end up with an economic cycle that is much more extreme than it would be otherwise, and a growing government debt, precisely when new demand for more fixes pushes government to be larger still. So everything ends up leveraged, and releveraged, to that same capital bet. It creates an artificially exaggerated economic cycle.

Were taxes to fall on land, being of stable God-given supply and with prices that vary less than those of capital, the economic cycle is no longer so leveraged. Community revenues no longer depend upon our production guesses. And the added stresses of those fix-it programs are mostly eliminated.

"I know ... because people would always have access to arable land. And unfortunately for both of us, I don't see where your logic is faulty."

Maybe you will after another beer. Land-value tax unleverages the economic cycle. Government's role becomes one of protecting opportunities present in the playing field and filling in for where the free market doesn't work. Not guaranteeing our successes, just our opportunities. This is a far cry from the government today: redistributing capital to try to create opportunities and to feed the economically lost. Instead of inadvertently designing poverty through faulty laws and then trying to fix it, government can focus on preserving the full gamut of our freedom. The government we know today is stuck in its own distractions to fix what amounts to a society riddled with missing opportunities for its citizens.

"You're talking about such a cultural shift, though. Wouldn't it be easier to lower taxes to get government out of the way?"

Actually, Sam, if the revenues from taxes aren't enough to meet the needs of the community, then taxes aren't high enough.

"You are going to feel very alone out there, you know."

If taxation is driven by community needs, policies that cause the needs are the problem, not the amount of tax. Every community must decide what sort of life its worst-off members deserve and how much we're willing to pay for it. Some nations ignore the question, but that's just a way of deciding that some lives can be pretty bleak. Our country happens to pay attention. Deciding and redeciding this takes up the bulk of our political energy. If we wish to shrink our tax burden, then we must either shrink the real need behind the programs it funds or choose to allow more citizens to suffer. Tax levels are set by our collective expectation of the living standards we have for fellow citizens.

If taxes had been on land value all along, our government wouldn't need as much revenue as it currently does, and the poor would have better lives. Compared to an idealized version of our present, then yes, Sam, taxes are too high. But our economic imbalances, caused by poor tax policies, have presented us with a very needy reality. Reducing the size of government is not about cutting spending; it's about cutting the need for spending. Taxes are too high compared to an ideal scenario, but they aren't too high for a tax code that's improper to begin with.

"In saying taxes shouldn't distort the free market, you're referring to your rule of thumb—if man didn't create it, man can't own it?"

Yes. Wait, no. Not quite. It's not if man didn't create it ... it's if *a* man or woman didn't create it. That little word "a" means all the difference. What I've been saying all along is that all men and women, collectively, own the land as citizens of a nation. But "a" man cannot own land. Conversely, "a" person does own what they create, not the community. Individuals can use the land for the tranquility of a home, or the bustle of a business, and wallow in every bit of those rewards. But it's the community that owns the ground.

"Okay. I'll try to be more careful in my language."

It can be important.

"So I see. Again, sorry."

No need for sorry, Sam, please ... so, would you like another?

CHAPTER 11

Marginal Matters

"How can you know in advance what a free market can't do?"

If there's fair opportunity and unfettered choice present in the situation, the free market can handle it. Without those conditions, a free market won't work. The economic forces will operate, as always of course, but without the right conditions, they won't produce a market that's fair and efficient; they'll produce problems that need fixing. Ignorance of this is what makes government seem ineffective and costly.

"Wait. We've talked about this, these conditions, haven't we?"

I'm glad you remember.

"I mean ... the land-tenancy system—community ownership, as you've said—is fundamental."

Without question.

"And the oh-so-esteemed unfettered no has to be available to everyone."

Absolutely.

"And people don't have to play ... the competitive game, the rat race. They can drop out without becoming a drain on the rest of us."

Correct.

"And, let's see ... it has to be able to be policed, but you just mentioned that. Was there anything else?"

No, that's it. When it comes to how a true free market operates, those are the conditions we've discussed.

"Huh. Not bad. That's pretty simple. But now you're saying there's more?"

Not more conditions, no. But there's more to appreciate about them. Because they're not only necessary to keep markets from breaking down, they also describe what government's role needs to be.

So, given that people are people, our competition can be fierce. We have to be vigilant about maintaining free-market conditions. People will attempt to change them, to change the rules to gain advantages. And they'll use wealth to do it. It's like lobbying to changing the rules of the game in the off season to favor your team's particular skill set, or failing that, to get the referee to look the other way, for your benefit. But greenmail, blackmail, extortion, and bribery are all economic distortions. They hurt innocent people, consumers and competitors alike. The laws guiding a true free market should not be shifted by whims or desires.

Let me be clear. It's natural that some people become wealthier than others. It's natural that some companies become wealthier than others. And it's natural that the wealthy can do more for causes they believe in. It's even natural that with wealth comes an ability to buy political influence or government services. But what's not natural is for politics and economics to share the same rules.

What today passes for political debate is often just jockeying to catch dollops of capital funneling through our political infrastructure. This makes our markets vulnerable to corruption by politics. By design, free markets sort for profits, not policy ideas. They're not designed for sifting through lies and half-truths either. We spoke yesterday about how falsehoods distort economic outcomes ... with the example of Carom's cut knee. And we spoke of emotion, how a satisfying tale can lead us away from truth. When freedom is at stake—and freedom is always at stake— measuring a man's voice by its economic reach is to flirt with corruption. Political laws, unlike economic laws, are well written if they prevent technological amplification from working too well. Arguing through paid media is a fun-house mirror distorting sincere debate. The practice endures because only the winning politicians make the laws upon which we play. They'll understandably tend to reinforce what worked for them. Besides, if a moneyed interest helped them get there, the same moneyed interest will help them "think" about reform.

Sam, you see how the conditions needed for a true free market are simple. To stay that way though, economic laws have to work on the most fundamental levels of markets. They can't be guided by special interests. They can't, as corrupting laws do, address only particular entities or classes. As with good taxes, good law also needs to reach all of us.

"Nice words, Jorge, but they're not reasonable. You really want politicians to be given money to win and then not give their supporters anything in return? I mean, forgive me, but it sounds sort of crazy. You're saying, in effect, the government needs to avoid corruption by avoiding corruption. Technically, it's a tautology. Practically, it's ridiculous. It's a fantasy. It's not going to happen. Corruption is always going to be part of the game."

You're right. After all, it is a shortcut to profit. But its influence could be minimized if we, as a community, understood the difference between valid and invalid economic law. If we understood the boundary defining what a true free market is from what it is not, we could clearly see when our government is acting to nourish the fairness of the market and when it's not. When we understand economic fairness, laws that attempt to steer outcomes, rather than make proper efforts to maintain a level playing field, will generate an outcry. The opportunities for corruption would dramatically shrink.

"What makes you think there would be an outcry? People don't pay attention. Most people aren't going to do anything about anything unless they're already up to their eyeballs in the problem. And when some do get vocal about something, they're labeled 'extreme' or 'fringe' because they're a minority. The majority rarely feels a need to get involved, so they don't."

You're right again, Sam. I'm not so sure of that outcry either. I'll grant you, it's more of a hope. Perhaps it's not for today, but if we ever hold a community-wide understanding of what economic freedom can mean, a bonding of strangers through a culture of dignity, it could come. If we had that understanding right now, maybe there would be an outcry.

"How can you say we don't understand freedom? We're the land of the free! Freedom is most of what we talk about! I mean, in the daily news, a violation of freedom pretty much makes something a story."

We definitely use the word "freedom" frequently, but I don't think we really share an understanding of what it means. It means something different to the ignorant than it does to the educated. It's something different for the rich than it is for the poor. It's certainly different for the religious than for the secular. At least by becoming clear on simple economic freedom, we'll better see the subtle threats made against it.

"And if this nirvana ever arrived, you think corruption would just go away?"

No. But its opportunities would shrink. If corruption thrives in the murk left by biased definitions of facts and concepts, then the more clarity we share across our community, the less vulnerable to corruption we're going to be.

We've chosen two great ideological constructs to guide us toward freedom: capitalism and democracy. But democracy, as just an idea, is not what will get us an honest vote tally, any more than the mere thought of a free market will achieve one. What gets us to real freedom is our clarity in properly harnessing the fundamental forces, through our laws, to construct it. Logically, we'll find the right design for freedom faster if we know what the destination looks like and why it should look that way.

"But ..."

Hold on, Sam. I understand that the appeal of an imagined destination is subjective. A true free market is only one picture of economic freedom. You can want to go there or not. But there's nothing subjective in how the fundamental forces operate. Our potential rests squarely on how well we harness them.

We're social beings, so we make our choices to harness them with politics. That's where we make society's rules. So it happens that capitalism needs democracy to write its rules. But in turn, democracy needs capitalism to invent its dreams. This doesn't mean the internal dynamics of the two are interchangeable. Democracy is a separate idea from capitalism, with different forces at play. So if truth is ever going to guide us, if truth is ever going to be a viable antidote to ignorance, we must know that these forces clearly mark the distinction between a marketing campaign, which is a free-market construct, and a debate, which is a political one.

The clatter of a dropped tray dominated the restaurant, but only for a blink and a stare. Conversations everywhere quickly resumed.

Truth can be as demonstrable as gold in the ground, if we make the effort to see it. But when its value is being debated from border to border, as it periodically must be in a democracy, it deserves a forum, especially for debates. Free markets can find profits with aplomb, but they aren't designed to find truths. Truths are not test marketed or designed to be popular. So they are distorted, to be product-like, when they're communicated through the mechanisms of a competitive market. A demonstrable truth, with an importance wholly unconnected to sales, is suddenly subject to the quality of its marketing.

Free markets seek a balance between supply and demand. But physical and fiscal reality means both supply and demand are constrained by limited resources. Supplies have to be reordered, and sales have to fit within budgets. But in politics, ideas aren't constrained by anything but desire. They're not capital, because ideas cost nothing to buy. And an idea can be distributed to every conscious mind without ever having to restock an inventory. So if political debate is conducted as a marketing campaign, in a fiscal showdown, truth and fantasy become equivalent nebulous products. We already know that free markets fail at sifting out honesty. So political truths are likely to flounder, there among exaggerations and deceptions, as often as not.

And sure, some speech delivered for politics might sound similar to some speech made for profit, but we shouldn't be fooled. Both types of speech deserve their own bespoke playing fields, with rules designed to find communal truths in the one forum and rules for profit in the other.

Because what the wealthy gain from their economic leverage can be deployed, when our laws allow it, to gain yet more leverage through politics. That is corruption. When money is knitting society's fabric, the needle penetrates deep.

"I'm not going to need another drink, am I?"

Up to you. And by the way, I'm still buying.

We know well-told lies are a relatively cheap pathway to the bank. Since truth is not a product, profiting can occur without it. So while profit inspires action in a free market, if it is gained unhinged from truth, it will ultimately destroy that market. It's why market police are needed, to help ferret out the lies.

"Are you saying political speech needs to be policed too?"

No. I didn't mean to. Political speech is something else. It is opinion. But if its goal is to determine what's best for the country, its arguments need to be truthful. In a free society, opinions need a fair field too. That requires a fair debate. Since opinions cannot be legislated away or policed by the government of a free nation, it's up to journalists to keep them grounded.

Good journalists are like mechanics that can tell when something is off in society's engine and know where to find the problem. They understand how it ought to be, are immune to unseemly persuasions, and are vigilant in communicating to the rest of us.

Really, we need the truth-seeking work of both police and journalists. Together, their efforts are like inoculations against the corruptions of our ideals. But they must keep at it, for corruption is like a virus; it will shift and evolve to find our weaknesses. It's easy for it to hide in complexity, for example. When there are extra steps and convoluted practices in our rule making and rule keeping, they are likely gilded pathways to confuse or frustrate somebody. They only serve to create ignorance. And ignorance is a pretty calm ocean of opportunity for both profiteers and politicians.

Transparency, simplicity, and wisdom are our tools to get things right. All attempts to weaken them—clouding transparency, adding complexity, or walling off wisdom—can only steer us to places where what sadly passes for freedom is parceled out inside of closed rooms.

"Oh my God, where's that drink? Could you be any more depressing? You've also really gotten away from economics, haven't you?"

No. It's all economics.

"Journalism? Last time I checked, that's not economics."

It is, though. It's an important part. Maybe it'll be helpful to think of society as a zoo. Imagine it: no matter what we do, we all have a place within the zoo. But instead of being caged according to what we eat, or whether we have horns, or claws, or flippers, we're in sections according to our economic style. Competitive people spend most of their time exchanging goods or services in the very large center. And a ring around them is for the people who mostly keep to themselves. The areas are different, but people occasionally cross to the other. But government workers are milling everywhere, both inside and outside this great cage, keeping order. And journalists watch over the government. So both government and journalists together are the zookeepers, acting as needed to make sure the free market contains fair opportunity and to clean up after it. The journalists tell government where attention is needed. And they help us understand how good or bad a job the government is doing. But they also tell us what our neighbors do, so we can better understand our choices.

"Okay, I see. Journalism is like a feedback loop for the government and the economy."

Yes.

"But none of what you describe stops lies or corruption. I mean ... if you think about it, corruption is inherently in the cage. Because the free market is what creates the wealth that's used to manipulate people. So life is not a zoo. No real lion can throw the zookeeper an extra hundred grand to get extra meat. But people? People will do that. I think the analogy falls apart."

It's not that corruption is eliminated, Sam. That's not my point. But the ability to act in corrupting ways can easily be minimized. There are three factors of a true free market that work in freedom's favor.

"If the wealthiest beast in the cage can bribe the zookeeper, then it's going to get extra meat."

Yes. That will happen. No question. There will always be some of us who offer or accept bribes. But it can happen less. What I'm talking about is minimizing the opportunity for that behavior and the damage it does when it occurs.

The first factor of the three is that regulators are worth more to the community than the regulated.

"What? Government regulators are worth more than businessmen? Come on."

Absolutely. Regulators are worth more to the community than the regulated.

"You're killing me ..."

Why?

"You're being deliberately provocative, right? So I'm not going to raise my voice. No way is a regulator worth more than the guy in business. Business is the accelerator of the economy. A regulator's the brake. Any banker is worth way more than his regulators."

On the other hand, you can go faster confidently when you have a brake.

"You know what I mean."

I do. Which is why public scrutiny can do almost all of the regulating for financial industries. We discussed that yesterday. We, as a mass of people, aren't going to let a bank get too crazy with our money, not when we can see what it's doing.

"Oh. Right."

What I'm talking about now are material designs, like for the transportation or storage of chemicals, where, if they break, they can hurt the environment. Or manufacturing systems where, if it's faulty, the product can literally hurt people. I'm talking about actions that can physically damage the playing field or us players. Regulators of those industries are worth as much to us as any CEO of those industries. But yes, Sam, an entire industry is worth more to a nation's economy than a government department, hopefully by a lot. But when it comes to matching the values of a job against a job, person to person, if the regulator's work avoids disasters, then the value of a regulator is worth more to society than any CEO.

"See how I'm not raising my voice? But you are going to need to keep talking and explain. Like, right away. I thought you were a free-market guy."

I am ... for fair opportunity. But there's no opportunity in poisoned land.

"But overdoing regulation kills jobs."

Don't put your view of our capital-taxed, hopefully-one-day-quondam economy on what I'm saying. Preserving jobs is what I'm talking about. Jobs are lost when land or water is soiled to the point where it's out of productive use altogether. How is freedom preserved when a third party's action forces a family to move or makes them ill?

"I'm trying to keep an open mind."

The task of a CEO is to deliver product. And that's fine. But the task of a regulator is to prevent disaster. And that's fine too. From the community's point of view, disasters can be far more harmful and costly than the potential profit of a product is beneficial. Land-value tax is a powerful incentive to prevent poisonous runoff from soiling the drinking water for tens of thousands of people. But imagine a medically unproven batch of pills that has harmful effects on thousands of people. What will stop that from happening? Or imagine how the testing and licensing of professionals prevents hundreds of thousands of people from being injured by fake doctors, or by the false practice of law, or the unskilled at anything else, be it architecture, or electrical wiring, or driving, or piloting, or plumbing. The value of that particular regulator's task can be worth more to the community, by preventing disaster, than the value of any one man in the industry being regulated. So what I'm saying is that a regulator's pay ought to be commensurate with his or her potential to avoid the disaster. That type of respect, defined monetarily, would go a long way to keeping regulators on an honest path. Giving them what they're due is one way to fight corruption. Do you see?

"You want to raise their wages ... the regulators?"

By a lot. To match their wealthy counterparts across the table.

"To make it harder for the wealthiest beast in the cage to bribe the caretaker ..."

Harder, yes. When it's easier for the regulator to say no, it's more likely she will. But, as you suggest, bribery would still be possible.

"Well, and the other two factors? You said there were three?"

They just happen to be part of a properly functioning free market.

"What are they? Or do I already know them?"

Well, we know that a free market doesn't handle dishonesty well. So this is the second factor: where there's dishonest intent, we must make it a regretfully painful exercise for the people involved. Any violation of the ethics of a free market is a serious offense to all of us. If economics is to be a means to our liberty, then economic justice demands more than money. Paying restitution is just returning the stolen property and maybe the value of time and effort the pillaging caused. But anything less is no penalty at all. Anything less, and restitution merely becomes a cost of operations. Real justice requires that an abuse of liberty be matched with a loss of liberty. Liberty abused is a crime; therefore, liberty lost is an appropriate punishment. And jail time will always matter to anyone serving it, even if a particular amount of money doesn't.

The third factor is that laws themselves must operate only on the most basic, fundamental levels, such that there can be no question of their uniform effect upon industry.

"What does that mean?"

Regulation should not be more specific than is required for the task. Otherwise it unnecessarily burdens business with effort or cost. For example, it may not matter exactly how something is sealed, only that it is sufficiently sealed. It may not matter how something is backed up, so long as the backup system will accomplish the proscribed task. If we all understood that a failure to comply with the standard would be met by fierce justice, whether or not the disaster actually occurs, the details would take care of themselves.

"You mean, even if there was no problem, at the moment, if a regulator found something in a condition to lead to a problem, there'd be consequences? Like jail?"

Yes. And any misrepresentations made by the regulated party would only add to the punishment.

"You really love to punish. I had no idea."

If the idea is to prevent disaster, there's no other way to be.

Sam, the fundamental forces already point this way. When the unfettered no is available, laborers can choose what situations they desire to enter. Workers will have the ability to choose a company, instead of the other way around. A company's reputation for safety, respectfulness, and generosity become important factors to attract workers. The need for most labor regulation would, therefore, disappear. Not all, mind you, but much of it.

"Minimum wage laws?"

Not needed. Life on free land becomes the minimum lifestyle. Wages from employment will always have to offer something better, or employers won't be able to hire.

"Oh yeah. You told me that yesterday."

And the free-land lifestyle, as opposed to a specified-wage lifestyle, is immune to inflation. Growing carrots and raising chickens, or whatever one does on free land, will remain a stable style of living.

Also, the "you break it, you own it" aspect of land-value tax makes much of the need for regulation go away.

"I remember."

So regulation can truly be minimal, and consequently, there'll be a great narrowing of the paths of corruption.

"I didn't realize how powerful land-value tax is as a regulating force. The pollution stuff I got before, but not the corruption aspect. Am I hearing myself? It makes sense."

In a land-value-based capitalism, there is a simplicity and obviousness to our obligations. It's not like someone can take land and leave it overseas, or put it in a safe, or fail to declare it. It's always there for all to see. The government would simply send the secured user a bill for the rent due. No more gathering scraps and statements and numbers and filling out forms.

"I like that. And free land users wouldn't even get a bill?"

Correct.

"Free at last. Free at last."

In terms of choice. But even freedom needs rules. Since the Internal Revenue Service would no longer be tracking income types, deductions, gains, losses, interest, amortizations, or depreciations and the like, it would become more of a land-management operation. And local police could help make sure that those on free land are not abusing the system. Free-land users need to be monitored like any neighborhood, but also to make sure that no one takes advantage of the tax-free situation.

"I'm not sure if I'd ever want to live on free land. But I can definitely see situations where it gets complicated. Is it inheritable? What happens when parents live there, but their adult child has a job and sends money home? How would police know if someone's working out of their bedroom? What if an old person can't work the land anymore?"

Ah, good questions. Hmmm. Forgive me if I forget to answer one.

"I'll remind you."

I'm sure you will. A working child sending money home is not an issue, so long as the parents tend their land. There is no income tax, so shifting income around isn't cheating. Someone could even be a billionaire and live on free land with a Rolls Royce parked in front, but he or she would still have to tend the land themselves without hiring others to do it. That's the deal—you must work the land in exchange for getting it for free. Basically, if you're going to drop out of the competitive free market, you can't still depend on services that come from that market. Then again, if you don't want to give up the luxuries a competitive market offers, then pay rent and live somewhere that will make you happy. On free land, you have to get your hands dirty.

"Would you really get arrested for hiring others?"

I hope this is obvious, Sam, but on competitively valued lands—like a ranch, farm, or suburban backyard—hiring others is perfectly appropriate. But the purpose of free land is to establish a living standard. It must function as a home for those who choose to be outside the competitive workforce. But its lifestyle has to be true self-sufficiency in order to keep the competitive market at bay. Otherwise desperation will worm its way into the community, and government will be asked to fix it. And our current problems will return.

"Why would the competitive market encroach on free land if it's there because the competitive market didn't need it in the first place?"

You're just giving me a hard time now, right? You said the opposite yesterday.

"I did?"

You said, "If you could get something for nothing, wouldn't you take it?" Or something like that.

"Maybe I did say that. But I'm not trying to give you a hard time. I'm trying to find a way to feel secure in what you're saying. It's not easy."

Well, I can appreciate that. But it's true. Once the price is free, and with no further obligation attached, those with one foot in the competitive market would take all that they could. And the choice for workers to say no would evaporate with each new claim. That's why it's important that there be two different contracts with the community. On competitive land, one pays to use the land as one sees fit. But on noncompetitive land, one must use the land personally in order to not pay for it. Preserving the unfettered no necessitates preserving the lifestyle that comes from having said it. And the requirement to personally tend free land will keep speculators away.

"But jail?"

Absolutely. If you muck around with freedom, you're hurting innocent people. Maybe violators will lose access to any free land anywhere, for a good long time. And owe restitution to the community too. A payment equaling the cumulative total of all salaries paid by violators to those they hired while using free land might be a minimal start.

"Wow. You make it sound like a federal offense. Why is it such a crime?"

It undermines the market, which is all of us. It's stealing opportunity from someone who needed that choice. Free land is a fulcrum on which a fair economy balances. Everyone's affected when that balance is tilted. Access to free land is what vanquishes economic desperation. If desperation is allowed to return, we'll all pay for it.

"But to make hiring someone a crime? How anti-capitalist can you get?"

On free land, the larger view has to win the day. Free land creates an open economy where we can choose to be in the competitive marketplace or not. If profit-driven competitiveness controls all uses of land, it will destroy our potential for choice, for freedom.

"What if someone wants to open a store?"

This is the start of a dream. It should be encouraged. But if a free-land user wishes to enter the competitive market, she can find a place that is valued by it and pay rent. A store can never be on free land, or it will usurp land that represents freedom for others.

"This is some kind of mega-zoning rule?"

Well, yes. A business is for the competitive market. Free land is for those who opt out of the competition.

"How could someone living this free-land lifestyle afford to pay rent or buy inventory to even start a store?"

Normally a bank would help finance it. But the community could choose to accommodate new entrepreneurs as well, especially since in that economy, the government will be financially flush. We might allow a brief period before charging rent, for example. The property would likely be of low value, anyway.

"Not bad."

The community would also dictate the period required for the new storeowner to leave their home on free land and move to competitive property. That would complete their emergence from the margin—to be working and living in the competitive marketplace.

"Seems like the government is doing a lot of mucking around there, except for the tax break, of course. Isn't the rest of it intrusive?"

You could call it that, I suppose. But if rules are needed for a competitive market, rules are needed to transition to one too. I don't think encouraging capitalism is such a bad thing, so long as it's fair. But communities can decide the particulars for these issues.

And by the way, the government could determine that overall demand for free land was weak—so weak that it wouldn't cause harm to shrink the pool of it. If this were the case, people on free land who wanted to start businesses could initiate a transparent, public process that would be capped by an auction. The hopeful storeowner would have the right to match the highest bid on their intended property. This is the only way a free parcel could join the competitive market.

"You're showing a lot of faith in the free market, Jorge."

If a market has the right rules, it's trustworthy. It's not faith really, so much as principles.

"If the population continues to grow ... eventually, wouldn't the competitive market use up all the land?"

You could reasonably think so. But I would ask you to think this through carefully. It's not likely.

"No? We'll soon be adding a billion people to this planet with every generation!"

Yes. And in a land-value-based economy, communities will grow efficiently. Cities will grow taller faster than they'll grow wider. Suburban sprawl, or any sprawl, won't be economically attractive. Community footprints will be as small as possible. Comparing community designs and efficiencies to what's in our capital-taxed economy today will be comparing apples to oranges.

"But what about billions of new people? They're going to make the competitive market so large that it will have to take all the land. Besides, who's going to feed them?"

I can't tell you precisely why it won't be an issue, even though your concern is very rational. But it won't be an issue.

"If I'm being rational, and we're disagreeing, then you're the one being irrational. What makes you say it won't be an issue?"

History. The broad sweep of history shows that buildings have been gradually built higher. Farmers have gradually become more efficient. Fuel use has gradually become more efficient. Transportation systems, from sailing ships to rails to jets, have gradually allowed for a more effective allocation of resources. History's tale is that we can expect to successfully embrace many more people on the land we already use, without needing more of it.

"Wow. That's so optimistic …"

I understand. But over time, the population has always grown—except during the occasional plague or war—and the pessimists who feared an unsustainable end have always been wrong.

"But now, with the numbers we're talking about … we've never had so many people on the planet before. It just seems impossible to end well."

The worst is always clear to a pessimist.

"Well, the best is always clear to an optimist."

Nice parry. But I'm simply following the line of history, Sam. Where it leads us isn't clear. Not to me, anyway. What is clear, though, is that we do get better at making things. So that's the line I follow. While you say it seems impossible to end well, I don't see that it has to end. We are capable of making good choices. We've made them before.

"We've also made bad ones. Isn't that your whole point about our economy?"

Well, aren't we here now, talking? Given that every economic system benefits someone, the questions are always who and how many? Whoever is benefitting at the moment isn't going to want to change anything. That's natural. But issues about our very survivability, from population growth or whatever, put all of us in the same boat. Who really benefits then?

"Jorge … most people don't care about ideas, especially subtle ones. They care about feelings, guts."

So then we'll care when we understand that it matters, when we feel the potential. These things ebb and flow. Eventually, every issue will have its time.

"Eventually, we'll also be dead. But I really hope you're right. I really hope I'm wrong."

In the meantime, at least, we can try to make good choices.

CHAPTER 12

Bodies and Minds

You had asked about old people, injured and the sick, who are living on free land.

"And you thought you'd forget."

People who physically or mentally can't work the land need our help. So, if they don't have family to do it, the government will take care of them.

"Just like that?"

What would you rather happen to them?

"So you want to socialize medicine?"

Well, yes and no. The health-care industry is an oddity, sort of an economic mutt. Parts of it can operate as a competitive market. But in parts of it the conditions for a free market don't exist. Those parts need to be socialized.

If every life is to be considered equally, critical care can't offer cheap and expensive versions to patients. In a free market, you can choose a cheap or expensive stove. But is it fair to demand that choice for a heart operation?

"Why not? Not to be crass, but why can't there be price points for critical care? Why should every life be valued equally in health care when the law values lives differently? You know, legal settlements depend upon a person's age and prospects for future earnings. So why should health care value life equally when the law doesn't?"

When it handles a case, the law is seeking compensation for harm. The practice of health care is supposed to do no harm. Health-care providers take that as an oath. If health care offers both cheap procedures and expensive procedures, and the expensive ones are distinctly better, isn't the doctor who offers less than the best effectively doing harm?

"No. If you're not making the patient worse, then you're not doing harm."

If a poor person has two broken legs, and the doctor only fixes one, the patient's not worse, but has the doctor done harm? And besides, economically, is there really an unfettered no in the situation for the patient? Someone who is forced to choose the greater harm to themselves, or the greater risk, isn't making a free choice. So it's not a truly free market that's operating there. But society can make the choice to establish its morality where the market can't. A true free market is man-made after all and, therefore, is a moral construct.

But you're right that there are valid pricing mechanisms in health care. Because there's no unfettered no for patients, the lifestyles of doctors, nurses, and administrators are easily protected by sending bills that account for the capital taxes they pay. So, just like in any other industry, health care becomes a higher cost for the poor than it would be otherwise. And what's unique to health care is the fact that the insured can afford to spend more on it than they otherwise would, so health-care pricing can ratchet higher still. Supply and demand is irrelevant to pricing critical care, because demand isn't by choice. So yes, with no true free market possible, critical care should be socialized. If it were, we'd have an efficient health-care delivery system, with costs rising in proportion to demographic trends.

The other side to health care is competitive. Elective procedures are, by definition, a choice. They are free-market events. When shopping for a surgeon to get wrinkles removed, the unfettered no is inherent.

But in an emergency, shopping is not possible. Or even in health maintenance, with prescriptions and the like, there is fundamentally no free market.

"For emergency care, I can see why I might not have a choice about shopping. I could just wake up in a hospital and not know how I got there. But for health maintenance ... that means checkups, right? Why couldn't I shop for that?"

You can shop for a doctor by reputation or with whatever criteria you want. But regular checkups are another means of preserving life. So if the system itself requires doctors to "do no harm," checkups cannot be doled out to the highest bidder. And if the doctor tells you what tests to take or what pills to swallow, you can't reasonably say no to any of it without potentially causing harm to yourself. Typically, a doctor has all the leverage over a patient. It's not a free-market environment.

"That's why there's an Internet. Ada's always looking stuff up, especially when I'm foolish enough to admit to a pain. She's always looking for new drugs and gadgets."

Well, the knowledge a doctor acquires—through years of advanced schooling and subsequent years of practice—can't reasonably be approximated by a patient, even one like Ada, who conducts searches. Or even a patient who's had months to study. It is not reasonable to expect a doctor's education from a sick patient. And it's not fair for the market to require one. There's too much at stake.

Look, when you go to an auto mechanic, you don't need to understand how the engine works or how every other system affects it. Your choice in him can come from personal experience, from his reputation, or from the price. You'll know approximately what it will cost. And you only need a reasonable expectation that the mechanic will fix it at a fair price. The same reasonableness applies to any free market transaction. When you're a patient, it ought to be enough to shake hands, so to speak, with an expert of sufficient repute.

And while a mechanic will give you an estimate that you can accept or reject before starting the job, doctors don't feel that kind of competition because patients are often in no position to reject a treatment without accepting some harm or risk to themselves. Besides, how is someone in pain, unconscious, or frightened in a fair position to say no to a medical professional? Or to know which, when there are different opinions offered, is right?

"Yes, Jorge, but this is why there's health insurance. They'll decide. And when you can't say no, the costs are covered ... except for a deductible or a copay."

They do decide. And that's the problem. Private insurance companies are profit-driven. They strive to take enough money from you, over your lifetime, so they can have a profit even after paying your health bills. The only thing assured with insurance is that their incentives are not aligned with yours. Sure, if you're lucky enough to have a common medical condition, an insurance company will take care of you, but not so much because it's you. It's more to preserve their reputation to sell more policies to others when you live and don't become a statistic. But if your condition is very rare, so rare that you could be seen to have won some hellish lottery, and your friends and neighbors would never see themselves being so unfortunate, then the insurance company might halt your expensive treatments. Their incentive is to pay as little as possible on your behalf whenever they can get away with doing so. There's no other way for them to profit. Few of us imagine contracting the most rare or worst of conditions. But if it happens, the free market won't be on your side.

"My insurance has been pretty good."

But it's not that way for everyone, not without special laws to fix it. The conditions for a free market aren't there: hospitals enjoy a pricing power that has little to do with economic competition, and insurance companies likely care more about their profits than your well-being.

"What about nonprofit hospitals?"

Nonprofit hospitals still have to hire administrators and staff in what is a competitive hiring environment. So the salary levels they offer are effectively set by for-profit facilities. And, their equipment is bought from for-profit companies. Nonprofits really have to generate a similar amount of revenue as for-profit hospitals, unless they're funded by charity.

And by the way, Sam, do you really want what happens to you being decided by revenue-minded parties? How would you know when the insurance company's desire for profit, or the hospital's need to pay the staff, overrules your desire for good and efficient care? In health care, maximizing profit and maximizing personal well-being are pieces from two very different puzzles. They're not a natural fit. When forced together, the resulting market can only be flawed.

We're free to treat the whole health-care industry as a free market. But if the conditions for a true free market aren't there, then inefficiencies will follow. As will a growing economic instability of the industry and a growing inequality of treatment across community members. No person should be seen as a profit center when that person has no choice but to participate.

"But socialized? I hate that idea."

It's an ongoing need within the community. And nonelective care doesn't fit the criteria for a true free market. So it is a natural role for government to fulfill. Anytime there's an ongoing need that doesn't slip, without contortions, into the operation of a true free market, it's government's obligation to meet that need.

"Why must it be government?"

It's then that government is more efficient. It saves costs overall.

"How is it more efficient?"

Applying the profit motive to an inherently noncompetitive situation ultimately drives expenditures unnecessarily high. Hospitals might claim their prices are high because some people can't pay at all, and they're absorbing that expense. But high prices only shift the hospital's supposed charity to patients and companies who pay those prices. They're the ones who end up paying for the hospital's "charity."

Then, of course, the forces are at work. As prices are driven higher, more people can't afford to pay, which drives prices higher still because people need hospitals anyway, and so on. This, in turn, will create calls for government to "fix" things. But when the root cause isn't being addressed—in this case, forcing a free market to operate where it doesn't fit—things only get worse. So it's least costly for the community to let government handle it and stop pretending there's a viable free market there to begin with.

"If health-care providers were transparent about their pricing, wouldn't that drive costs down?"

It could drive prices down from woefully inefficient heights, but they could never attain the level of a true free market's efficiency. There'd never be an unfettered no for patients. And to price shop, people would have to be willing to choose a service provider in advance for every contingency. But the unexpected will happen anyway, and the unexpected will distort the market.

"How do we know what's naturally handled by a free market and what's not?"

The principles tell us. An unfettered no must be present. A reasonable potential for equivalent knowledge between the buyer and seller must be present. And honesty must be police-able.

"When would honesty not be police-able?"

Well, with pay-for-service, for example. It can be difficult to know if a doctor is ordering a test to benefit the patient's diagnosis or her own finances. It's kind of ironic that the doctor's financial incentive is almost opposite the insurance company's; one wants more services, one wants less, yet neither is incented to care only about the patient. Some doctors—the better ones—can ignore their financial incentive. But if human nature is any guide, they will be a minority of doctors. Still, second-guessing a doctor's choices doesn't lend itself to black-or-white judgments. It's hard to know what someone's thinking without them telling you.

So, to finally answer your question—

"About time. I don't even remember my question."

Are you kidding? Don't you remember the lone person living on free land who gets old or sick? In the absence of a family willing to do so, he or she is taken care of by the community.

"And what if he doesn't recover? And if he has children?"

The surviving spouse would soldier through a difficult situation. They'll stay in their home. But without an able spouse or other adult to tend the land, the children would go with other family members. And failing that, a community orphan program would house them. Then, when they became adults, they could choose to enter the competitive market and pay rent ... or take free land of their own.

"What happens to their family's land?"

With no family adult able or willing to tend the property, the land would revert to the community's pool of free properties. It becomes available free land. We're talking about an immediate family member here, not a second-cousin-removed sort of thing.

On leased land, though, just to be clear, families can stay for as long as they can afford it.

"So long as their rent was paid."

Yes.

"Speaking of choices, if you're living on free land but want to send your child to a private school, can you do that?"

So long as you are tending your land with your own hands, you can do as you like for your child.

"Aha! Then that's hiring someone!"

Education is another economic mutt of an industry, like health care. Some of it fits a free market, some doesn't. But what's always true is that a broad education adds to individual freedom. So it's worth a minute to see where the free market works, to explore the conditions that good educational facilities require to thrive: sufficient population density and educational purpose.

A competitive market in education can't exist without enough people around. In rural or sparsely populated areas, there may not be enough children to make a school economically viable, let alone a second one to compete with it. So if the population density doesn't support a free market in education, then we have to ask, as a community, if it's appropriate to provide the service. And for that, we need consensus on the purpose of education.

"Is the purpose in doubt?"

It might not be to you and me. But there are those who feel government has no role in offering education, not even in rural communities. If those arguments are voiced, they would have to be overcome for public schools to get built.

It could be that those arguing against government-funded schools believe that government should only protect us from invaders or from each other. That any attempt by government to do more merely usurps our freedom. But if our community is going to be structured upon freedom for all, then there has to be an ability to choose, to some degree, one's own path in life.

"Of course."

If economic freedom means one isn't mired in the circumstance of their birth, then education must offer a wider berth as well. A solid education allows for greater opportunity by exposing a child to what lays beyond the experience of her immediate home. By offering the wider world of ideas to children, we'll all be better off. If our grown neighbors are making better choices for themselves, they are more likely to succeed in their endeavors. The whole community will benefit.

"So if the population is too thin, government should supply a school."

Yes.

"Then I know what's next. You're going to say that when the population is dense enough, the market will build private schools."

Yes.

"You're slipping, Jorge. You're getting predictable."

I'm not worried. Actually, public schools will remain after we convert to a land-value tax. In time, though, in densely populated areas, public schools will be less and less needed. A free market in private schools will grow to meet a dense population's needs.

"Was that a pun?"

What?

"Schools for a dense population?"

Oh … ha … no. It just slipped out.

"Private schools would become awfully expensive. They already are now. But without free schools around, Jorge, tuitions would soar. Most parents would get priced out."

Not most. Only some. It's normal for city centers to support the most expensive schools … and the most expensive everything, for that matter. Land values are higher, by demand. So the wealth is there to match it. Schools built there can never be truly cheap. But without being forced to compete with free schools, moderately priced schools can develop.

"How does the absence of free schools make for cheaper private schools? Wouldn't private ones get even more expensive?"

For any product, including a school, there's a calculation of how much you get in return for the price you pay. The distinction is pretty stark when the comparison is between expensive and free. People who can afford it usually choose the expensive school, which economically may be counterintuitive. But many parents think smaller classrooms give children an advantage in learning. And advantages in life are gained by giving a young person reputation and connections. The connections to wealth those schools provide has value too. That's another of wealth's natural advantages.

Free schools, at least economically speaking, are purely of educational value. Almost any education that comes out of them is worth it because it's free. Please understand, I'm not judging free schools on their academic merit; many provide fine educations. I'm only speaking from an economic point of view. I mean, if you get something for nothing, that's a value!

There's a problem though in valuing a medium-priced school. It won't show a clear benefit over either the expensive or the free. A lesser reputation for education or connections isn't worth the cost, not when a similar reputation is available for free.

"You think government-run schools can be as good as private ones?"

Of course. The teachers can still be passionate and effective. I'm just saying that economically, "free" presents a value position that's difficult to compete with. Free schools are the result of government providing a service, separate and apart from the free market. The value of public education isn't subject to pricing by supply and demand, so the price—free—isn't a measure of free-market worth. Only schools that charge tuition are submitting to the judgment of the market.

Free schools makes offering a clear value-proposition difficult for a medium-priced school. It's possible to make that distinction, but parents who can afford the expensive schools will use them, and parents who can't will likely opt for the free. A true market develops when there is no "free," as choice between expensive and moderately priced schools becomes real.

"You're going to kill education in this country."

Quite the contrary: where the free market can work, it will make education more attuned to the needs of our society. Tuition will begin to reflect an education's usefulness.

Imagine driving out from a city center. As we drive further and further, cheaper land values will allow for lower-priced schools. And when it gets to the point where population densities are unable to support a school to teach about our wide, diversified world, government's obligation to maintain a level playing field requires it to provide the facility that the competitive market can't. And of a quality the competitive market would require.

"Why should families in cities have to pay more than taxes for school when families in rural areas don't? That doesn't seem fair."

If education is a factor in economic opportunity, then it has to be available to all. The question becomes: what is the most efficient way to educate a community? A free market has the answer. Where the free market works, let the free market work. Where it can't, the government needs to step in. Of course, assuming the goal is freedom for all.

"It still doesn't seem fair. It's redistributing wealth."

What's not fair?

"Some are forced to pay for education, and some are not. That's not fair."

Fairness is reflected in the land values. And, where does that come from?

"Land value? The activity of the community using it."

Exactly. So as we move out of city centers with expensive land, at some point, in areas of cheap or free land, even finding enough qualified teachers could be problematic. So the rural school can't be held to the same standards of academic diversity and expertise as a school in a city center. But don't rural residents have the same right to opportunity and education? It is a part of their having freedom. If equal opportunity is our community goal, what else but government can make up the difference?

"Can't rural schools have teachers just as good as any in the city?"

Of course. But in a city, there are many, many teachers and a wide choice of schools to sort through. Parents can expect good teachers with some regularity. But in rural areas, getting a fine teacher for your child is bit more about luck. And we don't want to institutionalize opportunity based on luck.

Equal opportunity is not about cost. It's about availability. Those living in city centers are already living on expensive land and can afford what the free market asks for their children's education. But for those living in sparsely populated areas, even if the family could afford it, a private school might not be near. Equal opportunity demands that they have access to a school. Other than having wealth at birth or a great business idea, education is the best ticket to freedom.

"So the poor in cities? What happens to them?"

The number of poor people in cities would shrink, in part because there would be no working poor. But schools would appear that many of them could afford.

"How do you know?"

Affordable schooling will be a cause for some teachers, a market niche. And for those parents who find that even a modest tuition is a burden, well, public schools will be around for a number of years, until the change settles out economically. When that period passes, they can always choose cheaper land with cheaper schools, or free land with free schools.

"So you're going to piss them off too … making poor people leave."

Why would they be angry? They'll have a real choice about where to live … a viable, dignified choice. As the job market becomes more efficient—and without government's intrusions—city living will become their true choice, rather than a necessity to receive social services. Besides, in a meritocracy, living in unaffordable neighborhoods is not a right; expensive neighborhoods are a reward.

"How long will the transition away from public schools take?"

I don't know. Until people are mostly comfortable with it.

"That's not an easy pill, Jorge. People will need some major convincing."

Yup.

"And with college? The same principles apply?"

The same principles always apply.

"I knew you would say that. But college seems different to me."

Why would it be different?

"For little kids, education is local. Most families don't want their little ones going far away to school. But once in college, kids travel. Eighteen-year-olds aren't limited to what's local. Doesn't that change the competition?"

Travel makes for a different market puzzle, yes. But the principles used to solve it are the same. So with a true free market, we have to realize that not everyone must go to college; regardless of the economy's sophistication or technological advances, a living wage could be earned without it.

And since companies will be competing for workers, larger companies might find it advantageous to establish their own schools. Such programs, if offered for free, would certainly attract future employees. So another thing to realize about a true free market is that not everyone who wants a higher education will have to pay for it. The competitive market will find ways to have the quality of worker it requires.

And finally, a true free market is never stagnant; industries are dynamic, and job descriptions are always changing. So the last realization is that education will more closely reflect that shifting gamut and offer a wide assortment of goals and tuition costs for students. Sophisticated companies will have sophisticated colleges and universities to feed their employment needs, while other companies will find employees from the education market's generic mix of schools.

"Sounds like some people's education would be awfully narrow. If your future employer is schooling you for one specific job, how much of anything else are you going to learn?"

Schooling will be a company's investment in their employees. They aren't going to educate people to be limited in scope, not when future employees will want to see viable career paths within the organization. Companies will come to see establishing fine schools as a competitive incentive, in that well-rounded employees have a better chance to bring the company success. The school might well be where future managers come from.

"But why free schools? Traditional colleges and universities will still serve the competitive market, won't they?"

Sure. So most students will have wide-ranging choices. And importantly, Sam, because government does what the free market can't, any service that government provides will require schools to train people for those services. Expertise is needed for government jobs, just as much as it is for private sector jobs.

"If nonelective health care is socialized, does that mean medical schools would be run by the government?"

Yes.

"Really? You're killing me, Jorge! There's no competition in government. Without competition, how will doctors keep their edge? Innovation will go by the wayside."

Because politicians want to keep their jobs, government has incentive to minimize costs and be more efficient. Government will work to reduce the long-term costs of providing care. And private research will continue to look for profits. So there is competition. And who said government will run all the medical schools?

"You did."

I said the government will run medical schools. I didn't say all of them. Private health care will still exist. Don't forget about elective care. Lots of future doctors will prefer a private path, focused on elective procedures, to the public one for critical care. And they'd have private colleges to choose from. Free government schools and tuition schools would be available for students looking for public or private careers.

"So if, say, you wanted your body sculpted, your doctor will have gone to a private school?"

Yes. Private schools will train doctors in elective specialties, the competitive part of health care. And government schools will train them for preventative and emergency care, which are not competitive.

"And the government schools are free?"

They are. But government schools wouldn't just be for health care, Sam. They'd teach every field that government work demands. So government schools could be more like universities, offering programs in engineering, financial services, energy, transportation, criminal justice, medical research … whatever the economy demanded.

"And what would stop someone from getting the free education at a government school and then going to the private side?"

A commitment to public service would be required for receiving that free education. Just as a company-sponsored school could require employment at that company. But the incentive to leave government work won't be strong when it's offering a competitive standard of living.

"You really believe in paying government workers well."

I do. There's no reason government work shouldn't be paid according to private standards, including higher pay in areas with higher land-rents.

"I can see why government schools would teach things like finance and engineering and medicine. But why research? If the competitive market is the engine for innovation, wouldn't the best research be there?"

Research in the competitive market has a different agenda than research the government or a nonprofit lab would do. Profit seeking steers research to find profits. I mean, we've seen normal moods, like sadness, become treatable conditions, obesity be called an illness, and old age be seen as a disease. Old age! Because it's in the best interest of drug companies to find new conditions to treat. People conducting science for profit tend to find results or interpretations that support the profit. The danger is that profit-seeking science can easily distort the truth. We've been through this. Free markets aren't great at finding truth. It's best to allow a financially neutral party to seek the truth. That's a nonprofit standard.

Not-for-profit is the only kind of research that can honestly assess what might be seen as disruptive to current markets. In our debate about climate change, for example, one industry wants to find one cause for it, and other industry wants to find another. But the science can't be resolved by industries dueling for profits. There is no valid free market for determining the truth in global phenomena. The highest reaches of the atmosphere and the darkest depths of the ocean are invisible to company accountants. Only government or charity has the potential to find a long-term, hard-to-see truth without bias. And charity, being seeded by the private sector, can't be counted on to have sufficient funding early enough to stay ahead of far-reaching issues or to truly be unbiased. Preserving our life on Earth actually needs our nonprofit governments to be here.

"Government is biased too. Different politicians have different beliefs. Whoever is in charge is going to impose a bias. Why would government be neutral when a charity or a for-profit company wouldn't be?"

You're right. The neutrality of government can be distorted as easily as in the marketplace. The issue for government is whether people who respect science are put in charge, or if people who don't are put in charge. A nation can always choose to ignore science. But that doesn't make science any less valid. And it doesn't mean phenomena and their causes are going to go away. Not seeing gravity doesn't mean it stops holding us down.

If it's in the interest of government to protect its citizens, then respecting truth gives it the best chance to do so. Fiction can offer appealing, short-term illusions of safety. And a nation is free to make illusory choices. But there will still be long-term perils. Good leadership sometimes requires taking people to where they wouldn't go otherwise. Global events and concerns need to be met. They get met, or in that wake of failed leadership, the interests of the nation are left vulnerable. And, potentially, the fate of all nations.

"This sounds a bit sketchy to me. You're saying government will do right when the reins are given to people who believe in science. You might as well demand they believe in the tooth fairy. How do we know they're not anarchists or communists? Or out to line their own pockets? And, Jorge, it doesn't mean they won't waste our money. Frankly, it seems naive to depend on that—that the people running the show believe in the right things at heart."

It's up to us, as voters, to take an interest in the people we hire. That's trite, but it's true. The Catholic Church isn't going to pick an atheist to be pope, not without undermining the Church. So we have to pick people who won't undermine our government.

"Government screws up a lot, Jorge. It's not the be-all and end-all. We've all heard of colossal failures, wastes of money, when government picks a failing business to support."

It's not the be-all and end-all, but we need it to do what the free market can't. It has to support companies to develop products that are critical to our future. And profitability is irrelevant. Those decisions have to be guided by science, not profit, especially when there can be such a huge effect on our nation. We can't depend on quarterly profits to prevent epidemics or to find us some clean and enduring power source in a timely fashion. But government can. Government can anticipate such long-range concerns and then support a skilled company with lending, regulation, or grants. If it's done for the right reasons, not political favors, we could all be better off for it.

"Huge wastes, Jorge. Our tax money. It's in the record books. That's no myth."

It's true that government efforts fail. But so do private efforts. Federal programs can be much larger than typical private endeavors and so are more visible in their failures. But government is no less efficient, in percentage terms, than private industry. Private companies fail or go bankrupt all the time, especially new ones. Restaurants close. Rockets crash. Most start-up businesses fail.[vii] That's also a fact. It's a minority that survives beyond a few years. Just watch the number of stores that come and go near your home. And then think of how many you don't see, trying to make a go of it out of a back room, or on an upper floor where the rent is cheaper, and how many of those fail within a few years of starting. Even large companies start programs and cancel programs as their potential, or lack of it, becomes apparent, sometimes after spending hundreds of millions of dollars. So put it in context, government-led or –supported projects are subject to that same calculation, except they're usually done in riskier areas. Good leadership has to take risks to meet the changing long-term needs of the world.

"Private investment is at least someone's choice that's not using my money. It's my money the government's using when it chooses where to invest, and I don't get that choice."

That's why we have elections. If you want some say-so on the projects government invests in, vote.

"I vote, Jorge. I'm just not so sure it matters. Government ends up everywhere anyway, like butter melting into an English muffin."

CHAPTER 13

I'll Trade You?

Sam, that's why it's critical to understand what a true free market is and what it's not. So government doesn't seep into every nook and cranny of the economy. Government work should really be restricted to what the free market can't do for itself.

"That it's not is what's so depressing."

We're both fine with government engaging for national defense, right?

"Of course."

So if government sees a security risk, and the free market is not addressing it, it really behooves government to contract with a company or two that has the know-how to work on it. And we could see those investments as being smart? Not a distortion?

"We could. Yes."

The flip side of the coin is when governments require us citizens to invest. It's a problem, because we're being mandated to seek profit. That's a distortion to the economy.

"The way you say it, it sounds like a distortion."

Requiring stocks or bonds for our retirement accounts certainly favors publicly traded companies over private ones. It's another expression of a government's fondness for capital formation when its revenues come from capital. But anytime government fiddles with capital, it has a tendency to make things worse over time.

"Then why doesn't fiddling for defense make things worse? Weapon systems are capital too."

They are. But government is developing them and buying them to meet geo-political needs. Government is ultimately acting as a customer for weapon manufacturers. But mandating our personal investment in stocks and bonds is making us be customers when we weren't shopping.

"But in retirement accounts, how is it bad if private people are making their own investments?"

It's only bad if it's government-mandated activity. Listing a company on a stock market is done for one of two reasons: either it's to allow the company another way to raise funds, or it's to give the company owners more liquidity for when they want out. Mandated investment creates a working pool of money that would otherwise remain neutral or indifferent to those listings. It makes the investment pool larger for the owners of these companies than it would otherwise be. And their wealth is ultimately made greater than it would otherwise be. The community is investing more than it otherwise would only because of the mandate. Market valuations have to be affected. This is a clear distortion that then encourages even more companies to list. Only a government that depended upon capital formation for its own revenues would legislate such behavior.

"There's nothing wrong with a stock market, is there?"

Not in principle; not at all. A stock market is a natural outgrowth of a mature competitive marketplace. It's really an iteration of the competitive free market itself. And like any free market, the government needs to regulate it but not participate in it.

"Some would say regulating it is the same as participating."

That's like saying the referee is actually playing the sport. Any market requires fairness. So for example, a capital market, like a stock market, exists to match up the positions of buyers and sellers. Fairness makes it seem that there ought to be a line ... a basic first-come, first-served line to place trades, with no cutting. A regulator would make sure of that.

But capital exchanges that choose to boost their own profitability will naturally cater to larger players and start showing no more pretenses to fairness than a nightclub using velvet ropes and bouncers to pick its crowd. But with capital markets, we're talking about people being given advantages in wealth creation, not mere social cachet.

"The exchanges would say they need to be competitive, that if they didn't accommodate the wishes of those larger players, their business would just go elsewhere, to another trading system or even another country. Someone else will always be happy to accommodate them."

Then the question becomes: can there be a free market in supplying free markets? A true free market is a platform. Once the platform itself is seen as a generator of profit, it becomes a product, with the fairness integral to a true platform sacrificed to the game. So would you rather maintain the integrity of competition within our public markets or sacrifice that integrity to maximize profit?

"The free market is all about maximizing profit. That's all it's ever about."

Yes, but fairness is the measure of a platform, and profit is the measure of a product. When the platform itself is engineered to maximize profit instead of equal opportunity, someone's gain from being allowed to skip to the front of the line is necessarily someone else's loss.

"Yes, Jorge, I realize … but what if the stock market used parallel lines? What if there's one line for larger players and one line for smaller ones? Wouldn't that be fair?"

That question reminds me of the separate-but-equal arguments used in the 1900s to preserve the status quo of racial segregation. It doesn't work. Separate facilities are inherently unequal.

"I can see that when you're talking about people's skin color. But why would it apply to different-sized piles of money?"

Because it's establishing a preferred customer. Preferred customers are fine for a business like a bank or a nightclub. Companies can do what they like to compete. But the market itself is the playing field for making those choices. It's not the product. A true free market doesn't accommodate preferred customers differently; it's structured for all customers equally. Any regional bank would scream if banking rules were designed to give even the slightest advantage to a competitor.

Investment banks and brokerage houses compete for profit in capital markets. However, the fair capital market itself is not entered into that competition. The community is best served when government either regulates markets or runs them as a platform.

What's not so much depressing but is frustrating is that we tout the ideal of free markets, even as we've conjoined them with government. We'll foolishly see a free market as the answer to problems, even when poor conditions guarantee that it won't work. And when conditions are actually right, we can't leave well enough alone.

"And you think democracy is going to save us. Voters are the same people who think what you are saying is wrong."

Well, it has the potential.

"How does democracy have potential, Jorge? You've said you don't want a free market for politics. So how are candidates, especially the good ones, supposed to get their message out if they can't advertise? If they were selling your ideas, I bet you wouldn't mind the money spent on it."

Your question is exactly what I'm talking about. People think that campaign politics is a free-market activity. It is not. An economic trade must include an exchange of goods or services. There is no such thing in politics.

"Buying ads. Booking halls for speeches. Those are free-market trades."

They are. And that's what makes it confusing. They're the parts that get pieced together to build a campaign. But, Sam, in terms of politics itself—the pure thrust of a candidate running for office—what is being traded? What is the candidate after by running?

"The vote. I vote for someone in exchange for letting them run things."

Exactly. So, economically, what of value is being exchanged? If there's an economic trade taking place, there must be a swap of a value for a value.

"Confidence, maybe. People with a reputation can trade on confidence. Politicians too. They give me confidence; I give them my vote. But I don't really know, honestly. Politicians sell themselves. Then I vote."

If it's an economic market, then there must be a product. What is the product in politics?

"Power. And votes. It's the majority vote given in exchange for their power over everything else."

What kind of power? To do what?

"Geez, Jorge, I have to think. Impose an economic philosophy? A morality or social code? How we interact with other countries around the world? Should I go on?"

No, that's good. What you're saying is the power we give politicians is the power to impose ideas. Policy ideas.

"Yes. That's what campaign politics is—debating ideas in an effort to get power."

But is it an economic trade, votes for power?

"Sure. Like you said, we're picking the referees."

Does anyone own policy ideas?

"Own them? Like with patents or intellectual property? No."

So how can they be product, with definable economic value?

"Well, it matters what course a country takes. I don't know how you put a number on that, but it matters."

It does matter. Sam, absolutely, it matters. Still, if they're going to compete on an economic playing field, the question must be how to value them. Because that's what markets do: value things. One could put political ideas in a book, but we're not going to pick our leadership by how they rank on a bestsellers list.

"No."

We want our politics to be a debate.

"Sure. But now I'm more confused."

Remember—markets are designed for seeking profits. They're not designed for seeking truth. So if politics happens in the realm of ideas, and ideas aren't products, why should a campaign be considered a free-market activity?

"I realize you want me to say it shouldn't, Jorge. But politicians have to freely make their points. How do you have a robust democracy if the campaigns aren't free to do what they need to do to win?"

They do have to be free, but their freedom is in speech, to debate their ideas. Why should campaigns be run like marketing campaigns if political ideas are not a product? I wholly agree that free speech is important. It's of fundamental importance. But political debate can't play on the same field as for-profit products. Campaigns demand an arena of their own, a set of rules that lets truth be worthy, not an arena where it can be practically irrelevant.

Imagine a sports league where we could vote for the referees. But teams were allowed to pick the candidates and use their team's funds to campaign for them. After fans voted, who but the richest team would have the most referees working for them? Could we believe these referees would be unbiased during games? Could teams that didn't fund the referees on the field have a fair chance of winning?

We couldn't even be certain that the best referees were on the field. Some of the best would have enough integrity that they couldn't be bought. Their names wouldn't be on the ballot.

"I suppose. But even if you're right about this, how do you distinguish between where the free market ends and politics begins?"

How do you mean?

"Well, you're saying they're different, but where's the line? Take the media. You say politics and commerce should play by different rules, but broadcasters, even journalists, are allowed to have a point of view. It doesn't matter if there's a campaign in progress or not. Newspapers and broadcasters have political views. You can't just turn that off when it's election season."

You're right. There can't be rules about which opinions can or cannot be expressed. Free journalism and free speech are paramount to a free society. But media is an industry squarely in the competitive market. Opinions are part of its product, to attract subscriptions or advertising or both. Industry winners and losers are determined by normal economic metrics—the most revenues, the most profit, the most listeners or readers. The difference, Sam, is in the product. Journalists have one. Politicians don't.

"Come on, Jorge. Every candidate that's taken seriously is marketed just like a product. They advertise and hire public relations teams. The campaign is pitching product, be it the candidate or the philosophy, every time they make a speech or print a bumper sticker. Maybe a vote isn't money, but it is the way we buy political product."

Yes. But that again illustrates the confusion I'm talking about. Selling products is a legitimate free-market exercise. But political points of view are only packaged that way. Saying red is a better color than blue is not a position anyone can, economically speaking, own.

"Of course political ideas are products. Ideas and the way they're presented are what attract campaign contributions. That's the market saying, 'I like this product.'"

Those are contributions to the campaign, not purchases of a product. In politics, votes are the currency, and as you just said, they aren't money. Even if you see some semblance of a trade there, it's not an economic one. The winner of an election conducted in a competitive market can only claim to have won a marketing war. A battle of ideas can't be won. Actually, it's not even being fought if it's in a forum that is as responsive to fiction as to fact.

And, Sam, even if you still disagree that a policy isn't a product, you'd have to agree that it's like no other product. Majority rule affects all of us. You can vote no and still have to live as if you voted yes. No capital product does that, unless it's a very dangerous one. Name a product that affects the whole community, even if half the people didn't buy it.

"I can't ..."

But that's politics. Kindred spirits can join to uphold ideals. But when campaigns cost thousands of times the salary an office holder will get, it's clear that some contributors see candidates as vessels to acquire more wealth. Elected representatives can only comply by changing the rules of the economy. "Free-market political campaign" is an oxymoron.

"Well, obviously, all that spending isn't just to get some legislator a salary. Government contracts get awarded, appointments made, laws passed; that's how it works."

It does work that way. But as a community, we can aspire to more—to achieve an equality of opportunity, not only within our economy but also for the politicians who'll referee it.

"What is equality of opportunity for politics? If free land is it for economics ..."

That's for communities to decide. It's not the place of economics.

"Really? That's a cop-out."

I'm sorry you feel that way. All I'm saying is that there's no fundamental basis for campaign politics to use the rules of economics. And doing so can lead to some foul-smelling rules.

"Does it really make such a difference if people are going to try to influence and cajole politicians anyway? The increment of corruption, to coin a phrase, can't be that much worse, can it?"

Should the referees of a sport be chosen by how well they play it? If the referees of capitalism were chosen according to their business success, they'd be chosen for their ability to deliver profits, not for their ability to deliver fairness. Those are distinctly different skill sets.

"What if one country actually had a true free market, but it traded with a country that didn't?"

That depends on how the rules between the two economies differed. But there would be a space within the differences for economic inefficiencies that could leach into either economy. Diplomacy would determine how well corruption was kept from filling that space.

"I recently read about some lousy plasterboard that was shipped here from overseas. It turned out it ruined the homes that used it. People couldn't live in them anymore."

Oh, I remember hearing about that.

"Such a junky product should never have been here, in our market, in the first place. Would that have happened if we had had a true free market?"

Probably, I'm afraid. Yes. Markets aren't good at finding liars and cheats. Economics could only impose a loss of future orders on that supplier. So, again, it has to be up to government and the law to impose a sort of preventative scheme or to seek punishment. But in some nations, with bad law, no real restitution is available.

Nations can compete with the quality of their laws. It's a third arrow in the economic quiver, alongside natural resources and the quality of infrastructure. Bad law allows inferior products to have their profit, with no consequence for the harm that's done. But given a choice, buyers will stay clear—stay away from nations that allow deliberately inferior materials to erect homes, or contaminated or phony pills to be swallowed by already ill citizens. Given a choice, who would choose a trading partner whose rules allow for that?

"A company in a country with equally bad law?"

Exactly! Economic laws give us a foundation to take care of ourselves when the market can't do it for us. Diplomacy needs to keep international avenues open to make sure there are options for our corporate buyers, in different countries, so that they can say no. The competition between suppliers, between nations, would go a long way to avoiding this problem in the first place. Not eliminate the problems, but it would certainly help.

"I don't know. There's a profit at stake; morality isn't going to drive international trade."

No, not morality—legal efficiency. Legal efficiency equals cheaper; in the long run, more profit. And competition among nations can slowly create those efficiencies in law. Look at the history of trade. There you'll find a clear tendency to cheat, scam, or take advantage of people when there is little prospect for a relationship. This was true for travelling snake oil salesmen, and it's true today. Remember that free markets can't protect people before the harm is obvious. So a body of law that does that can help win us international customers. And wouldn't we prefer to trade with a nation that did the same? Really, culture should permeate across borders, if only for the sake of trade.

"How can government do that? The world's filled with nations that don't want outsiders telling them what to do."

Of course they don't. But every nation wants an opportunity to have more wealth. International trade is such an opportunity. And we don't have to tell them what to do. If treaties promoted fair competition, each nation could figure it out for themselves. Years or decades might pass before change occurred, but lucrative trade would be a persistent inspiration. And good diplomacy a constant prod.

"It doesn't have to be about laws or politics, Jorge. Sometimes a company will just cheat, or worse, even with good cultural relations."

People cheat from home. People cheat from away. You're right; it won't go away. But cheating is much less likely when cultures cross-pollinate. Both governments and companies can use cultural preferences to build relations with their international partners. It's a clear role for government to be constructing, treaty by treaty, the groundwork for international trade.

And the nature of a truly free market allows a nation confidence in the face of expanding trade, even foreign investment, because growing land's value benefits the community. There wouldn't be political pressure to protect an industry with tariffs on what comes in, or with subsidies on what goes out, when land values are rising.

"What if foreigners are getting government subsidies that let them price goods so low it undermines our industry? Don't our companies deserve protection?"

Subsidized prices definitely cause distortions on salaries and productive capacities. It's a manipulative economic action that's best met with exogenous economic tools, like diplomacy, or we must be willing to walk away. Even nations need an unfettered no. It's only prudent for us to find, across the world, multiple suppliers for our industries. If we aren't dependent on a single supplier, then dumping and other economic schemes will lose their effectiveness.

"But wouldn't walking away cost jobs? You make it seem like the benefits of honest international trade are obvious. Maybe the benefits aren't so obvious. What about jobs?"

Remember—with a true free market, we'll have an efficient job market with extremely low unemployment. But distortions can only play out in fundamental ways. Unfortunately, when economic principles are violated, it's labor that suffers.

"Umm ... is that an answer to my question?"

Not really. Not yet. But if the point of a true free market is a universally free population, under a government that is unintrusive as is fairly possible, then liberty means workers can go where they see better opportunity. But across the world, we enforce laws of oppression. Countries hold duopolistic delusions that government should tax capital, and individuals should own land, when the opposite is what's right. The result is populations forced by starvation or pestilence into slavish, inhumane jobs. And, unfortunately, the wages paid to them will always be lower than what's paid to workers in a true free market. It follows that their products can be priced lower too. To the extent their products infiltrate a true free market, to the extent they sell, the low prices realized by an oppressed labor force will usurp the lifestyles of fairly paid labor.

"Then we do have to protect our jobs."

That's a quick conclusion, and it seems intuitively right. But it's a fruitless path. Attempts to protect our jobs from barbaric economics elsewhere only doom our markets to unintended effects. It's better to just ban the immorally created product than try to compensate for it with some economic tweak like a tariff. A tweak, even if from good intentions, creates a distortion, which will just lead to more distorting laws to try to fix things. Protecting jobs with tweaks is the path to going backward. The principled path is to avoid the artificially cheap product outright.

While saying no is a powerful economic tool, it might well be hard to do. But we can never gain freedom by turning away from principle. If free-market forces are allowed to play out, which I'll admit is easier said than done, they'll eventually have a corrective effect.

"Will we still be alive to see it?"

Transparency is the key. To improve the quality of international trade, governments need to create transparency. It might seem odd, but consumers being repulsed by barbarism actually benefits our long-term interest, because the more those products fail, the less abusing labor will be tried. But until the benefit of true freedom for workers is seen, it would likely take a really roiling backlash, like the rest of the world saying no, or the unusually beneficent will of a government unwed to power, for a nation to foster change that placed human dignity above corporate profit.

So, until all nations abide by truly free markets, nations and the businesses they shelter will have a choice: to profit by maximizing liberty or to profit by oppression. Unfortunately, most nations alone couldn't sustain the politics of freedom, not while the cheap prices clawed from oppressive practices seep into their economy. But a resounding, collective, international no could give them enough strength. Though helped by the world, that nation would symbolize the shining city on a hill.

"If there were a shining city, more people would be attracted to it. And if we were it, they'd come here. In fact, they already do. And so again, I have to ask about jobs …"

Of course people will come. Who wouldn't want to live in such a place? But, Sam, the more robust the unfettered no, the less joblessness will be an issue. Nations need to see their way to saying yes to the no.

"Immigrants would be flooding in. Isn't limiting them a reasonable way to protect jobs?"

Using the word "reasonable" is an interesting way to phrase it. You know, or at least I hope you know by now, that my freedom obsession is going to keep me in favor of open immigration policies.

"You're so damn predictable, Jorge. Again, you didn't answer the question."

If a free market is about equal opportunity, worker mobility is integral.

"But worker mobility is different than immigration. People moving within our economy is fine, no problem, but people crossing international borders … they'll suck up all the jobs."

That's your fear, Sam, not what's fundamental. People are alike in the eyes of economics. It doesn't matter where they're from. It's land access that defines opportunity. So immigration policy can avoid the emotions and much of the associated politics by paying attention to the unfettered no.

"How does that work?"

Government, as manager of the free lands, is sensitive to the pulse of our economy. When demand for free land begins to grow beyond the community's ability to absorb it, and that demand is from immigrants, it then becomes appropriate for visa pathways to be more restrictive until equilibrium is reestablished. Free-land supply and demand tells us what we can tolerate economically. It's up to our community to heed the message. So in the short run, the answer is yes, limiting immigration will maintain more robust job opportunities for citizens. But only in the short run.

In the long run, the issue is not about protecting jobs. It's about protecting wages. A wave of immigration larger than an economy can absorb will drive the average wage down. But this will have no effect on the lifestyles of people living off the land, as they're not getting a wage. And so long as free lands are properly managed, low wage earners won't be affected either. That's because the lowest wage has to provide a lifestyle better than living off the land, or employers won't be able to attract workers. So the most vulnerable to a surge in immigration is the middle class and their wages.

"I don't understand …"

An unfettered no allows for the bargaining power to demand a living wage. So low-end wages are secure; any lower, and workers would opt for free land instead.

"I follow."

But the middle-class lifestyle doesn't have that bargaining power. With no cushion of great wealth on the one hand, and what would be a downgraded lifestyle to free land on the other, they have no easy way to tell their employers no. A sustained wave of immigration would hit their wages the hardest. The middle class is the canary in capitalism's coalmine. When it is dying in proportion to the population, the economy has a problem.

But that's the case for a flood of people. If immigration is managed at the right pace, according to the demands on free land, it will drive middle-class wages higher.

"Higher?"

Free markets thrive on new ideas and new products. And new people improve the chances of hearing new ideas. Plus, every person adds to general economic activity. Immigration is a net plus to the community when it's managed right, enhancing community wealth and the value of land. So over time, rising land values will push wages higher too. Employers will have to abide with higher pay if they want to keep their valued workers. In the long run, Sam, a smart immigration policy pressures the average wage up.

So, to your question—"Is it reasonable?"—the answer is yes. Capping immigration will work for the short term. But in the long run, it means lost opportunities for all of us. And it violates the notion of a true free market.

"Free land won't get used up eventually?"

Not when its availability is guiding immigration in the first place. Since free land is the rock of economic freedom, if it's allowed to disappear, it affects everyone. So when the availability of free land is threatened, it's a sign the nation's doors must temporarily close. But as the economy adjusts, and free land finds its equilibrium again, a smart nation will reopen its doors.

Of course, if all nations abided by free-market principles, the incentives to emigrate would be minimal. The only factors to drive immigration would be war, disease, or a change in a nation's productivity due to a changing climate. These will always be international concerns. Otherwise, the global adoption of true free-market principles would eliminate immigration as a disruptive force. It would hardly be on the political radar.

"Jorge, I'm sorry. You know the fate of your scheme might not be so grand."

We'll see. I've been pushing the applications a bit, I'll admit. But at heart, it is a practical prescription for a world like ours, where opportunity in proportion to people is rare. If governments everywhere worked to promote free-market principles, then no nation would need to build gates against immigration. But you're not going to tell me, Sam, that we can fight with our lives for the full liberty of people born here while not allowing those less fortunate to share in our graces. Especially when, managed properly, they will boost our wages.

A boat will hold just so many people before it's likely to sink. But if we abide by its physical capacity, the same boat can make many, many trips. And if we can shrink the need for people to wait at the dock in the first place, everybody wins.

"By shrinking the need for people to wait at the dock, you're saying that if the nations of the world could all recognize and respect basic economic principles, it would make the cost of governing much cheaper for everyone."

Yes. But what you just said sounds better than the way I said it.

"Jorge, you do know this is a pipe dream, right? No offense."

Well, everything is a pipe dream until it gets done. Going to the moon seemed a pipe dream. But then we began to understand and apply the principles of physics. A truly free market requires no more from the principles of economics. At some point, nations will realize that when they trade using different economic rules, neither country's system can remain unaffected. Opportunities for cheating will multiply. Or the laws passed to prevent cheating will create their own problems. Common rules would be far cheaper, in the long run, for everyone. It's not crazy to hope for, as long as there's diplomacy and trade among nations.

"Well, I'm skeptical, but know I'm not rooting against you."

Gee. Appreciate it.

CHAPTER 14

Brother, Can You Spare a Currency?

"So, using the same rationale, couldn't we say it would be more efficient if every nation used the same currency? The way it is now, with conversion costs and all the manipulating that countries engage in—wouldn't the world be more stable and efficient if everyone adopted the same currency, like gold?"

Sam, a currency's value is built upon two things: a set of codified economic rules and the quality of the economic activity that uses those rules. A common currency across nations can only endure if the nations uphold the same set of rules. If differences in rules and practices have a big effect on labor values, well, they have an even larger effect on currency values. It might be nice to imagine a world with a single currency, but even I know that dream is unstable when economics is practiced in different ways.

"But gold has universal appeal as it is. Wouldn't gold, or a gold-based currency, sort it out?"

Not at all.

"Come on."

Gold has only limited use as a currency.

"Gold has been around forever as a currency!"

It certainly has a long history as currency. But so does silver. So does copper. Yards of cloth had a long run. And bushels of grain. Even shells and notched sticks. And today it's paper. History teaches us there is nothing unique or special about gold being a currency.

"I didn't mean that gold itself would be used as the medium. But what if a paper currency was pegged to gold? What if the value of a dollar, or yuan, or whatever, was set to be a certain weight of gold? Currency values would have to be more stable that way than what we're experiencing with this fiat system we have."

By currency value, do you mean an equivalent weight of gold or in relation to other currencies?

"I mean both. Being on a gold standard would stabilize the value of our currency so it doesn't lose value to inflation. And it would stabilize the exchange rate of our money against the rest of the world's currencies."

A single concocted law can be used to equate anything to a specific value. However, over time, as economic forces inevitably exert themselves, lawmakers would find themselves stressed to continue following it.

"Why?"

A government assigning value to something, even a unit of currency, is market intrusion. A true free market doesn't have its tools priced by politics. It discovers value through its own transactions.

"But paper money, free-floating fiat money, loses its value over time. At least gold holds its value."

Since when is it the function of money to hold value over time?

"Well, that's what money is, isn't it? A store of value?"

But what is being stored? And for how long?

"I don't follow you. It's value that's being stored."

The value of what, though?

"The dollar."

But what drives the value of a dollar?

"Government policies."

In a secondary way, yes. But primarily, the value of any currency is born through work.

"Work?"

Money holds the value of work, be it a salary from labor or a price from a product. Money is only useful because people make things. If we didn't make anything, if we didn't make jars or clothing or grow crops, there wouldn't be a need for money. Its role is to hold the value of those efforts.

"Then it should store that. And not let the value inflate away."

Let's follow the forces. Money, for example, is used to buy workers. Money is a worker's income. And when a bank offers a loan, it expects to be repaid because of either the borrower's ongoing income, expectation of income, or potential to create income. Now a bank might gamble by supporting the start of a business because of the plan and people involved, or it might play it safe by demanding collateral. But either way, the loan is made against work—either the applicant's current work, work from her past as represented by her assets, or work in her future as what rewards her new business might bring. Can you see that money is an empty vessel without work backing it? Money is used to value work.

"It still shouldn't inflate away."

Sam, for how long will your company value the work you did last week?

"That report I wrote? Why? I don't know … maybe a month? Six months before it's completely stale. By then, they'll be on to something else, anyway."

So you have to keep working to keep earning?

"Of course."

You have to keep working to maintain your value to the company.

"Sure."

So the value of your work fades, yet the money you're paid for it should last forever?

"What are you getting at?"

Is there anything you've bought lately that you expect to last beyond your lifetime? I mean, without maintaining it somehow?

"I don't know. I bought a desk … a huge, old rolltop desk. That's going to outlive me, for sure."

What's it made of?

"Wood. Rosewood and mahogany, I think. Ada picked it. But what are you getting at?"

It will need maintenance, won't it? I'm not an expert, but I believe it can't be allowed to dry out, or the wood will start to crack. At the very least, it has to be kept indoors and protected from the weather. And if you use it and care about keeping it in perfect condition, it will likely need refinishing at some point, if only to fix the inevitable nicks and scratches.

"I get it. You're saying all that requires work."

I am.

"What if I just keep it in the house and never touch it?"

Your house will require maintenance to keep a roof over the desk, won't it? The years won't pass without something in your house needing fixing. The roof will start to leak. A pipe will burst. A window will break. The water heater will need replacing. All that will need to be done over time, and all that contributes to keeping your desk protected.

So the result of someone's work requires additional ongoing work to maintain its value. Even a beautiful video screen requires the ongoing efforts of other people to give you something to watch, or it wouldn't be worth the space on your wall.

"That's not always true. Suppose, in the future, my desk became an antique. It could become more valuable than when I bought it."

As an antique, your desk will have acquired a value that outstrips the cost of maintenance. But, it's the rarity and quality of the craft in it that's being valued. That's akin to valuing art.

"And quality, high quality, is rare."

Very. So can we accept as fact that anything we make—with rarity value being the exception—loses value over time, is consumed, or requires ongoing efforts to maintain it?

"I suppose."

Then why should money, which is also a creation of humans, be any different? Shouldn't money also require ongoing efforts to maintain its value?

"You work, you get paid. That is the value everybody agrees to. Why should compensation become devalued later?"

You did the work for your report, but as you said, its value isn't lasting. So if someone bought that report from you, like your employer effectively did, why should it lose value over time while what he gave you to do it maintains the same value forever?

"How could I even begin to plan my life without some stability in the value of what I earn?"

Stability isn't the same as holding a value forever. Inflation is what erodes the value of your salary over time, right?

"Yes. If the cost of everything I buy rises, sure."

But that's to be expected, isn't it? Especially when we know there is an ongoing degrading to the products of our efforts. Foods quickly spoil or need some added effort like refrigeration to preserve them. Buildings need maintenance. It's as if capital decay is Brownian motion in an economy. It's always there. And the level of it suggests an appropriate level of inflation.

"But inflation has been high and low. My food hasn't rotted any faster or slower."

Of course not. But across the whole economic community, there's an average expected durability to the value of products. Part of that value is in the stuff to make the product, our capital, and part is in the cost of labor to make it. To keep it simple, let's assume that at the time a product needs replacing, the value of labor in it is wiped out, while the stuff of the product can be sold for scrap. When labor costs are low, there is a smaller value of labor built into the final cost of a given amount of stuff. There is less value to decay. Inflation is low as a result. But when labor costs are high for the same amount of stuff, the same decay eats up a higher percentage of the product's value, simply because there's more labor in it as a percentage of the product's value. So inflation is higher too.

"So inflation is driven by the relative value of labor?"

Yes. And it should normally approximate the average, community-wide decay rate. But inflation can become unwieldy in a capital-taxed economy because of all the leveraging forces at play, from distorting the value of work to distorting the value of capital itself. Inflation can swing wildly. However, in a land-value economy, those wild swings go away, because manipulations to the value of labor are eliminated.

I'm not saying inflation then won't ever be a problem. Our expectations for it can become a self-fulfilling prophecy. Too much inflation hurts the poor, even creates more of them, especially in a closed economy. And too little is unsustainable because of the natural decay of products. But at a moderate, near rate-of-decay level, inflation presents nothing to fear.

"Even at a low level, it gnaws at the quality of my life."

The amount of money in a community is proportionate to the total goods and services within it. As the population grows, as new industries form, as new products allow for the creation of other new products, the pool of money should naturally grow. There's nothing that says a dollar earned fifty years ago should be worth the same as a dollar earned today, any more than the precise work done fifty years ago would be valued in the same way today, unless it became valued for rarity like an antique. Money has to work to maintain its value, just as you have to work to maintain your value to the company. Money has to be economically engaged to maintain its value, just like any other tradable product.

"What does that mean, money has to be engaged like a product? Money's a product?"

Sure. Tools are products. And money is a tool for the economy, used to expedite trade. Tools clearly have value in being used, in being engaged. But they also have a cost in not being used. You might keep a hammer in the tool shed, but while you're not using it, you're still maintaining that tool shed to protect the hammer from the elements. Fifty years later, your hammer can still drive a nail into a wall, but storage costs have eaten away its value, and new, better materials found to forge hammers in the interim have also made yours relatively less valuable. Time and economic progress will erode the value of any tool, money included. So money needs to be put to work, engaged with the economy, to grow with its economy over time.

"Well, that doesn't happen for gold. Or for diamonds."

What doesn't happen?

"The storage costs don't eat away the value. When I found my grandmother's engagement ring after my mother died, I can promise you storage costs didn't eat away a bit. It was worth a whole lot more than what my grandfather paid for it. More than inflation too."

I'm sure that's true. But there's a particular form of supply and demand at work there, Sam. How old was your grandmother when she got engaged? In her twenties?

"Probably. Yes. Definitely. Twenty-two."

Then there have been three or four ever-larger generations of people to come into the world since then. And the amount of wealth in the world has vastly increased because of all those additional people. Even if the wealth is concentrated in a relative few, there are still many more people alive today who can afford discretionary spending than there were in your grandmother's youth. Demand for diamonds has grown greatly. And miners can manipulate the supply, by slowing their output, to ensure rising prices.

"Wouldn't gold be subject to those same forces?"

Of course.

"Then it can hold its value. And that's my point. So why can't it work as a currency?"

You just said why, Sam. The same forces are at play. Gold can gain significant value just by being harder and harder to find over time. Or if the number of people who want it grows over time. So gold is subject to being valued by rarity. It can gain value when it's disengaged, just sitting in a vault. But competitive markets strive for profit. The goal there is to sell more, not to maintain the value of the product. Most products are ultimately disposable. There's a mismatch between that purpose and what you're saying is the purpose of a currency. Gold value can be uncorrelated to economic activity. But a currency needs correlation to its economy.

Even so, let's grant your wish. Poof! Gold is adopted as currency. Suddenly new gold has to be mined as the economy grows; costs of land, labor, and equipment have to be folded into its value. If the supply of gold did not match the pace of economic growth, its rarity value would begin to outweigh its currency value. If that happens, it means that people who had been able to store it, successful or lucky people, would have an unearned advantage over those who were still working to save it. That mismatch is inevitable. So, in the long run, because its supply is finite, gold cannot work as a currency any more than oil can be the world's main fuel forever.

"How is that analogous? Oil gets burned up. Gold doesn't. Gold can last forever."

Economies using gold as a currency can easily outgrow potential supplies of it. Eventually we'll run out, just as we'll run out of new supplies of oil. At that point, the rarity value will completely take over. That gives great advantage to those who have stored gold over those who continue to work for it. It's unfair ... and no way to run an economy.

"So if gold isn't the answer, how is money supposed to work, or be put to work?"

Money, in a way, is like people. Its uses are almost as diverse as we are. After all, it's an invention spurred by our own desire for conveniences. We've given it our traits that way. So just as an active person is going to maintain strength and stamina far longer than someone who spends their waking hours on a couch, money put to work in economic activity is going to maintain its value better than money resting in a mattress. Both money and humans need to be active to maintain their strength. But, in money's case, the strength is called purchasing power. Exercise is to people what investment is to money. The only difference is that money doesn't sweat.

"Well, I do. It'd be nice if they'd invent a gym that didn't make you tired. My old love handles have turned into body-length bannisters."

You don't look so bad. But just to finish this point, let's keep focused on the community. Money invested in an economy will maintain its long-term value in accord, on average, with the fortunes of that economy. As long as the economy grows, invested funds will, over time, have greater value than money held away from economic productivity.

"That sounds a bit risky. I think a lot of people would be scared by what you're saying."

If investments reflect the risk in the economy overall, then the risk is no greater than the chance of that economy collapsing. Obviously, if you're investing for a greater return than that, then you have to take on greater risk. But no transaction is risk-free. Looking to store value in a mattress isn't risk-free either. Anyone who chooses to enter the competitive market by working for someone or by building her own business is taking a risk in the company's prospects. Anyone who has saved for retirement has earned those savings from having taken risk, be it through employment or investing. Even retirement only means that one has left the labor pool; it doesn't mean one has left the risk pool. But a well-designed economy will minimize risk for everyone. Remember—an economy based on true free-market principles is cyclically muted, a relatively stable economy. It's not as scary as our capital-taxed system with such oversized booms and busts.

"Do you guys want to see the menu?" *The dark-eyed waitress appeared again, lips still unsmiling.*

Sam gave a quick glance to Jorge, just to be sure. "No thanks," *he said.* "I think we drank our appetites."

Her face went flat and unmoving like a paper cutout, as her body was already gliding for more lucrative tables.

"So, given what you've laid out, it seems like the biggest risk to an economy is from the people who govern it."

It is.

"You've been pretty clear about it. When they pass a law that doesn't jibe with free-market forces, we're all going to suffer in the long run."

We will. And thank you for thinking I've been clear, even though you think I've been dreaming.

"I didn't mean …"

Don't worry. I'm just pulling your leg.

"So, then the solution is for government to be as small as possible, with fewer fingers in the fewest pies."

Yes, government should be as small as possible. But that's not a solution in and of itself; that's a result that stems from a solution. Land-value tax is a solution because it minimizes the needs government needs to address. So government can be as small as possible. And understanding where free markets work and where they don't minimizes bad decisions. But all this really depends upon what is meant by "as small as possible."

"As small as possible means no larger than what is needed, like you said."

Okay. Well, what is needed?

"Watch this, Jorge. I've been listening. Let's see … what's needed is whatever the free market can't do for itself."

Not bad. Good to know I haven't wasted your time.

"Not at all. You bought me beer."

Gee, glad I could fill the time while you drink.

"Hey. Here's to you. So, with everything else you bashed, you bashed gold as a currency. Then that leaves us with paper currency."

Well, fiat currency. It doesn't have to be paper.

"Okay. Either way, the point is, why is that good? It doesn't seem very free market–like to have treasury departments and central banks intervening all the time."

My only point has been that precious metals or other physical elements are not a long-term solution because of their potential rarity. Nothing says money has to be tangible. For a currency to be workable, there mostly has to be sufficient trust. I can see a day when we no longer use paper. But the need for intervention … it's only a result of the rules we've chosen.

There is a valid need to keep the nation's books, collect taxes, and issue currency. A treasury department has its place. A trustworthy nation with a strong military might even be asked to store treasure for other, weaker nations.

"The treasury department would be in charge of that?"

Yes. Ours does that every day. We hold gold for many nations.

"Imagine ... a treasury that actually stores treasure."

The need for a central bank, though, is less straightforward. Its manipulations—raising or lowering interest rates, or guiding lending levels—are born of our decision to tax capital. In the world today, interest rates need to be managed because a government tapping capital for revenues is nervous about fluctuations in the nation's capital base.

Interest rates are effectively the cost of that capital, a blending of the varying values of labor with the need for a bit of profit. And capital levels are further leveraged by taxation. Therefore, a central bank is needed to manage and massage a nation's debt, to achieve specific results from the economy. You're right in that, by definition, a central bank as a manipulative entity goes against the nature of free markets. But in the world of true free markets, those centrally orchestrated manipulations wouldn't be needed, because capital would not be the source of government funds.

"Remind me why land value is not capital."

Land is not a product of man.

"Ah. Right. Sorry."

This isn't a gym. Don't sweat it.

"Would central banks exist then?"

In a true free market? Yes. But by rights, the manipulation of a nation's debt ought to come from policy—to create debt if it's needed to pay for a response to a crisis or a war. A central bank would rightly act as a backup lender for emergencies. And their major role would be in managing the audits required to make sure the nation's financial entities fully reveal their activities to the public.

"We talked about that yesterday. The government does the audit. The public does the interpreting."

Yes.

"But what about the national debt?"

What about it?

"The debt is now so large. I mean ... it's frightening to think a mistake by the central bank can have massive, horrible consequences. And the mistake might not show for years."

Today's central banks have the powers they do—to manipulate currency values and spark inflations—because of the economic leverage that comes with taxing capital. The ominous size of our national debt, as we've discussed, stems from that too. But debt is not necessarily the monster some fear. In and of itself, debt is not that scary.

"Are you kidding me?"

I'm not kidding. It's likely debt was the spark of all economic growth, although it took a while for the spark to actually light a fire. Indulge me in a story. Imagine a long time ago when communities were very small and relatively isolated; people knew each other and usually when they would see each other again. This allowed them to trust each other. If someone needed a garment, the shoeing of a horse, a meal, or whatever, it was okay to let him or her pay later, because reputations mattered. But saying someone can pay later is really issuing a debt. Those personal debts made it so a craftsman didn't have to go about town hauling wood or stone behind him, ready to perform his service just to buy a new pair of pants. And a farmer could take care of his family's needs all year, when he was trusted to repay his debts from the next harvest. Debt allowed people to do their business unencumbered.

Then an idea caught on that improved debt as a tool. People started keeping records. This simple act, the marking of a debt, encouraged economies to diversify and grow. Records of debts allowed debts to be traded. When everyone in town knew the blacksmith by name, everyone in town could also know his debts were good. With a written IOU from Jack the blacksmith, you could trade that, his debt, to a neighbor to receive whatever the neighbor had to offer. Your neighbor could make that trade because he too either knew Jack personally or knew Jack's reputation for always making good on his debts.

But as populations grew to the point where some of the people in your store were strangers, things had to change. It's one thing to trade among people you know and regularly see. It's quite another when you interact with strangers. One isn't going to grant a debt to someone who isn't likely to be seen again. Strangers were therefore as likely as not to be ones to take advantage of or to rob. But, and this is the point of the story, if the recording of debts could be trusted, even among strangers, the temptation to cheat would shrink. The record could be trusted even if the person couldn't be. This is where one smart king founded an important function. Government could promote the growth of a larger economy—not only to stop crime but also to have a real financial role by consolidating records and enforcing both debts and ownership. Or maybe a clever king just saw a way to enhance his power. After all, stoking a more robust economy, holding ownership records of property, and formalizing debts would mean no less.

That could be how governmental economic authority began. I don't really know. But however it started, it meant that the economic rules of your own small village also applied to other towns in the realm, to people you didn't know. Common rules and expectations for transactions meant that strangers didn't have to be seen through wary eyes. When government began to record debts and referee the marketplace, it allowed one to deal with strangers and believe repayment would come. This general acceptance of who owned what and what was owed to whom, as enforced by government, was fundamental to the development of markets.

A centralized government enforcing common rules is what allowed for the spread of trading. Relatively civilized market behavior could begin to replace more unceremonious acts, like pillaging, as a means of seeking wealth and empire. But it also allowed kings and their ilk to grow their personal wealth by assigning costs to their subjects' personal stakes, costs like fees or taxes. I've been talking about kings, but it could have been churches too. Tithing to the churches, taxes to the kings.

"Wait. So debt was money?"

Debt was money—the very first form of money. And it's still money. It will always be money. Debt is a declaration of trust bestowed on the borrower, given by the lender, and usually under some government regulation. It's no accident that our money has the word "trust" printed on it. Instead of recording specific tasks, like cooking a meal, hanging a door, and valuing those IOUs for use in trade, a system of credits was created. It's easier to give credits and far more efficient than maintaining lists of performed services and chores. Credits, naturally, became universally accepted within the community. And the form of the credit itself became more universal. Even today, currency is still just an expedient way of sharing the benefits of our credits and debts.

A banker's real work—as opposed to the easier task of providing storage services for wealth—is to find the entrepreneurial spirit in the community. And the entrepreneur's initial task is to present herself as worthy of the banker's trust. A banker is paid to take a chance on the entrepreneur. When a bank sizes her up to give her a loan, even when there's nothing to her name but the business plan—which is what a proper bank does to support growth in its community—that banker is showing not only faith in the validity of that plan but also in her ability to execute it. In other words, that banker is putting faith in the entrepreneur, believing her future work will generate the money to pay him back. Her loan— money effectively created out of trust—increases the money supply of the whole community. It goes into the community as she spends it. Issuing her debt has created money.

"Banking doesn't work that way. And if it once did, it doesn't anymore. Today everyone is just a credit score or a pile of assets."

Sam, I haven't been trying to describe "what is." I've only been trying to describe the most effective form of economic community. To the extent we already do whatever, that's great. But it'd be nice to get all of the economy on board. I understand that people have been reduced to numbers. It's far from an ideal situation.

But, however banks do what they do, it's debt that allows economic creativity to flourish. How else can an entrepreneur create a business where none existed? Without debt, an economy would be a very stagnant thing. In their way, banks curate our economic future.

"But when it's the nation that's in debt, and the debt is so large … I mean, how much is too much? How do you know?"

It's too much when people who purchase it stop believing the nation's goods and services can ever pay them back. This is the point where a new issuance of national debt goes unsold, or the interest rate demanded for purchasing it quickly soars.

It's also crucial to realize the significant difference between a nation's debt and a personal debt. People are expected to die. Nations don't have to. Personal loans are based on a foreseeable path for repayment, generally within a person's lifetime. But if not, their estate will be obliged. Nations are different. A nation's debt, in theory, can carry on for eternity. So when investors assess the potentials of a nation, the scale can extend well beyond a single lifetime. There's potential in the cumulative value of every good and service generated over a very long future. The effect is that a nation believed to be fiscally strong can carry a far larger debt than a nation of equivalent wealth and population that is perceived to be weak.

"But no one lives for an eternity. So why would a debt buyer care about the distant future of a nation?"

If the long-term future of a nation seems viable, then she can more easily believe the nation's current debts will be paid. She might be looking to establish a stable source of income. Or perhaps she just wants balance for the financial risks she holds elsewhere.

There is a taught power that goes with giving a loan. I don't mean an individual lending to a government is going to hold sway over that nation. But when governments lend to individuals, or individuals lend to each other, the power calculus changes. The lender, assuming they're financially sound, is acquiring leverage over the debtor.

This power was likely abused at first and then for a long time after. Only a few generations ago, we used debtors' prisons. And it used to be, a long time before that, that unpaid debts were paid with physical harm, even death, or by providing a family member to be a slave. The ability to command violence, with the state's support, assured a lender of coming out on top without caring whether the loan could be repaid. In this way, slaves were created, manufactured by offers of unwieldy loans. We have become more civilized of late; at least the threat of violence or loss of liberty is no longer required to satisfy a loan. However, in a true free market, lending would progress even further. It would view offering and receiving loans as actions of equal economic weight.

"But you said there was a power that comes to the lender."

Only because governments made it that way. Looking at it, strictly economically, a loan is a transaction of equivalent risk for the creditor and debtor. The bank, or other lender, makes an assessment of the person and her company's plans. By giving the loan, the bank is declaring that trust in her and in her company is warranted. Investors do similar work: making assessments of people, companies, and nations, and choosing whether to trust in their future. In a true free market, the risk is borne equally on both sides. Should there be a default—meaning the debt terms pass without repayment in full—the amount unpaid becomes a loss to the bank or investor. And it becomes a loss of reputation for the debtor, while public recording makes sure that the story of her failure is available to all future lenders.

The best plans can fail for unforeseen reasons or honest mistakes. But fraud is difficult to forgive. If the lender's trust was abused, meaning the intention to repay the loan was misrepresented, then the matter belongs in court for a jury's consideration. A purveyor of fraud deserves to end up in jail, in addition to repaying her loan in full to her lender, along with penalties and associated costs. Fraud demands a far worse fate than failure.

"The abuse of freedom warrants the loss of freedom. I think that's what you said."

Yes. So it's a matter for the legal system to rectify. The economic system can't. Economies are our collective decisions to trade or not to trade. But there is nothing in economics that guarantees such decisions, once made, are wise.

"Speaking of wise, I get that debt was money ... is money. But I want to know, how does real money come into it? The currency we can carry around? You mentioned credits ..."

Well, there's more story here. We can easily imagine the world used to be a very violent place. Kings desired treasures from neighboring places while needing to protect their own. Naturally, maintaining standing armies made sense. And the way to keep an army loyal was by offering them an entertaining fight every now and again and a bit of prosperity.

A competent king realized he couldn't keep all the riches of victory without risking revolt from his army. Soldiers had to be fairly paid. But it was awkward to do that with found treasures, with so many sizes and weights of candlesticks, plates, jewelry, and the like. The easiest way to share would have been to melt it all down, or what remained after the king plucked for himself, and reform the loot into small, pocket-sized pieces. Then a fair division among soldiers was simple.

And perhaps the king would want to remind his soldiers of who was paying them. Perhaps the king's own face could be stamped upon the metal pieces. At that point, we have the coin as we now know it.

But paying an army caused continuing incentive to conquer and acquire more treasure. The only alternatives were to war some more, mine for gold and the like, or tax the kingdom's subjects. But warring too much was risky. And miners needed to be paid too ... unless the miners were slaves. Wiser kings, not necessarily good people ... but wiser kings, realized that slaves could be acquired when his subjects were in debt. And debt could be created when subjects were unable to pay their taxes.

If this is how the notion of taxing capital started, then it's also the roots of our economy's flaws.

"But how do you think we got to fiat currencies, without any metal backing them? I know ending the Bretton Woods system did that in the 1970s. I can't imagine why anyone thought it was a good idea."

A world emerged with many coins, each from competing kingdoms and stamped with an image of their king. Of course, because gold is gold, coins could be used anywhere. But realms didn't respect rival stamps and probably didn't trust the stated value; the coin, away from home, was worth only the raw value of the metal. So a small value was accrued to using a home coin—a slight premium above the value of the metal alone. Shall we call that the value of trust? It was an early sign that currency need not be valued by material. There was something more than the physical that made a currency worthwhile.

"You're saying that's what led to fiat currency?"

Yes. Not that fiat currency happened then, if that history is right, but the potential for it was born then.

"I have to say, it seems like a mass illusion to me, fiat currency. It's just collective acceptance, with nothing real to bolster it. It's destined to fail. Maybe not in my lifetime, but that old saying about a dollar not being worth the paper it's printed on is going to come true one day. That could never happen to gold. Why don't you see that?"

I do see that. It's a clear possibility. We've seen in history how it works. We've seen countries using fiat currency mismanage things to the point where their paper became almost worthless. But we've also seen how specie currencies need to be managed. When gold was chosen to be currency, mining operations had to be severely regulated. Why? A large, new gold discovery or a period of overly exuberant mining could collapse its value. Storage facilities needed not only to be built but protected, as they were obvious targets for envious nations and criminals. Private ownership of gold has even been made illegal at times, or limited, in attempts to protect the value of the metal or the money based on it. My point is that any system, fiat or specie, needs to be run thoughtfully. Any system can be bungled or mismanaged.

But only fiat currency has the natural elasticity to track closely to the expansions of its economy. Having trust in its value is no different than the trust required to believe in Jack the blacksmith's reputation. It's no different than the faith required to issue or to buy debt. And it's no different than having faith in a free market. If debt reflects a value of expected goods or services, then so does currency. Both are forms of money, after all. So fundamentally, as long as the printing of currency is proportionate to the growth of goods and services in the economy, the value of that paper currency will be secure.

And when I say secure, I mean it in the same sense that the value of your work, at work, is secure. If money is a fair trade for your employment, then it's also fair that both you and money have to keep working to maintain your respective values.

"But boom-and-bust cycles happen because people get overly optimistic about future demand and then overly pessimistic when it fails to materialize. Isn't currency creation from debt subject to that? Lenders are people, right?"

They are. Sam, a true free market isn't immune to economic cycles. It's just that the cycles won't be as severe in their ups and downs because we won't be taxing capital.

"I hear you, Jorge. But government is people. And paper money is so easy to make, to physically print the stuff. Isn't it tempting for governments to print and print to keep their people happy?"

Actually, most money isn't printed like that. Far and away, debts create more. And it's important to remember that nations practicing true free-market principles won't find themselves in debt. So with government out of the way, the free market will a have a practical monopoly on debt creation. And therefore the money supply.

International currency values will always be in relation to other countries' economic predictability and stresses. But at least the delicate balancing act of government issuing additional currency for an already debt-ridden economy will not be tried, except in times few and far between.

The rules need to come from government, not money. Only government is capable of instituting and enforcing rules over large areas without bias. Geographically diverse economies like ours can only share a single currency when government provides a playing field that encompasses the whole. A currency can only work across diverse state and local governments when there's a common belief that the rules will be upheld. If these beliefs begin to decay, so, too, will the value of a currency as a tool.

"Now you're saying money is a tool. Before you were saying it equaled work, in the amount of goods or services. Which is it?"

Money is valued by work, but it's a tool. It's a tool to measure the value of man's work, like a ruler is a tool that measures distance. A ruler is not of any particular form or distance; it could be a yardstick, a tape measure, or a laser. Its function is to mark a specific distance, which is information for other uses. Money is similar in that it is not defined as particular goods or services, but it marks the value of a specific amount of work. Then that value can be transferred to other uses.

Currencies are tools that we invented to make our efforts more efficient. They are as natural as inventing garments to keep us warm. And like any tool, currencies require some maintenance. But they are not of a piece with the platform of free markets. They are merely tools that result from the economic design we choose. Our rules establish the stability of any currency that results. But treating currency as part of that economic platform only encourages mistakes ... like instituting a gold standard.

* * *

Can you accept that money is a proxy for the value of man's work?

"As of now, yes."

Then should the law treat it otherwise?

"Well, by definition, no."

So it follows that money cannot be treated as anything else by law. Not without distorting the value of that thing and warping the use of money.

"Ah, we're back on politics."

Sam, the heat of politics is where economic distortions are forged.

"I know. I get it. You're talking about money as speech."

And it's important. Speech is naturally from a person or from the masses. Its power stems from the quality of the message or from the sheer numbers making its sound. But when its connection to a speaker is lost, speech becomes something else. It's then like an airport announcement but with a policy agenda; it becomes propaganda.

"Propaganda's been around forever. It's not going anywhere."

True. And neither is money. By design, money is disembodied. Its value is meant to be interchangeable among people, through the will of those people. Speech, though, by design, is embodied. It has an identifiable voice. Its voice is not interchangeable. Money can buy equipment for disseminating speech, but those technologies are not speech. They are products to entice exchanges for profit. Advertisements are economic products too. But if what's being advertised doesn't lead you to something you can purchase, then it's no longer economic. It's propaganda.

Decreeing money to be speech, as we have done, is deeming it fair to see the work of hundreds of miners, the profits of which flow to the company owner, be taken out of economics and turned into propaganda. Consecrating money as speech allows profiteers to dominate debates with wage earners. It enhances the value of profit as it diminishes the value of wages, by weakening the power of natural speech.

"How does it weaken natural speech?"

It allows a message, bought by one person or company, to be louder than a natural gathering of thousands. Understanding economics, the wheres and whens of its application, is ultimately what protects our individual freedom. Politically equating money and speech effectively transfers the labor of every employee in the competitive market into political power for their company's leaders. By defining money as speech, employees lose part of their voice. It may seem subtle, but it's so. Conflating money and speech is akin to legalizing a mild degree of slavery.

"Jorge, that's harsh. With DNA, I get the creeping slavery thing. But with this, no one is owning a piece of anyone else."

Not harsh, Sam—accurate. Slaves are people who, through the force of law or the weakness of law, have had their voices taken. When money is deemed to be speech, a man's work is essentially yielding his voice to his employer in the form of profits. Employees are left without a monetarily equivalent voice to match it. Few workers have enough money left over to put speech on their shopping list after spending for their daily needs. When turning money into speech, the law expands the voices of a select class of people by taking voices from other classes. It's a law that's parallel to slave law. It's a law of a principle that can't win an honest debate on freedom.

A political voice needs to be measured by its integrity and resonance, not its marketing budget.

"The company owner earned that profit by providing jobs for all those miners. Can't they, the owners, spend their money as they see fit?"

You're speaking for the economics of it, Sam. Yes, in economics people can spend their money as they see fit. A yacht as large as can be afforded is an appropriate purchase, but as much propaganda as can be afforded is not. Again, politics is not economics. They require different rules. The search for profit and the search for truth require different tools.

"If money isn't the tool for politics, what is?"

Time, perhaps? In economics, money is spent to promote products. In politics, maybe it's time that's spent to promote positions? And maybe there could be a residency requirement to first enter the conversation so that outsiders can't distort it? It seems to me that representative government requires a representative debate. Admittedly, this isn't about economics as a system of wealth creation, but it is about who gets to define our economics.

Come to think of it, this is another function for labor unions. Not only do they protect workers' salaries in closed economies, but they work to restore a political voice to workers in those economies. They're a balance to the leverage granted owners when government allows money to be unconstrained in a realm for which it was not designed.

"You seem to be more excited by the politics than the economics."

Because politicians make the rules. And the rules are everything. Our freedom is in their hands. If we allow politicians to be chosen by the people with the most resources, they will tend to make rules that protect their economic interests, including the use of those resources. Ultimately and necessarily, this leads to a corrupting of the economy; rules start being made for favor rather than for fairness. Political spending weaves its way into the economy by buying ever-longer and stronger needles to ply and alter the pattern of our communal fabric.

"Jorge, yesterday, I would have disagreed. But I don't think I can argue after this weekend."

It makes sense for this misunderstanding to follow when we already misuse capital. If we use it to fund the government, then why shouldn't we use it to choose the government? But we can't allow that mixing. We can't allow a misused tool to guide our politics. Politics deserves a better conversation, where the incentive is to fix our flaws rather than to preserve them.

* * *

"So, can you get back to my question about central banks? Talking about politics and money made me remember it."

Remember what?

"I mentioned how scary it is to have central banks managing these huge piles of national debt, and you went off about the history of money."

Ah. Well, I had to put the answer in context.

"Had to? Please ..."

When a nation taxes its capital, it's taxing the people's work. It's taxing our profits, salaries, infrastructure usage, plants and equipment, purchases, and sales. Such taxes not only distort the true market value of those things, really of everything in the economy, but also create inefficiencies that give the economic cycle higher peaks and lower valleys than it would have otherwise. We've talked about this, but let's take it one step further.

When the economy is in the doldrums, the government starts seeing less revenue at the same time demands for its help are growing. This is how taxing capital worsens cyclical peaks and valleys, how capital taxes feed economic volatility. Public and private debts begin to rise together. It also becomes difficult for government to eliminate its debt because the population's needs only seem to grow, due to the forces we've talked about. So over time, long periods of time, the debt tends to grow.

Sometimes, a nation in debt can recover if there's an extraordinary growth spurt in the economy, as can happen when significant new trade agreements are first implemented, or a bold new technology catches fire. Then tax revenues can rise while needs shrink, and the debt can be reduced. But these are not circumstances a government can readily plan for. Every dollar of government spending is meeting a need or desire. So to be able to reduce a nation's debt without diminishing the lifestyles of its citizens, some luck is required. And leaders need to be cognizant of that good fortune in order to capture it, or it could be generations before another lucky circumstance arrives.

So, aside from lucky times, national debts tend to grow. And this is why central banks, or government-run banks, have an important role. For governments that are leveraged to a nation's capital, it's risky not to manage its debt market. Since government debt itself is a market distortion, central banks are needed to provide stability for what can be a precarious balance.

"A balance? Between what and what?"

On the one hand, as debt grows larger, politicians see it as an ever-more-potent policy argument to cut programs. On the other hand, increasing debt gives exaggerated importance to the industries chosen to receive it and the economy's financial sector, by giving them a massive, unearned asset pool to work for profit. So central banks need to balance the politics of debt with the opportunities given to our financial foundries, to hone the good of the nation.

Also, recall that debt itself is issued in anticipation of future productivity. As more and more debt is issued, more and more emphasis is placed on that future. But no future can be seen with absolute certainty. Doubt makes debt more expensive, and a larger debt creates more doubt, so it makes sense, from the government's point of view, to have an entity that is devoted to trying to manipulate debt. Trying to make the financial future more predictable can seem like a good, or even a necessary, idea. It's no wonder intervening central banks came into being.

"Those manipulations often make people worry about inflation. But if inflation is what you say, about rates of decay and the relative value of labor, can a central bank really control it?"

With big, broad turns, in the sense of steering a huge cargo ship, yes. But not quickly, in the sense of steering a fine sports car. They can't alter the fact of decay, so central bank policy can only affect the relative value of labor. Artificially high interest rates will allow the value of labor to rise. Artificially low interest rates will keep it low. Losing control, or the perception of it losing control, is a central bank's biggest fear. Because uncontrolled deflation will put businesses out of business, and uncontrolled inflation will make lots of people unemployed and poor. Either way, financially ordinary people suffer. The leverage in a capital-taxed economy makes these scenarios quite scary. It would be better to have an unleveraged economy and not have to worry about artificially set interest rates.

"So that's why, historically, inflation is the central bank's biggest concern?"

Capital taxes have made it the problem we've flirted with most often over the years. A lender's investment won't have worked so well if inflation becomes too high. Naturally, then, if inflation is feared, lenders will start demanding ever-higher interest rates on their loans. They'll charge an interest rate that they think will compensate them for the expected loss in purchasing power. Higher interest rates make all debt, including government debt, more expensive. This makes a government that is dependent on debt rightfully concerned about inflation.

"I remember that when I was young, a loaf of bread cost a dollar. Now it costs three."

It's a good thing you're old, Sam. If that inflation happened quickly, it would be a big problem. When inflation rises too quickly, it harms one's lifestyle. Too quickly means more than the natural rate for it set by decay. Manufacturers can try to hide inflation by keeping the price the same but shrinking the amount of bread in a loaf. Or they can use cheaper ingredients. Or they can succumb and just raise the price. But central banks don't have those choices. If there were fears simmering around rising inflation, then the cost to borrowers would soar.

Outside of wars or emergencies, national debt levels are determined by the funding needs for government. So if our needs and desires drive that funding, to shrink the debt, higher taxes, lower spending, or both would have to follow. This almost guarantees rising animosity among the masses because the average life will feel the change. Either individuals will have less money, or money will buy less bread. Too much inflation is not a good thing for governments or for their populations.

"How do you know when it's too much?"

When a central bank needs to manage it, the threat of inflation is too high.

"Yes, but ..."

No. That's the truth. A true free market would not have the concern.

"But Jorge, inflation could still happen. Droughts and floods can throw off the supply and demand balance of food. An earthquake can shutter a mine, or lots of them. And if war draws raw materials out of the regular economy, just a hint of an expectation for war can start prices rising. So I don't see why inflation wouldn't be a concern to a true free market."

In a true free market, the natural state of governmental budgets would be balance. Only the private sector, the free market, would issue debt, presumably in the amount needed to keep the economy growing. Government would simply print enough currency to make sure that people's petty cash needs were covered ... enough to make small and spontaneous transactions cost-effective, but that's all. Currency is only a small percentage of total money, anyway. Most, by far, is in the form of debts.

Remember the analogy of the zoo? Feeding the free market inside that huge cage is part of the government's job. That happens with the establishment and issuance of currency. The small amount needed for light economic bites isn't hard to manage.

It's the free market itself that creates the rest—the big monetary meals and banquets. Perhaps one day, government can get out of the business altogether; there'll be a technology that allows the free market—alone—to accommodate all of our monetary needs. When money is created in proportion to the needs within the free market, and who would know better than the market, currency manipulation is eliminated.

As for your inflation from a shrinking supply of goods, I'm sorry, but if it's due to devastating weather or war, economics can't solve it.

"Why? Why can't economics deal with inflation from weather or war?"

Economics can only react to needs or desires for product within its universe. Hits from outside that universe can throw an economy off kilter. It's the same reason immigration needs to be managed. It takes science, conducted without concern for profit or reward, to guide our expectations for extremes in weather. And it takes diplomacy, conducted calmly and respectfully, to manage our expectations of war.

It might seem ironic, but economics—as wonderfully as it might ever be practiced to bring liberty and satisfaction to the largest number of people—is always going to be at the mercy of the wisdom or ignorance of people outside its bounds. The free market can't solve all of our problems. Ultimately, for the long run, our scientists and diplomats are needed to guide us.

"You're denigrating the free market? After all this time spent promoting its virtues, you say it's not that great?"

I'm not denigrating it. I'm realistic about its limitations. However wonderful it is, it has them. A free market can be the greatest platform ever devised to accommodate mankind, with all our range of ambitions, in a fair and efficient way. But the time frame for scientific understanding does not coincide, except by chance, with the time frame for profit. The drive to profit needs to work within the useful years of a person's lifetime. This dissuades the patience and humility that good science requires. Business can't be expected to work on the time scale for national or global concerns because long-term implications do not cheaply translate to the year's profit statements. A free market needs guidance to address long-term concerns. Private parties can be hired to do it but only when they aren't looking for profit and when the well-being of a nation is paramount to everything else. In other words, parties very much like a government.

War is also well outside the realm of the free market's control. One might think that if the nations of the world sought more economic integration—meaning that trading partners also understood each other's cultures—the need and desire for war would correspondingly shrink. If a nation can acquire what it needs through fair trade, it would be far cheaper to do that than to fight for it. But this integration is up to the diplomats and politicians of the world.

There is nothing economic forces can do but flow like water in channels defined by our laws. Diplomats and politicians have the power to steer that flow. Only their wisdom can avoid unnecessary pressures building up behind their legislated dams.

As I said yesterday, economics is not a panacea. But what it can do, and do very well, is provide a platform for the ever-expanding happiness of people—giving scientists, diplomats, and politicians a shared faith that their good work can have a real impact on our planet. Our many human personalities, talents, and ambitions can all be embraced with abiding respect when they're born from true liberty.

"I'm going to go now, Jorge. You should too. Your train back will be here in ... eighteen minutes. But you should know ... even though we've been talking economics, I feel a bit like I've been to a therapist."

Why, did we talk for fifty minutes?

"Hah. Fifty hours maybe! I'm kidding. Just kidding. But when we started yesterday, I was feeling uncertain—dissatisfied, really—with the state of the world. And I still feel that way … but now, somehow, it's actually different. I thought I knew what I knew; now I'm not sure. I have to digest this. What I thought was freedom seems to be a bit constrained. It feels bigger now. It's like you freed up freedom itself somehow. Not that I think what you're talking about will ever happen, but I'm glad for this talk. Am I even making sense? It's all a lot to think about."

Sam, if we can begin to see what to do with our desires for change, isn't there hope in that?

"I guess so. Sure."

Well, hope is exactly what economics is for—to find a way to fairly give each and every one of us a safe place to pursue our dreams. *Jorge placed three twenty-dollar bills on the table.*

"Good one, Jorge. Hey, I'm glad we found the time. Thank you."

Me too, Sam. And thank you. Where are you headed now?

"Home. Ada will be waiting. Take care, Mr. Olduvai."

Be well, Mr. Rueul. And give my best to Ada.

"We'll have you over for a barbecue soon, both you and Carom. You can see the new deck."

That would be great.

Exit—Commencement

The first European immigrants to American shores encountered people holding an ideology of land use that was very different from their own. The Native American belief that land belonged to no individual must have seemed bizarre, a philosophical shock. As such, it was also a chance for the new arrivals to rethink the place of land in economic society. But any reorientation was not to be. The wild-looking natives were not considered equals. And the modesty of their simple tents was downright uninspiring compared to the elaborate grandeur of cathedrals and castles back home. A vast, fruitful countryside seemed to beckon, a draw soon bolstered when the confidence given by bullets over arrows finally quashed any inklings of debate. A reexamination did not occur. That rare moment for new understanding passed.

This is not to say that the Native American view on land is ideal. It doesn't unleash development and human ingenuity the way capitalism does. But allowing a different view into the conversations of the day might well have allowed for a better form of capitalism to foster.

A Suquamish chief known as Chief Seattle elegantly summarized the Native American view of land. This is a translation[viii] of his 1854 speech, given in response to a young nation's offer to buy his tribe's territory around Puget Sound:

> The president in Washington sends word that he wishes to buy our land. But how can you buy or sell the sky? The land? The idea is strange to us. If we do not own the freshness of the air and the sparkle of the water, how can you buy them?

Every part of the earth is sacred to my people. Every shining pine needle, every sandy shore, every mist in the dark woods, every meadow, every humming insect. All are holy in the memory and experience of my people.

We know the sap which courses through the trees as we know the blood that courses through our veins. We are part of the earth, and it is part of us. The perfumed flowers are our sisters. The bear, the deer, the great eagle, these are our brothers. The rocky crests, the dew in the meadow, the body heat of the pony, and man all belong to the same family.

The shining water that moves in the streams and rivers is not just water but the blood of our ancestors. If we sell you our land, you must remember that it is sacred. Each glossy reflection in the clear waters of the lakes tells of events and memories in the life of my people. The water's murmur is the voice of my father's father.

The rivers are our brothers. They quench our thirst. They carry our canoes and feed our children. So you must give the rivers the kindness that you would give any brother.

If we sell you our land, remember that the air is precious to us, that the air shares its spirit with all the life that it supports. The wind that gave our grandfather his first breath also received his last sigh. The wind also gives our children the spirit of life. So if we sell our land, you must keep it apart and sacred, as a place where man can go to taste the wind that is sweetened by the meadow flowers.

Will you teach your children what we have taught our children? That the earth is our mother? What befalls the earth befalls all the sons of the earth. This we know: the earth does not belong to man; man belongs to the earth. All things are connected like the blood that unites us all. Man did not weave the web of life; he is merely a strand in it. Whatever he does to the web, he does to himself.

One thing we know: our God is also your God. The earth is precious to him, and to harm the earth is to heap contempt on its creator.

Your destiny is a mystery to us. What will happen when the buffalo are all slaughtered? The wild horses tamed? What will happen when the secret corners of the forest are heavy with the scent of many men and the view of the ripe hills is blotted with talking wires? Where will the thicket be? Gone! Where will the eagle be? Gone! And what is to say good-bye to the swift pony and then hunt? The end of living and the beginning of survival.

When the last Red man has vanished with this wilderness, and his memory is only the shadow of a cloud moving across the prairie, will these shores and forests still be here? Will there be any of the spirit of my people left?

We love this earth as a newborn loves its mother's heartbeat. So if we sell you our land, love it as we have loved it. Care for it as we have cared for it. Hold in your mind the memory of the land as it is when you receive it. Preserve the land for all children and love it as God loves us.

As we are part of the land, you too are part of the land. This earth is precious to us. It is also precious to you.

One thing we know: there is only one God. No man, be he Red man or White man, can be apart. We ARE all brothers after all.

Clearly, this is a different relationship to land than the one brought from across the ocean. But it is not wholly incompatible with capitalism. Sam Rueul and Jorge Olduvai discussed how respect for Earth could be integral to capitalism through a land-value tax. If the economy that resulted from it and the innovation that bloomed would be unrecognizable to Chief Seattle, the reverence for land underlying it all would be warmly familiar to him. Our economy can simultaneously become more efficient and liberating. President Lincoln, in his Gettysburg Address, said that even a nation conceived in liberty sometimes demands "a new birth of freedom." Is this today, our time?

Views of land tenancy that are different from our own have been around for millennia:

From the Holy Bible, Leviticus 25:23: "The land shall not be sold forever; for the land is mine, for you are strangers and sojourners with me."

From the Qur'an, 2:22: "Who made the earth a resting place for you and the heaven a canopy and [who] sends down rain from the cloud, then brings forth with it subsistence for you of the fruits; therefore do not set up rivals to Allah while you know."

And from the Bhagavad Gita, 15.12–13: "The light that coming from the sun illumines the whole world; and which is in the moon, and in the fire; know that light to be Mine. Entering the earth I support all beings with My energy; becoming the sap-giving moon I nourish all the plants."

They are three of the world's most popular religions. Different as they are in the ways of worship, they agree that land is for our use. Yet, similar to what the Suquamish thought, they also see individual decrees of land ownership inevitably coming into conflict with Him, whichever form of *Him* one has chosen.

That our economic relation to the land is chosen means we are accepting enduring consequences for our choice, whether they are visible to us or not. Even unseen, the effects of a land-tenancy system can be a powerful, anonymous motivator. The movement that Reverend Martin Luther King Jr. led during the 1960s began as a quest to secure economic justice for the poor. The poverty he witnessed was rightly seen as immoral. The cause of it, however, was only partly understood.

Although most African Americans were poor, even those with assets had no viable political voice. Their prospects for casting votes were locally diverse adventures, often unsuccessful. It was soon realized that the poor needed their voice in politics in order to try to find their justice. And so the great civil rights movement grew. Great strides were taken, guided by great men. Achievements of the time were nationally legislated and institutionalized.

Yet the solution to poverty was never found. Poverty persisted because it wasn't understood that economic growth alone could never lift all the poor so long as capital was taxed and land wasn't freely available. But now we can see why, if those are the field conditions on which capitalism is made to play, the need for government poverty programs, the exaggeration of economic cycles, and those nerve-racking community-born deficits will endure.

The economic world and the values it reflects are always our creation. From the impoverished to the wealthy, we jointly decide if money will be needed to buy our freedom, or if freedom is to be like air, already surrounding us.

Each choice we make includes a weighing of courage with fear. Whether it's how fast to drive or what food to try, the result derives from some preponderance of one trait over the other. Courage and fear also fuel our politics, with one party promoting a message of economic courage needing less government and the other speaking to economic fear needing more. It's this politics that tilts the balance between our nation changing or remaining the same.

If our grand ideal is to structure communities as lotteries, with freedom as the prize for a lucky few, then we have succeeded in finding our balance. Of course, we've incurred costs to clean up after the holders of all those losing tickets, overlooked stark indignities given to our poor, and forgiven much liberty lost to the rest of us. But we have succeeded. We've employed economic laws that leverage capital such that some of us end up devoid of wealth while others reap more than their share. We have effectively chosen to fundamentally manipulate economics to satisfy what can only be a deep and domineering desire for a rigged inequality.

Whether or not this system is forged from ancient impulses to exert dominance over fellow men and claim control of the Earth, it is based on laws designed to attain and maintain power for a very few—laws crafted willfully to prevent widespread access to economic freedom. Whether or not the fundamental forces of economics have been twisted or ignored from the stark beginning of civilization, or sometime later, it has now been so long—and the masses have been struggling for freedom ever since— that those harmful twists and slights have come to be seen as normal.

If Shakespeare was right, and all the world's a stage, then the presentation of our current economic arrangement is a theatrical carousel of alternatively rising and falling horses, turning, ever spinning, forcing riders up and down by design. The economic system itself, although despotically disinterested in any one of us, has the power to cowrite each of our individual parts. It forces us into its version of drama, scripting great trials of perseverance or tests of ingenuity for some, and the vigil of great leisure for others. It tries our economic acting with melodramatic highs and lows. This system's innate ability to cowrite our lives defines our loss of liberty.

A different system, a better system for the sake of freedom, would let each of us write our own stories. The economy itself would be demoted from cowriter to the mere stage it was always supposed to be. This ideal society would structure communities more as economic theaters where the talented, driven, or lucky can exert themselves, succeeding or failing without favors from government. And the equivalent of a chorus, living on free land, need not be part of the drama. If this is our goal, then we have not begun to create it.

The freedom to test and be responsible for finding one's own satisfactions has little to do with winning or losing, or being dominant or submissive. Economic freedom is rather the unhindered ability to discover our personal talents, or lack thereof, in a public and fair audition. It's opportunity.

But opportunity is not attained if one's only choice is to take a job. True opportunity is having the ability to say no to a job. It's the condition of self-sufficiency that doesn't require a boss's approval or aid from a community fund. True opportunity gives a person liberty to engage the world with universal respect—for where we each begin our economic journey, for where we each arrive, and for the vagaries of the path in between. A market offering true opportunity presents a dignified circumstance for any aspiration at every stage in life.

Instead, we have transformed a great debate between economic courage and economic fears into a war between capitalism and democracy. Factions of our culture see one or the other as an enemy, when neither represents the problem. It seems almost ironic in today's milieu of adversity, but capitalism and democracy need each other. Capitalism needs democracy to keep it morally grounded, and democracy needs capitalism to inspire our greater freedom. If the political efforts to hold each one at bay were instead directed toward achieving a true free market, then both could find satisfaction in the cause.

Courageous free marketers can attain their dream when we stop taxing capital and start respecting the economic role of land. The only way to make government as small as they would like, without targeting any financial class, is giving government fewer self-created tragedies to address. Intrusive and manipulative government programs can be eliminated when the needs that inspire them are themselves eliminated. We've just heard Misters Rueul and Olduvai discover a means of accomplishing this by governing in accord with true free-market principles.

Once implemented, these principles will also vanquish the doubt from wary capitalists. We have learned why their concerns and fixes are legitimate in our faulty system. Poverty created by the taxation of capital and the lack of an unfettered no invisibly stir rationales for their fears. But the vast economic programs this politics requires are only bandages for the injuries caused by its flaws. To doubters of free markets, a true free market offers a way to believe that both humanity and fairness can be found in capitalism.

The idea of a true free market is one both sides can agree on. Eliminating taxation of capital brings the true value of products, labor, and land to the fore. The unfettered no unshackles the freedom to work and incarcerates unfair inequalities. Capturing land value for the community also incentivizes good care of our planet, without overwrought regulation. A truly free economy provides a calmer future, without exaggerated cycles of highs and lows. And most importantly, it relieves the pressures of poverty that suppress an ever-growing segment of our population. In sum, it maximizes our freedom and minimizes our government.

A step toward a true free market can be made by creating mock auctions to recognize the value of our land. Such a program would value parcel by parcel over time, perhaps ten years. Free lands will be identified as the acreage of arable, low, or no-value land grows. And when the free market is given the auctions for real, land-value tax can be slowly raised on competitive properties while all other taxes proportionately fall. By a specified final date, the transition would finish, and land-value tax could rise to the level where what remains of all other taxes falls to zero. That will be the day our greatest economic freedom is born. For on that day, when someone wants to sell her property, the land underneath it will be leased from the community. A true free market will have begun.

Perhaps the fear of disenfranchisement will be strong in current owners of underused and cheaper lands. But if the community has decided to move to a land-value system, the community's great majority will understand that enfranchisement in those properties was the result of years of mistaken practice—that what those owners are losing is not a hard-won birthright but an unfair advantage over the rest of us.

Even so, these landowners would not be evicted. Leased lands would be available at fair auction prices. Free lands could be kept by accepting the terms for free land use.

Federally sponsored retirement programs could be phased out through attrition and by limiting beneficiaries to those who qualified before the transition date. Government welfare programs could then be scaled back to serving only the physically and mentally needy. The economy could soon reach a full employment as defined by humanity, not by statistics.

The needs for public education would be also identified and addressed over the transition period and, perhaps, for some years to come. And the health-care industry will begin its economic division into lifesaving and elective-care markets.

In their conversation, Misters Rueul and Olduvai never mentioned the idea that revenues would be divided among federal, state, and local governments. Had they discussed it, they might have found that current proportions of government spending would be maintained among the various entities. These levels could be adjusted over time as the need for different community programs shrank or grew. Over time, the proportions of revenue needed would stabilize and allow for confident, long-term, land-based budgeting.

It bears repeating: an economy is a reflection of a community's values. If our core values are personal responsibility and fairness, then a true free market will satisfy us. When economic forces are better understood, the time and effort of political wrangling over trying one approach or another and adjusting budgetary numbers to patch the economic issues of our day will be moot.

At that time, too, it will seem silly for capitalism and democracy to be at odds. Each works best when they work together in caring for our country. United, they embody the fulfillment of Chief Seattle's wishes as well as those of the great philosophical economists who, even in their disagreements, only attempted to defend our dignity. In their true forms, capitalism and democracy's joint blueprint for freedom will confidently display our individualities yet keep our unhindered ambitions from abusing the earthen gift that nourishes us.

We know what we need from the Earth to care for our loved ones. We also know what the Earth needs from us to continue to shelter and nurture our children, and their children, and their children, and their children …

A true free market can be ours to enjoy. We only need to make it.

Acknowledgments

Several people read bits and pieces of early drafts of this book and were willing to discuss their reactions. I would like to thank Bill Ain, Bill Rossen, Debra Brancato, Masood Bhatti, Ayesha Pande and the late Mitchell Newmark, either for their encouragement or for their courage to suggest improvements. I would also like to thank Signe Hammer, Brenda Rusch, and the people at iUniverse for their valuable editorial attention.

Significant written inspiration came from many sources, including several works of Plato, Henry George's *Progress and Poverty*, Adam Smith's *The Wealth of Nations*, David Ricardo's *On the Principles of Political Economy and Taxation*, Charles Mackay's *Extraordinary Popular Delusions and the Madness of Crowds*, and David Graeber's *Debt: The First 5,000 Years*. I would also like to thank the US government for keeping its receipts.

Mostly, though, I would like to thank my wife, Jessica, for her years of patience in granting the personal space I needed to work on this project, and for her undying support of the effort.

To continue the conversation,
contact me via steve@atruefreemarket.com

Endnotes

i   http://www.irs.gov/uac/SOI-Tax-Stats-Historical-Table-23; http://www.irs.gov/
uac/SOI-Tax-Stats-Historical-Table-24

ii   Estimates of national land value vary widely:
http://academics.wellesley.edu/Economics/case/PDFs/LandValue.mar2007.pdf
http://www.slate.com/blogs/moneybox/2013/12/20/value_of_all_land_
in_the_united_states.html
http://www.federalreserve.gov/pubs/feds/2010/201016/201016pap.pdf
http://www.lincolninst.edu/subcenters/land-values/price-and-quantity.asp

iii   http://www.thenatureofcities.com/2012/08/21/vacant-land-in-cities-could-
provide-important-social-and-ecological-benefits/
http://content.knowledgeplex.org/kp2/kp/facts_and_figures/facts_and_figures/
relfiles/bi_pagano_vacant_land.pdf
http://www.brookings.edu/research/reports/2001/01/01-vacant-land-pagano

iv   http://www.newworldencyclopedia.org/entry/Fran%C3%A7ois_Quesnay
http://www.econlib.org/library/Enc1/bios/Quesnay.html

v   http://www.thenatureofcities.com/2012/08/21/vacant-land-in-cities-could-
provide-important-social-and-ecological-benefits/
http://content.knowledgeplex.org/kp2/kp/facts_and_figures/facts_and_figures/
relfiles/bi_pagano_vacant_land.pdf
http://www.brookings.edu/research/reports/2001/01/01-vacant-land-pagano

vi   http://www.irs.gov/uac/SOI-Tax-Stats-Historical-Table-24
http://www.irs.gov/uac/SOI-Tax-Stats-Historical-Table-23

vii   After ten years:
http://www.wsj.com/articles/SB1000087239639044372020457800498047 6
    429190
http://www.statisticbrain.com/startup-failure-by-industry/

viii   http://www.csun.edu/~vcpsy00h/seattle.htm

Open Book Editions
A Berrett-Koehler Partner

Open Book Editions is a joint venture between Berrett-Koehler Publishers and Author Solutions, the market leader in self-publishing. There are many more aspiring authors who share Berrett-Koehler's mission than we can sustainably publish. To serve these authors, Open Book Editions offers a comprehensive self-publishing opportunity.

A Shared Mission

Open Book Editions welcomes authors who share the Berrett-Koehler mission— Creating a World That Works for All. We believe that to truly create a better world, action is needed at all levels—individual, organizational, and societal. At the individual level, our publications help people align their lives with their values and with their aspirations for a better world. At the organizational level, we promote progressive leadership and management practices, socially responsible approaches to business, and humane and effective organizations. At the societal level, we publish content that advances social and economic justice, shared prosperity, sustainability, and new solutions to national and global issues.

Open Book Editions represents a new way to further the BK mission and expand our community. We look forward to helping more authors challenge conventional thinking, introduce new ideas, and foster positive change.

For more information, see the Open Book Editions website:
http://www.iuniverse.com/Packages/OpenBookEditions.aspx

Join the BK Community! See exclusive author videos, join discussion groups, find out about upcoming events, read author blogs, and much more! http://bkcommunity.com/

www.ingramcontent.com/pod-product-compliance
Lightning Source LLC
Chambersburg PA
CBHW020737180526
45163CB00001B/272